MY BROTHER GEORGE SEFERIS

George Seferis in Paris, 1921

IOANNA TSATSOS

MY BROTHER GEORGE SEFERIS

TRANSLATED FROM THE ORIGINAL GREEK BY
JEAN DEMOS

WITH A PREFACE BY
EUGENE CURRENT-GARCIA

A NOSTOS BOOK
North Central Publishing Company
1982

Copyright © 1982 Nostos
All Rights Reserved
Library of Congress Card Number: 81-86342
ISBN: 0-935476-10-5

This volume is number three in a series of translations dealing with modern Greek history and culture, under the auspices of *Nostos*, the Society for the Study of Greek Life and Thought, Minneapolis, Minnesota

Theofanis G. Stavrou, *General Editor*

Poems followed by page references quoted in this volume are from *George Seferis: Collected Poems 1924–1955*, translated, edited, and introduced by Edmund Keeley and Philip Sherrard (Princeton University Press, 1967), reprinted by permission of Princeton University Press.
Passages in French are retained from the original Greek edition.

Cover photograph of George Seferis.
Frontispiece photograph of George Seferis in his room, in Paris in 1921, preparing his speech on Jean Moréas.
Jacket flap photograph of Ioanna Tsatsos.

TABLE OF CONTENTS

PREFACE   v

A FEW WORDS   xv

I
1912–1918
ANOTHER ERA   1

II
1919–1922
OUR NATIVE COUNTRY FREE   29

III
1922–1925
THE DOOM OF IONIA   109

IV
1926–1931
OUR EXILE RETURNED   159

V
1931–1934
LONDON   193

VI
1935–1941
POETRY AND POLITICS   219

BIOGRAPHICAL NOTE   251

INDEX   253

PREFACE

Within the past twenty years a number of dedicated classicists and neohellenists have made available for English and American readers excellent translations of the works of George Seferis (1900–1971), now widely known as one of the greatest Greek poets of the century and winner of the Nobel Prize for literature in 1963. Among the most helpful of these translations — helpful in the sense that they faithfully convey the form and spirit of a subtle, complex body of writings and thus clarify for those who do not read modern Greek the reasons why Seferis' poetry and prose were so deservedly honored — are Rex Warner's two collections, *George Seferis: Poems* (1960) and *On The Greek Style: Selected Essays in Poetry and Hellenism* (1966); Edmund Keeley and Philip Sherrard, *George Seferis: Collected Poems, 1924–1955* (1967); Walter Kaiser, *Three Secret Poems by George Seferis* (1969); and most recently, Athan Anagnostopoulos, *A Poet's Journal* (1974), which also contains another splendid introduction by Walter Kaiser. The introductory comments in each of these volumes, in fact, provide insights not only into the structure and content of Seferis' writings, but also into the rich resources of his mind and heart. As Mr. Kaiser observes, speaking of the small portion of the *Journal* now available (i.e., 1945–1951), "it tells us not so much what its author did day by day as who he was and who he became as those days went by."

In the present volume, *My Brother George Seferis*, we have what must surely rank as both the fullest and the most sensitive record of who he was and who he became as the days of his youth led inevitably to those of his maturity and renown. For this book is the loving distillate of a life-long relationship, beautifully composed by the one person who knew the poet best of all — his "little sister" Ioanna, a poet in her own right, also known in her native land as Ioanna Constantine Tsatsos, former First Lady of the Greek Republic. To those who have been fortunate enough to know her earlier book, *The Sword's Fierce Edge: A Journal of the Occupation of Greece, 1941–1944* (1969), the beauty of this tribute will come as no surprise; both books are sensitively translated by Jean Demos, and the lyric intensity of the earlier volume glows on every page of the present one. Nor need one read beyond the opening "few words" of *My Brother George Seferis* to recognize the touch of a poet. Its tenderness is an augury of muted enlightenment suffusing the pages to come. "I shall not write about George the Laureate," she says:

> I shall write rather about George the young boy who wakened in a darkened world, surrounded by high mountains, where poetry was the only glimmer of light. About the young man, born with an open wound of sensitivity with which he faced the difficulties of life. About the craftsman who wrestled to subdue his material, to find his means of expression.

Here the haunting images of encirclement, of darkness and light, suffering and struggle are a virtual pledge that this will be no ordinary compilation of biographical minutiae, but a work of art painstakingly wrought from a lifetime of inchoate memories. And so it is, indeed, a work not unlike that of Seferis' own *Journal*, in which memory is the keynote, binding together as in a tapestry a variety of disparate themes.

The basic details of Seferis' career as a diplomat, lecturer, and writer may be quickly scanned in the biographical note at the end of this volume. The varied forces that shaped and molded that career — primarily those that contributed most to the growth and flowering of a rare poetic talent — are the dominant themes in *My Brother George Seferis*. These forces are, first, family loyalty and cohesiveness; then, devotion to one's native land, its traditions and ideals; courage and intellectual integrity in the midst of international turmoil; and above all, an abiding personal love, freely exchanged between the poet and the men and women closest to him — particularly his younger brother Angelos and his sister Ioanna. Because he was Greek, born at a time when Greece was still partially subjugated and at a spot which was to be the scene of the nation's greatest modern disaster, and because he lived to serve that nation through the turbulence of two World Wars, coups, and dictatorships; and to see it torn apart still later by dissension and civil strife, it is hardly surprising that Seferis' "open wound of sensitivity" is emphasized at the outset or that later his sister refers to him as "a tragic person." Given his background and the tensions that ruled his emotions from childhood on, how otherwise could he have become a poet at all?

The key to those tensions is in the letters themselves, so subtly suggested at the outset in the fluid imagery of the one from Paris in 1923. Letters in the brief opening section between George and his father, the stern yet kindly authoritarian idealist, serve to highlight an ambivalent relationship which will develop throughout the years as pressure from father to son, urging the priority of professional study, seemingly impedes the spontaneity of creative expression. And this relationship is counterpointed in the next brief section by the swift narrative of events during World War I; by the impact of those events on the family of Stelios Seferiadis as they moved from Smyrna to Athens to Paris. Then in the long section (II: 1919–1922) come the many new tensions which will complicate all relationships between the lonely young law student-poet and his family: involvement with Suzanne, first of several disillusioning liaisons; uncertainty whether to attempt writing his poems in French or in Greek — or, indeed, writing them at all; concern over ominous political events at home; quarrels with an ever more demanding father; involvement with Kirsten and despair over losing her; thoughts of suicide; identification with the nineteenth-century Greek poet turned Frenchman, Jean Moréas; pressures from forthcoming law examinations — all are summed up in his tormented cries:

> If I could open my heart, I think there would be written there on one side inevitable separation, on the other impossible love, and in between unattainable beauty . . .

And again:

> . . . how can I choose the first road when the second says to me "I am your life," and the first, tragic irony, is only a plate of lentils to fill my belly . . . ?

To their father's angry warning that "a man can't live on literature," one can appreciate his sister's dry response years later: "It was not easy to be a diplomat, a wage-earner and a poet."

Luckily for Seferis, the one person who had infinite faith in his capacity to be a great poet was his sister, even though she recognized that at age twenty-two he had as yet produced nothing remarkable — save, perhaps, his lecture on Moréas delivered in Demotic Greek to the Greek students in Paris. She realized that despite his loneliness, doubts, fatigue, and insecurity, the poetic dream was there, needing only to be encouraged and nurtured to become a reality: "I remember that I was always writing to him, again and again in a thousand ways: 'George, go on being yourself. Don't give up and lose the poetry you have inside you.'" This advice, we have to remind ourselves, was from a young girl in her teens, who was enjoying in Paris with her family what she recalls fifty years later as their last complete moment before being "plunged into the titanic wave of general disaster."

There is general agreement with Ioanna Tsatsos' conviction that the evil of the Ionian catastrophe, "penetrating the fibres of his soul," galvanized Seferis' creative imagination and led to the making of his finest poetry. In the next long section of her book (III: 1922–1925) she writes: "the wounds of his country were his most grievous personal wounds. He felt them one upon the other, past and present. And he lay awake foreseeing those of the future." But it was not the "woe of Hellenism" alone that eventually gave tangible poetic form to Seferis' turbulent emotions. At this crucial period of his life other more personal woes likewise impinged painfully upon his consciousness: concern over his family's straitened circumstances, his own and his brother Angelos' lack of sufficient funds to live decently while studying in Paris, the breakdown of his mother's fragile health, and perhaps most painful of all, the agony of his unfulfilled relationship with Jacqueline. Noting that the six student years spent in Paris "laid the foundation for his attitude toward life," the author employs her most interesting strategy in this chapter to illustrate the complexity of those shaping forces. To clarify more pointedly the connection between past, present, and future concerns she shifts kaleidoscopically from developments of 1923–1926 to specific events of the 1940s–1960s, even to the point of her brother's dying hours, and back again to the 1920s. Thus, the cumulative impact of a half century's experiences is swiftly dramatized in a manner comparable to the technique of T. S. Eliot's *Four Quartets* — and nowhere more poignantly than in her treatment of Seferis' love poem, *Erotikos Logos*. *L'affaire* Jacqueline, in fact, reappears now and then like a sad refrain in subsequent pages, even in reference to a poem inspired by a chapter in Edgar Allan Poe's *Narrative of A. Gordon Pym*.

But while the burden of the story up to the mid-1920s has been on the young man's "open wound of sensitivity," from there on it shifts to that of the craftsman finding his means of expression. With doctorate examinations behind him and a career in the Foreign Service successfully launched, Seferis was free to follow the road that was his life, as well as the one that would meagerly fill his belly. Translating the poetry of Valéry into Demotic Greek, preparing for the publication of *Turning Point*, his first poetry collection, and hard at work fashioning his more mature poems — *Erotikos Logos*, *Mythistorema*, *The Cistern*, *Mr. Stratis Thalassinos* — now in the 1930s he was "his own master . . . functioning on his own with self-assurance." While in London he had the time also to become thoroughly familiar with — and to admire — the poetry of T. S. Eliot, as well as to rejoice over his sister's marriage and to compose cheerful notes in English to her infant daughter. The brief period of the mid-1930s while he was back in Athens, living with his father and the Tsatsos family in the same new house at 9 Kydathineon Street, must have been among the most soul-satisfying of his entire career — its solace reflected in the muted tones of "A Word for Summer" and "Epiphany, 1937," written while he was virtually exiled at the Consulate in Albania.

Although Seferis' greater poems, "Thrush" and those in the *Logbooks* I, II, and III, were yet to be written, by the end of the 1930s he had found his means of expression. As he himself would assert later in his own *Journal*: "Until 1936 the years were very difficult . . . But now — these days when I am fifty — I know what I am. I know who may accept me and who reject me." And so his sister's task, announced at the start, has now been fulfilled. With great delicacy and the deepest affection, she has shown how the warp and woof of his life were woven to form the product of his unique style. Fifteen years ago Professors Keeley and Sherrard, in comparing Seferis' poetic genius to that of Yeats and Eliot, noted that its most distinguishing feature "has always been his ability to make out of a local politics, out of a personal history or mythology, some sort of general statement or metaphor; his long Odyssean voyage on rotten timbers to those islands ever slightly out of reach has the same force of definitive, general insight that we find in Yeats' voyage to Byzantium or Eliot's journey over desert country to a fragmentary salvation." With her own Wordsworthian touch ("Yet we are three") Ioanna Tsatsos transfigures this tribute, showing in the coda of her concluding pages how the bitterest memories of personal loss become transmuted into poetry — "A speck of love cast into the chaos."

Auburn, Alabama	EUGENE CURRENT-GARCIA

August 1, 1981

Paris, 13 February 1923

Dear little sister. . . . The letters I have written to you are my whole life. If by chance some day I read them again, drop by drop the moments of my life will pass before my eyes. I am reading your letters now — I have put them all in order, beloved pages that make me forget how hard life is, and also make me hold on to it. . . .

GEORGE

A FEW WORDS

It is hard for me to write this book.
It is a life which lives and yet it has passed away.

You were still looking at me, but you had gone.
Then time took pity on me. Suddenly I saw it turn back, and there you were again. From that moment I live both with time past and time to come.

I had two brothers. Both were poets. The older, George, became famous. Prizes were conferred on him. Young people murmur his verses. During his long, torturing illness, the whole country suffered with him.

The younger, Angelos, always closed in himself, unknown, died quietly one night in a distant land. His poems were lost. He was wrapped in a silence full of messages, a silence like that of a starry night.

Only God understands His justice.

I write about the first brother, because the dialogue between us was never interrupted. Angelos, perhaps the best of us, chose silence.

I shall not write about George the Laureate. I shall write rather about George the young boy who wakened in a darkened world, surrounded by high mountains, where poetry was the only glimmer of light. About the young man, born with an open wound of sensitivity with which he faced the difficulties of life. About the craftsman who wrestled to subdue his material, to find his means of expression.

The established forms no longer sounded for him, did not move him. Never satisfied, he was obsessed by the unceasing quest for the genuine.

"Mediocre, everything mediocre; mediocrity turns me to ice."

And there were the shackles of life: logic, action, the future, studies, the daily round.

How is truth to be conveyed so that it remains true? To touch it at any point you must shoulder all its woe. Finally, awareness reaches its limit. Then perhaps grace is given to create true art and warm man's frozen soul.

Why did we three children always feel ourselves somehow responsible for the evil in the world? Why even in happy times did some inexplicable sadness lie in wait for us?

Perhaps the myth of Sikelianos is true that when the first-born of a family dies, his soul returns in those born after. It comes back grieving over the injustice, longing for the life which was given, but not allowed to live.

Our mother's first child had died. Perhaps that was our secret.

Is creation perhaps the law of some mysterious longing for the unfulfilled?

I dedicate these pages to the young people who loved Seferis. Perhaps they may help in difficult hours of doubt.

I
1912–1918

ANOTHER ERA

The forces that 'spoke to our souls' as children were certainly Mother and Father, but also our deep Greek roots, and the sea, especially the little harbor of Skala (Old Klazomenae).

Memories, one after the other, framed by the places which were their setting, by catastrophes — landmarks.

Mother was a Biblical figure of a woman. However much I try, I find no adjective which suits her better. As I see her in the Homeric framework of that household in Ionia, with her steadfast faith and her fear of God, she reminds me of figures in the Old Testament. She went forward with all her heart, and she never lost her way.

Her father, Captain George, was a rich landowner. From him she inherited a natural love for the soil.

I never again saw our house after my childhood. A big house of three stories with a broad mahogany staircase. In the basement, storerooms. There we put the year's harvest. On the first floor the big covered courtyard, the dining room with portraits of grandparents and deep armchairs, the drawing room, the parlor. There was also the small open-air courtyard with the splendid wisteria, the stone basin, the tap. On the second floor the room with the icons, and the bedrooms. On the street side a big room with a covered balcony toward the sea; there we children played. That was our kingdom. There all the pranks and quarrels took place.

George had his own room, with a small desk where he could study. Angelos and I had ours. Our beds were side by side. I remember how at night I would often hear the creaking of the wood. I would be frightened and would wake up Angelos. We chatted and thought it fun to be awake against the rules. Our words would get fewer, drowsiness would befuddle us, and again we would be sweetly asleep.

I cannot forget the 'icon room' as we called it. It was like a church. Bright, spacious, smelling of incense. On one wall, in the corner beside the window, the big icon stand, leaning on a table. The household saints naturally had precedence — St. Stylianos, St. George, St. John. On the other wall, the great miraculous silver Virgin and the other Virgin, Our Lady of Tenderness, hung with ex-voto offerings. The vigil light burned night and day. A candelabra for the tapers. There every evening before going to bed we three children said our prayers. Often when I was looking for Mother, I found her there on her knees. I would sit down on the step without speaking and wait for her. As she came out, she would take me up in her arms and press me to her.

At Christmas time, they would put the brass brazier in the middle of the room. Then, on top of the burning coals, day and night until Epiphany, they boiled apples stuck with cinnamon and cloves. The whole house was fragrant. The year's supply of incense was made from these apples. We needed plenty because every day in the morning and at twilight, Mother censed the icons.

Mother was fervently religious, but she also felt deeply a Christian's profound obligation to others. Every poor man who knocked at our door was kept for a meal. Even later in Athens, with very little money, she did not abandon this habit. It was not just kindness. It expressed her respect for the needy one.

I remember a September morning when she came down much disturbed. We ran in our nightgowns to the dining room where the household had gathered. There stood the boatman, Stephanos, in his baggy trousers (*vrakes*), surrounded by five little children and his wife with a baby in her arms. They had been up all night. As Mother was opening her window, she had seen them all lying in their boat. She brought them inside, and said to the man:

"Are you in your right mind, Stephanos, to spend the night in the boat with these little children? It is already September and the weather is cold."

He explained: he had not been able to pay his rent, and the landlord had thrown them out. What was he to do? He took refuge in his boat.

Mother was troubled. Why had she not forestalled this bad

situation? She set them up temporarily in a room at the back of our house. Then she made them the gift of a plot of land opposite St. Nicholas. She could do this because she owned land. Stephanos built a little house. The whole village helped him. Good is contagious, as is evil. One brought stones, another mortar. Every man of Skala had a hand in it. For us children this building was a great game. All around we planted morning glories which bloomed quickly. The walls looked well with the vines, and they echoed with our laughter.

How immediate, how wholehearted was her concern, and yet so gentle as to be almost apologetic. She identified herself with the unfortunate person. She shrank from insulting his humanity, from hurting his pride. She knew all the families in the village, even the most remote ones, and she knew every member by his first name. She went regularly in the morning to see them. She knew about the health of their children. George often slept in their homes.

Mother did not go along with the idea of governesses. The thought that she could not enter our rooms freely at any hour of the day or night was intolerable. She insisted on looking after us herself. It was not easy. George was full of mischief and the natural hero of us younger children. One day he climbed up on the shelves of the storeroom where the sweets were kept. He was looking for the jar of orange jam. The shelf gave way, and with a terrible clatter, George and a good many jars came crashing down. Mother was frightened. She came running and dragged her son out from the broken glass and syrup. When she saw that he was all right, she gave him a slap and put him into the bathtub. All that afternoon she did not speak to us. This was a heavy punishment. I remember my despair. We so needed the warmth of her love. All three of us were ready to become saints if only she would smile at us again.

She always looked like a queen as I watched her coming down the stairs, tall, erect. I would open my arms to her, and say, "Let me hug you, my sweet."

Without ever preaching, Mother left us a priceless inheritance: faith in God's presence. The boys with their masculine reserve did not express themselves easily, nor did they often go to church. But however little you knew them, you sensed that they breathed God's presence, that they lived in the fullness of Orthodoxy.

This faith supported George to the end of his life. The prayer which he learned as a child was always there. In critical hours, in fruitful hours, I would see this appeal as it rose from the depths to his eyes.

The single word *Dosmena* (*Poems Given*) says much. It was the word George gave as title to an important group of his poems.

"What a fine poem — The King of Asine!"
"It came from God."

He smiled when he gave me his translation of *The Revelation of St. John*.

"You see, Ioanna, each man has his own way of praying."

At the end, during his long illness in the hospital, in the ward for intensive care, I sat on a stool beside him, and with his bound hand he pressed mine, all eyes. When he could speak, he said,

"Light a candle for me."

In the evening we would wait in our beds for Father to say goodnight to us. When we were small, his tenderness toward us was unlimited. He spent hours carving little wooden boats for George with their holds, their masts, their movable tillers.

He was very skillful at this. He would choose a big walnut, empty it with his penknife, and — I can't imagine how — fashion for me a little box which would open and shut. We children stood round and watched him intently. As he worked he told us stories. He was a poet himself, and he knew how to select the legendary element that appeals to children. One of my earliest memories is that of sitting on his knee, George and Angelos beside us, while we listened to him ecstatically. In a lively simple way he explained how the great King Xerxes prepared his army and his bridges, and swept down to conquer Greece. He told us about the victory at Salamis. George, being a big boy, would ask:

"How many boats were there? Where did Xerxes take up his position?" As for me, I just wanted to hear what happened, indifferent to strategy.

How eagerly we waited for that hour with Father before the evening meal! As soon as he arrived home, we would run after him:

"What story will you tell us today?"

Angelos and I would bring him his slippers. He would sit down in his armchair with a mysterious smile on his face, as if he were conspiring with himself to find a way to bewitch us.

"So Alexander the Great, mounted on his fierce horse, galloped into Asia with his army, and was victorious, always victorious. Most men at that time learned Greek and could read Aesop's Fables — I was reading them to you the other day . . ."

And another time:

"So thousands of artisans and craftsmen built St. Sophia. And the master builder was a learned man. Painters who were saints painted the icons. There were votive lamps without number. How can such a church ever again come into being? The Virgin was enthroned there forever."

But when he came to the Fall of Constantinople, six childish eyes, filled with tears, were fixed on him:

"Couldn't the Emperor Constantine run away?"

"Of course he could, but he did not. He preferred to be killed."

"But why be killed?" we asked desperately.

"Because if he had run away, he would not have been turned into marble, and we would not be waiting now for him to come to life again."

Thus, day by day, he poured history into our eager hearts.

As children grow up, they become satiated with their parents' "virtues". The common daily life of the home reveals tiresome defects which they judge severely. Thus, as the years went on, we found our father's authoritarian attitude oppressive.

George felt it most of all. Father made big demands of him. He wanted George to be perfect in everything he did. I remember that in the big reservoir of Smyrna Father wanted to teach him high diving. He was made to jump from very high up. George was afraid and did not want to jump, but finally he did. I squeezed Mother's hand, trembling with fear lest he stay at the bottom.

Father's feeling of responsibility for our education was perhaps exaggerated. He followed George's studies closely. He stayed up at night with him. I sensed that my brother was troubled by all this, and I was sorry for him. But now, over the distance of the years, I look back at Father's efforts with gratitude. I remember him so well, and how I wish he had lived a few years longer to see his dream come to life — to see George ambassador to London. Here is what he wrote in June 1957:

> Dear Ioanna, Two words to show you that I think of you. Today at noon I presented my credentials to the Queen with the customary ceremony. . . . I think it went well (by Seferiadis-standards). . . . I am always looking into Aesop's mirror. . . .

Father was a man of high ideals. He was brought up to desire passionately the liberation of the nation in the ideology of The Great Idea. In his papers I still find writings about the history of Samos. In 1908 he went to the island to help Sophoulis. In the War of 1912 — so Mother told me — he was roused to the point of joining as a volunteer. What restrained him was the thought of what we, his children, who would have to remain in Smyrna, might suffer in consequence. He sang the praises of the warriors of 1912 in these lines:

> You boys who left school so as not to miss the battle
> Carry the light in the long evening of our race,
> The light that has never ceased to shine in our hearts.

Later he supported Venizelos in all his diplomatic contacts. When he saw with horror that The Great Idea was foundering, he attached himself to the League of Nations. He worked for this ideal, wrote about it. To such a point that at one time in Paris his name was discussed for the Nobel Peace Prize. Then came the Second World War, and once again everything collapsed.

At the age of seven Father had been left an orphan. The beautiful woman, his beloved mother, died at that most critical time. The little boy could not live except in her shadow. A secret adoration for her nested in his heart throughout his life. When he traveled, he took with him first her picture, and then his papers. To her he dedicated his poems (*From My Drawer*).

> As I go through this world
> If it is given me to sing
> A sorrow that will never heal,
> Know, dearest of mothers,
> That it was you who made me a singer
> At the moment of your death.

In how many of his poems do we find the heavy dregs of his orphanhood:

> Charon destroyed our home
> Strange hands locked us in our school room
> One rainy evening — little children,
> Pale, sick, with reddened eyes
> And black aprons.

While Father was a student at the Gymnasium, he met the girl whom he later married. She was in a lower grade. They fell in love. He went away to study law at Aix in France. He wrote to her, and when he was home during vacations, they saw each other. They were betrothed, and the six years of his studies passed. When he returned triumphantly with his doctor's degree, they married.

He lived for fifteen years in Smyrna as a lawyer, devoting much time to study. He wrote books about Law, following attentively the latest word on his subject. He was in regular contact with France and published articles and treatises in French. He served as legal advisor to foreign consulates. The environment was friendly. The intellectuals appreciated him, the simple people respected him. Neither competitive nor envious, nothing disturbed his natural nobility.

Father became a scholar of international standing. After Mother's death, I accompanied him to meetings of the Institute of International Law. I saw how closely they listened to him, how much they valued his opinion, how often it was he who provided the solution on a controversial subject. As late as 1966, fifteen years after his death, when I represented Greece on the Sixth Committee of the United Nations, distinguished international scholars greeted me warmly as his daughter.

He had most devoted friends, perhaps because there was nothing of the *arriviste* in him.

"I don't want their help," he would say. "It is enough that they should do me no harm." And he was not wrong.

But with what pleasure he addressed verses of Mimnermus and Anacreon to beautiful ladies! He himself had translated them, as he had Sophocles' *Oedipus the King* and *Electra*, as well as the songs of Byron about Greece. These are the best known of his translations. But he also turned into Modern Greek Sappho, Horace, and many French poets. Rhythm was instinctive with him.

He enjoyed his holidays at Skala. There he let his passion for poetry have free rein. Elsewhere he concealed it as if it were a sin. He thought his contemporaries looked down on poets. And when he published something literary, he chose romantic pseudonyms of the period so as not to be recognized. As a result nobody read him because nobody reads an unknown writer. Once Cavafy referred with admiration to his line:

> Laughter has died, and the children have grown old.

The friends of the Alexandrian poet were astonished. For the first time they heard of the poet Seferiadis.

His language was rich like that of the first demoticists. At that time they did not rummage about for their words as they do now. Every word had its freshness. His poem *To My Language* shows how faithful he was to it:

> The milk that I sucked has not become bile,
> Nor will I turn from the breast I sought as a child.
> I stamp into bits the newly shaped pitcher —
> Nor does it scare me if I bleed. . . .

Where did it come from, this power, this knowledge of the living language? All day Father worked in flawless Katharevousa or in French, writing about law. From what deep spring within him did this genuine Demotic well up?

> I remember her from childhood,
> How with lowered eyes she came
> Biblical, pale, most beautiful,
> Up the stone stairway to the church.
> As she passed, the village boys made way for her,

> While the beggars whispered blessings and apologies . . .

The sorrow of our servitude was always there in our house, silent, oppressive. It haunted our parents' every act. One evening the knocker of the outer door sounded urgently, persistently. Angelos and I ran to the banister. From there we could see the entrance. George was downstairs. He opened the door and in came Uncle Socrates holding a tall lady by the arm. If I remember correctly, the woman was wearing a long overcoat, a big hat, and a thick veil. Mother adjusted the veil slightly. Then she looked toward the staircase. Angelos and I went quickly back to bed. Much later we learned that the woman was a man wanted by the Turks.

The sails of our hearts were always filled with the breeze of the great ideal, the liberation of the race. The humiliation of slavery was unbearable. This ideal was not just an idea, but something burning within us, the anxiety of a great passion. In the ballade that Father wrote from Paris to his young son, then a student in Athens, he mourned this love:

> What has become of you, little primer?
> Smyrna, fields and earth and sky. . . .

Our passion for Greece overwhelmed us. Some saw it as utopia. But all of life is a search for utopia. Every great people has its myth. In us it was something still more.

When you have been brought up on the poetry of the centuries, on the art and expression of your fatherland, when Euripides' kingfisher comes to life on the bay of every island, when you feel that with such a sky and earth and sea you ought to be able to give form to feeling, then every blow to this solid trunk tears you to pieces. In us, children of Ionia that we were, all the complexity of the Greek world circulated in our blood. It was ours. We never felt ourselves *déraciné*. From the ancient temple to the basilicas, to the Byzantine chapel, to the monastery of Patmos, no surprise. Always the joy of recognition, of returning home.

The account of a life leads always to the pervading sadness of death. The only fresh breeze from the past is that first carefree innocence of the child, his play, the most precious work we ever do.

Skala, where we spent our summers, was not just a holiday countryside. It was a kind of magic land where we acted out our fantasies, where we escaped from the oppression of school. It solved our problems because there we had no problems. We were one with the sun and the seashore. It gave us a time of rich experience, always too short. Boredom was dispelled. We were free, free in a freedom of the rarest quality.

Skala did not have striking beauty. There were no forests, no high mountains. Tenderly it opened its embrace to the sea. On the one side, the villages of the shore, on the other the causeway to the island of Anaxagoras. Opposite were scattered little islands, like supernatural animals, faithful, resting there in the sea and guarding us. We felt their breath in the damp breeze. These islands are always there, deep in my consciousness, a safeguard, a refuge. To be sure they change form. Sometimes they are the poems I love, sometimes the journeys I dream of, sometimes loves, sometimes ideas, sometimes sacrifices. But they are always my islands. They keep the slime of ugliness away from me.

Along the beach, bamboo and bulrushes.

On the land side, endless expanse of vineyards and more vineyards. Many fig trees too. A hill with a little chapel on the summit. George always remembered climbing it with Father on St. Elias' Day. He wrote to Father from Athens in July 1918.

> Dear Papa,
> Today is Prophet Elias' Day. For the first time in years I am remembering that beautiful summer morning walk we used to take on this day. How we climbed up by that little road, and what joy when we stood on the top to look down on what seemed a great carpet, spreading from our feet to the sea and beyond, quivering with vineyards, valleys, islands, caïques — oh, what truly beautiful days! But let me not be sad! Next summer, God willing, I think we shall spend this day there at home . . .

There at Skala were all the country properties from Mother's side.

In Grandmother's garden the old plane tree, our great love. It made us dizzy with joy. Alive with sparrows and cicadas. And there was the wheel well.

The earth was frugal, but fertile. In August when they gathered the grapes and put them out to dry, they were full to the brim with juice. Who could have delighted more in those grapes, the Sultanas, the Muscatels, as we tasted them, spread them out? Their juice ran down our cheeks.

We had the chance, Angelos and I, to see Skala again with Mother, after World War I.

The earth gave forth measure and peace.

Loud knocking at the door, quick steps in the courtyard. In our playroom on the second floor, George had laid out on the table the watch Grandmother had given him. He took it apart screw by screw to see what was inside. He stopped to listen. Angelos and I did the same. We heard the triumphant voice of the coachman:

"The carriage is waiting."

We jumped up all three. The doors of Paradise were opening. George straddled the banister and in a moment he was at the bottom. We tried to do the same, but Mother appeared at that moment, took us firmly by the hand, and marched us down the stairs beside her.

We started for Skala. Big as it was, the carriage just managed to accommodate us. No one sat in his place for long. In a few moments George had climbed up beside the driver and was holding the reins.

How I admired him!

At last we arrived, dusty and hungry, and what a triumphant reception the little village gave us! Young and old, they were waiting for us. All the sunburnt fishermen, with their broad breeches, callouses on their palms, their friendly faces baked by the sea, the sun, and toil. They took me down from the carriage, lifted me high into the air, and I felt more secure than on my own feet. And there were the kerchiefed women with their big eyes, their children — all these were our companions.

Our house at Skala was long and narrow, built right on the shore. The first room was for our parents. The waves broke over it when the August winds were strong. There was the famous big bed, a real battlefield for the small ones.

How did George react to Skala? Now that I am thinking back over his entire life, I cannot remember him so friendly to the world around him, so fully himself, as he was there. He was aware of his body to the last cell. With her instinctive wisdom, Mother avoided the word "no". Everything was his, he made everything his own, above all through the sense of touch. The beaches, the soil, the rocks, the boats, the oars. We, his younger siblings, and his five cousins followed him everywhere. I remember the poor sluggish nursemaid who looked after our cousins. She happened one day to be taking her ease, seated in the middle of a dry ditch. George managed to go quietly to the well. One of the children held the 'tongue' so that the tak-tak of the water-wheel would not be heard, and the rest of us took the place of the horse. The water started to run. The nursemaid found herself suddenly drenched, without understanding how, and because she was fat, she could not get up. The world rang with her outcries and our laughter.

I liked the green figs which dripped 'milk'. When George wanted to climb the fig trees, he would take me with him. He would climb high up, settle himself on a limb, eat the ripe fruits, and pelt me with the green ones.

The quarrels we had always turned into unshakable solidarity at the mildest intervention from the adults. I remember one day when Mother was ready to slap George because he had reduced the mosquito net over the big bed to ribbons by wrestling with his friend Andreas. Tearfully I put out my hands to protect him, and Andreas said: "It's my fault, Kyria Despo, only mine."

His knees were always smeared with blood. He scraped them and then scraped them again. But the sea solved all the problems, both of mud and of blood. For no reason at all he would plunge in with his clothes on. He would pretend that he wanted to fasten an oar in its lock, to disentangle the lines, and then inadvertently he would fall into the sea. I would laugh heartily.

"Don't laugh, stupid!"

But when Uncle Socrates decided to take us by the little steamer to the islands, every minute seemed a century until we started. George was always in a great hurry. He would help by lifting the anchor, and then he would sit on the prow. The first island we reached was Aghia Markela, then we left it behind for the most distant one, Alata. There they would let us do as we liked for some hours. It was no simple matter to explore those secret beaches.

Where should we start? With the shells? What a big one I was holding!

"What's inside?" I would ask George.

"Let's break it and see."

"No, no! I want it for Eleanor's house." All the furnishings for my doll-house were made of shells.

Should we start with phosphorescent stones? We gathered them and piled them at the edge of the water. The wave would come gently and withdraw. The colors would come alive, and then fade again.

Those sheltered little harbors, gently caressing our childish hearts with their damp presence — these were our kingdom. In them we set the fairy tales which took form in our sleep.

And when we returned again to the islands, we went to look for the cities we had founded in the water the previous time.

The sea had become a part of us.

The Fifteenth of August at Skala was marvelous. Grapes and figs by the basket. We didn't mind fasting on Wednesday and Friday. We were preparing the Virgin's feast day, our mother's feast day. Cleaning house and making sweets. At last the great day arrived. We received communion at Saint Nicholas' Church, and then helped the women with small children so that they too could receive. We could not manage it by ourselves, but there was always someone to help us.

Afterward at home we wished Mother "many happy returns" as we celebrated her name day, and then waited anxiously. We waited to learn about the miracle, because in the great church at Vourla, the Virgin would perform her miracle. Kyrà Evangeline's paralytic child walked. Basil, the blind man, saw light. I listened ecstatically.

Then the motorboat from Smyrna would arrive, it too dressed with flags. And we three children would be on the lookout for Father. I remember Angelos saying eagerly:

"I tell you I saw him — with his mustache and his straw hat

and his cane." I too was looking and looking for him. George did not condescend to this childish behavior.

Father was with us every weekend. Also for the big feast days. From Smyrna he often sent cards to his older son.

> Dear George,
> I hope you are being careful and good and listening to your mother. Write me what we need for the caïque and how things are going. I kiss you fondly —

Again —

> Dear George,
> I am sending you some white twine to have braided for me. If it is fine, eight strands should be used. (For fishing lines.) Tomorrow I will send you more. I kiss you fondly, Papa

At Skala Father too had his fun. With his fishing lines and the tragedies of Sophocles, he would take our caïque and set out for the open sea.

He would return with a sea bass and some verses he thought good. He said them, said them again. And next day you might hear, now one child, now another, reciting mechanically choruses from *Oedipus*:

> Who bore thee, child?
> Who was thy mother?

At the end of 1961 in London, I was walking with George in Hyde Park. It was his first time out after minor surgery. He was weak, and leaned on my arm. We met a tall red-haired Englishman. George said jokingly:

> That blush of shame
> Proclaims thee Briton, once a noble name.

I laughed and continued:

> What more I owe let gratitude attest —
> Know, Alaric and Elgin did the rest.

We were quoting Father's lines from his translation of Byron's poem, *The Curse of Minerva*. We smiled at our connivance.

How eagerly George waited for Father to take him along for the night fishing!

Later in a moment of homesickness he wrote to Father (1918):

> I sit sometimes on the veranda as it grows dark. I see the first star putting its silver mark on the clear sky. I remember how we pulled up the nets — I remember — when the star came out, the caïque, the oar . . . I see the full moon like a great soap bubble. And I remember every beautiful return from our fishing, our net filled with several good-sized bream, and our hearts filled with the silver of the moon and the sea. . . .

These were our first years as I remember them, and as in later years we talked about them.

1914–1918

The atmosphere at home grew tense. The Turks were watching us. We were suspect. Heavy footsteps came and went in the street. Mother was nervous and anxious when anyone was late, and sometimes scolded us:

"Quiet, George. Don't talk so loud," and she would close the window quickly. She was always talking secretly with Father.

That summer we did not go to Skala. George lost his good humor. He no longer played with us. Angelos and I without much joy dug into old cupboards and looked through the books which had pictures. Our cousins, Aleko, Elli, Georgie, Stephen, Bebé, invited us often. Father, heavy-hearted, thoughtful, saw that war was coming. With our uncles he discussed the situation endlessly. One evening, when we heard again the menacing footsteps of our guards, he spoke the final word, and in obvious anger:

"Enough of slavery. We must leave here." He had thoroughly discussed it with Mother.

Chests, chests, — the three floors of our house were filled with chests, so it seemed to me then. With us we took all the books and such furniture as my parents considered indispensable. Silver and rugs to sell in time of possible need. Mother was silent, Father thoughtful. In spite of deep hope that we would soon return, the bitter taste of exile put an end to the grownups' laughter.

I remember nothing of the boat which took us to Greece.

We quickly made Athens our own. We played around the columns of the Olympian Zeus. Angelos gaped with wonder at the Apollo and Athena of the Academy. He said they came down from the sky. One Sunday I remember that Father had

George alone with him in his study. He was explaining something to him, showing him something. Then they went out together. That, I think, was the morning George went for the first time to the Acropolis.

Whenever we turned into a new street, we looked for the sea. A city without a seashore was a blind city, something unheard of, George said:

"Mother, we are going to suffocate unless we get some sea breeze." So poor Mother had to take us regularly to New Phaleron by train.

Our home at 10 Codrington Street was on the ground floor. There was a big veranda at the rear and a fenced-in space with a few trees. There we could play freely.

School began. George went to the First Gymnasium. He was fortunate in having a very good teacher, the famous Goudis. He took his students to the Museum, to the Acropolis, to the Kerameikos. He taught them the Ancient Greek language and at the same time the history of Classical Greece. He had the art of attracting students. Young people wanted never to miss his classes.

Angelos went to the elementary school, and I to Mme. Krikos.

Thus, little by little, we entered into a regular way of life. We found companions. George's best friend was Nikos Aronis. For Angelos it was Mitsos Tsatsos. Mother feared the influence of bad company on her boys. She was careful about our friends, and our house was always full of well-behaved children.

"I want my son to be first."

This ambition of Father's was a torment. He read all George's compositions. If he did not like them, he tore them up, and George would have to start again from the beginning. Mother would plead:

"But do let the child get some sleep." George would go on writing and grumbling. I sensed that he was unhappy, and I cried in bed under the covers.

In 1915, the Law School of the University of Athens unanimously elected Father to the chair of International Law. This must have brought some satisfaction to our parents' hearts. But for political reasons, he was not appointed. So passed another year of anxiety.

Now George began to be absent-minded. He was living in a world of his own. He did not answer when we spoke to him. In the street he could bump into a man without even noticing him. Father observed his son uneasily.

It was also unfortunate that I became very ill with pleurisy. I saw them all standing over me. I wanted to comfort them, to tell them that I was not going to die. Mother said quietly as she knitted her brows:

"The child needs a change of air, but how?"

Years later Mother told me that, during this period, for the first time the problem of daily life became a nightmare. They could not collect a single drachma from Smyrna. Their money grew less day by day. There were many expenses — illnesses, lessons. They sold what they could — the big rug, the silver.

And all the time the war, instead of coming to an end, was raging.

Again in 1916 we spent the summer shut up in Codrington Street. For a while we grumbled, but then we found an alternative — Father's library. We would choose a book, and prone on the floor, we would read for hours. We learned by heart the French Romantic poets. When George was not reading to himself, he would recite verses. I listened in admiration. How often I begged him: "George, do the Flambeau again."

And he, obligingly:

"Et nous les petits, les obscurs, les sans grade . . ."

Now the country was divided. Venizelos disagreed with the King and went to Salonica to form his own government. He was certain that the Allies would win, as was Father. King Constantine had his government in Athens. He believed that the Germans were invincible. George and all his Venizelist companions quarreled daily with the Royalists.

Hard days for our home. Mother was always pensive, economizing to the last drachma. Father was silent. There seemed no way out.

Suddenly something happened that changed our lives. A

ship owner entrusted an important case to Father — the defense of his rights in the international courts. His ship had been bombarded by the enemy and he was seeking compensation. This case took Father abroad. He won it. He was given others. Now he could stand on his own, could earn our living. He established himself in Paris.

I think it was in the summer of 1916 that George was in love with my friend, Melpo. At least he thought he was. Tall, chestnut-haired, beautiful, barely twelve years old, and a frequent visitor at our house. Everyone understood the situation except Melpo herself.

One evening we children held a conference and decided that it was proper for George to declare himself to her. He was embarrassed:

"Wouldn't it be better to write her a love-poem and read it to her?"

We studied the whole setting, how we would arrange things, what we would say in order to leave them alone on the veranda. Angelos and I, very quietly, without anyone knowing, climbed up on the service-stairway and hid behind the kitchen towels hanging there. Quite unseen, we could follow this earthshaking event.

No expression on her face. No movement. My heart was pounding. At last, in the evening when we were alone, came the anxious question:

"Then?"

"Then, after she had listened to the poem without interrupting me, she said to me 'how beautiful' and was silent."

Disillusion! I dare say George did not make a very great effort to win her over. It was a time when he was in love with love, not with the girl.

How we missed Father! We were always there, waiting for him.

1918–1919

The summer of 1918. Nobody had foreseen how long the war would last. We had lived on vain hopes for years.

Now Father wrote to Mother that the family was to move to Paris. His first thought certainly was of George. He had finished the gymnasium and was enrolled at the University of Athens, but Father very much wanted him to study in France as he himself had done.

And Mother, without hesitating, sold off what was in the house, took her three children, and started for France across seas infested with submarines and planted with mines. Later she often described her anxiety to me — she could not sleep while facing this grave decision. She was playing with our lives.

They carried me half asleep on to the ship. As a precaution we started in the middle of the night.

By order of the Captain, the few passengers were required to remain on deck. Otherwise, if we were torpedoed, we might not be able to reach the life-boats. They wrapped me in a heavy military overcoat. I clung close to Mother. In the complete darkness, a little sailor sat cross-legged on the deck and murmured a kind of song:
> Farewell to earth
> Farewell to life
> Here we are on our last journey.

We laughed. We did not yet believe in danger.

Corfu — like the capital of a great nation. An Allied base. Officers in various uniforms, elegant ladies, beautiful salons, carriages, colored umbrellas. Nothing to remind us of war. We went to the hotel. I fell asleep exhausted. I suppose my brothers did the same.

There we waited, waited for a boat to pass on its way to

Gallipoli, the nearest Italian port opposite. It must be a boat with room for civilians. Mother's little notebook records that we waited fifteen days on this flower-decked island. Our friends organized excursions for us. Life was pleasant enough, but we were in a hurry to reach Paris.

The trip to Gallipoli took place by day. The sea calm, the sun warm.

"Like going back to Skala," said George and breathed deeply.

The island of the Phaeacians brought recollections of Odysseus. George was now head of the family. He stood by Mother in everything — passports, tickets, baggage. He was looking after us. At dusk we disembarked in Gallipoli and went to an improvised hotel full of military personnel. Two English officers offered us their room. They could hardly believe that a lady, with three children, would be traveling in such times. Next day, on a miserable military train, we started for the French border. Faces glued to the windows, we were full of curiosity as we traveled across the fertile Italian countryside.

"France!" shouted Angelos. "Present arms!"

At Aix-les-Bains, a telegram from Father awaited us and told us not to proceed. Big Bertha was bombarding Paris from morning till night. Shells were falling everywhere, on stores, on houses. But we were impatient, and it all sounded as unlikely as a fairy tale. From the moment we left Athens we were always hearing about danger, and it finally became interesting. We thought it amusing to be heroic, but George was well aware of his parents' difficulties and tried to help.

Aix-les-Bains 28 June 1918
Dear Papa, We have been here a week today, but we haven't managed to join you although that was the purpose of our journey. I'm not blaming you. I understand that even since our departure from Athens, new dangers may have presented themselves, and that it would not be wise to face them immediately. But what can we do about it? Are we to remain apart forever? It's my feeling that we should go now to Paris where we set out for. Let's take our chances. We have been through plenty of danger by sea . . .

But Father could not decide to put his children under fire. Paris was being evacuated. Everyone who could do so was abandoning the city. He had rented a place near l'Étoile — the price seemed very low — a luxurious apartment with period furniture. No safety. Meanwhile we were waiting moment by moment for word that we should leave. On July 17, George wrote again, longing for reunion with his father:

> Dear Papa, We were ready to leave when we received your letter saying that you would come here. We are desperately impatient, counting the hours. . . .

Father did not come. We went to Paris. The day we arrived, shells fell on the big stores. It must have been the last days of July 1918.

We settled down in Avenue Wagram. Each of us had his own room.

A dry French spinster was hired to be my governess. It was my good luck that she did not sleep at home. In the evening after dinner, Angelos and I would take refuge in George's room. Those were our good moments. George read poetry to us tirelessly. At that time it was Solomos, Mavilis, and the French poets whom he loved, but he also read his own verses.

All these poets, legendary idols of our imagination, so familiar, so much our own.

That same year, the principal of my school came into our class one day and announced that Rostand had died. What a sudden misfortune it was for me! I wept inconsolably. My friend, Paulette, sitting beside me, asked:

"But was he a relative of yours? Did you know him?"

Sobbing, I shook my head. I could hardly explain to her what I myself did not understand.

In the autumn of 1918, George rented a student lodging near the Sorbonne. Angelos continued his Greek with Mother so as not to lose his year. As for me, I was sent to a French boarding school at Auteuil. The family was disbanded.

My school had a big garden. High walls all around.

The first week was hard for me. I felt lost. I was cold. Actually I had fever. The children looked at me with curiosity. I was "the foreigner". I wanted to leave. I wanted my mother. But I was ashamed to say so.

Then in a few days, with great sympathy, Amelia approached me, and later, Paulette, with her blond braids. Both were my classmates, and they became my friends. The others began to accept me. Life changed. Endless discussions at night after the study period. Our teachers, I think, were unique. Simple, solid people. They gave us of themselves. And I got good grades. I felt comfortable.

George came every Thursday to take me from school. On Sunday they expected us at home, but Thursdays were entirely our own. And he always had tickets for the matinée at the Comédie Française.

That is when I learned to love the classics. The first Thursday they played Racine's *Andromaque*. George tried for days in order to get good seats. The role of Orestes was played by the great De Max.

What an evening that was! I saw, I heard De Max, and discovered the meaning of charisma. I knew the play ahead of time, almost by heart. But now it was something quite other; it opened and broadened with a tragic intensity I had not sensed until that moment. And when at the end he hissed: "quels sont ces serpents qui sifflent sur ma tête . . ." and shook his red scarf, I felt that the whole stage was filled with snakes. Orestes could not sink more deeply into the madness of his despair. It was the first instant in my life when I was aware of the tragic absolute. There was a lump in my throat. I could not speak, overcome with wonder. And George the same.

"Let's walk for a while," he whispered.

We went toward the Pont Alexandre, plunged in silence. Eyes fixed on the current of the Seine, we continued to live this indescribable emotion. A perfect dialogue.

For me George was a teacher who did not teach. His presence always created for me an atmosphere where ideas and images came easily to life. Without words, we sensed that we were on the same course. Somewhere in our remote beginning, there must have been a flowing spring of common feeling. When we were together, it found its fullness and created harmony.

My Thursday afternoons with George were eagerly anticipated. We would walk for hours. We would sit on benches. He would recite verses to me, tell me of poems he was planning. That autumn I came to understand that for him poetry would mean suffering. He wrote lines, and then when he read them, he would tear them up. As for me, I knew from that moment that he was a great poet, and I kept and guarded every scrap of paper. As we sat under the Queens of the Luxembourg, he read me *Last Words of a Suicide*. They marked the first invasion of tragic feeling into the life of a carefree young man.

> Mediocre, everything mediocre, everywhere mediocrity.
> My loves, my passions, and what my heart feels,
> The soul's fantasy, and the mind's idol,
> The love of beauty and of the eternal,
> All mediocre, they smother me,
> Mediocrity turns me to ice.

Sometimes he would speak to me about girls in Athens who had attracted him.

> How well I recall you,
> My thought bending toward you,
> I feel your breath, the music, the light . . .

> You are all unforgettable,
> But how I remember You,
> Just You, my fair-haired one,
> In the darkness of memory . . .

He read me his translations, *Margaro's Lover, Parentheses* by Rostand.

But he still studied law conscientiously. The heavy obligation to his studies was his first concern. He did not suspect then with what tyranny art would later demand his time.

It was a difficult winter. War, snow, Spanish influenza, much work for all of us.

Suddenly, in November 1918, came the Armistice. Paris went mad. Women in black veils danced, sang, climbed trees. Music, celebration. A whole people in a frenzy, after the martyrdom it had passed through. I too wanted to be one of those gay, happy people, but how could I? That same day, my friend Paulette received the terrible news — her father, Major Dela-

croix, had fallen at the front just the evening before. She wept softly:
"If the Armistice had come one day earlier, he would be alive." . . . I stroked her blonde hair gently, I too in despair.

We did not yet know that sudden tragedy lurks in our every moment.

The holidays passed. We went back to studying. Fruitful hours. I loved my school with a vague gratitude. Every day opened a door to the fascination of some masterpiece. My French teacher enjoyed giving as much as I enjoyed receiving.

What the teacher builds, and what he can build, only he and the student know.

From then on, whenever I happen to find myself in the courtyard of an old monastery, a nostalgia stirs within me. An inner desire for an atmosphere of seclusion, quiet order, disciplined study. I am sure I owe it to the high walls of my school, to those months of fulfillment.

After the defeat of the Germans, all Greece leaned on Venizelos. He tried again, with all the prestige at his disposal as the ally of the winning side, to liberate the Greeks under subjection in Ionia.

Father had at last been appointed professor of International Law at the University of Athens. As Legal Adviser to the Foreign Office and member of the Committee for the Unemancipated, he had Venizelos' full confidence. His cooperation was immediate. The balancing of international interests, behind-the-scenes efforts, struggles, hopes.

Then, in the spring of 1919, came the great day. History owed it to us. We had paid dearly for it. How could the soul of man contain it!

My parents telephoned to me at school. George and Angelos would come to fetch me in the morning. We went directly to Sèvres. There we waited for hours outside a great building. Inside the men of power were discussing our fate. George was very pale — as I had not seen him before.

"Inside there," he murmured, "they are putting their signatures to our humanity."

Presently they came out in their frock coats and their high hats, Venizelos with his staff, and Father with them. They were smiling.

"Surely Ionia is free," George whispered as he squeezed my arm.

The final Treaty of Sèvres (1920) established in Smyrna and the area around it a local parliament elected under a system which the League of Nations would ratify. After five years this parliament would be able to vote for the union of Ionia with Greece. The Greek Government had the responsibility for order, maintaining the necessary military forces. (Articles 65–83).

George took me back to school. The trees bent affectionately above us, the people smiled at us.

When I was at home again, Father said to us:

"They shot Venizelos at the railroad station. He fell wounded into my arms. Fortunately the treaty had been signed."

Now as I relive the great moments of half a century, I see Father before me, his eyes always looking past me, beyond me, even when I went close to him seeking a caress. He measured every diplomatic move with caution, knowing that generations of Greeks would again have to pay for the smallest false step. At the time I could not understand his responsibility, but I saw it all vividly in his misty eyes when Venizelos lost the elections of 1920.

II
1919–1922

OUR NATIVE COUNTRY FREE

Examinations were coming. One morning George appeared at the school gate.

"What's happening? Why have you come?"

"Mother has had a small stroke. Don't be worried. She is better, but you must be near her. It isn't right to leave Angelos alone with her."

It was the end of May. The school year had almost ended. I did not go back to school.

Mother got well. We made plans. Our childhood dreams were to be fulfilled. We three would go back to Skala directly. George would remain to finish his examinations, and in July he would come with Father to join us.

For the first time I was separated from George. I forced back my tears, and clutched his picture in its small red leather frame. I would not be separated from that photograph. For the first time I was weighed down by a chilling sorrow which I could not throw off.

I remember the first days in Smyrna. Uncle Socrates was our host in his big house by the sea. He was a strong man, austere and just. We children were all afraid of him. They gave me a room to myself — heavily furnished, with family portraits all around. When I lay down on the wide bed, I was confronted by the angry look of some ancestor gazing at me persistently. I was frightened. I tried to be brave. I put out the candle. I closed my eyes. But even in the dark, I knew he continued to stare at me. Fear finally mastered me. I lighted the candle again, took George's picture, ran to Mother's room, and squeezed into her bed. She laughed.

"All right, my child, but why did you bring George?"

"What are you saying, Mama? Would you have me leave him with all those angry men who are after us?"

What a delight to rediscover the harbor of Smyrna. I had forgotten it. Its broad embrace held the whole Greek Fleet dressed with flags. Our battleships, the Limnos and the Averof. Many destroyers. Steam launches darting from one ship to another. A sea as thickly populated as the land.

Greek flags, one after another, on houses, on boats. Where had they found so many flags? For years everyone must have kept them in their chests, waiting for this day. The blue blinded my eyes.

The joy of liberation became delirium, madness. It took the form of love, of laughter, of play. On the quay, beautiful girls walked up and down. Their eyes sparkled with fun. They were all in love with the officers. I wasn't sure; did they love the man, or the Greek naval uniform?

Every cell of our bodies felt liberated from the oppression, the servitude, which our parents, our grandparents, our great-grandparents had suffered. The nightmare had ended. We breathed freely. We clasped the present moment, full of memory, full of hope.

And I, the restrained and melancholy one, felt for the first time this kind of madness. I remember that one Sunday Uncle Socrates invited the cadets who were in training aboard the battleship Limnos. They were young boys. My cousin Elli and I played hide-and-seek with them in all the corners of that big house, from the garden to the attic.

But why was George not there? This painful thought tormented me. I remember writing to him in this euphoria that it would be complete if only he were there with us, that he too would then believe in Life. But who knows? Perhaps the later catastrophe would have been even harder.

From the first day Mother wanted to pay her respects to Bishop Chrysostom. This was natural: before she left, she had had her stall in St. Photini's Church. She used to see the Bishop often, and he was regularly invited to our home. He once gave Mother a small Gospel which George always had with him.

Chrysostom had just returned from his exile. With great joy he saw his people again. He received us with fatherly affection, and said with a smile:

"Now that boundaries do not separate us, we shall see each other often." A gentle expression lighted up his eyes. He stroked my hair.

"How Ioanna has grown!"

Life is livable only because we do not know what will happen next.

At Skala Mother opened the outer door of our house with the big key. Its fading outer walls were still full of the letters, G.S. The last time they were whitewashed, George had put his initials as far up as he was able to climb. The house was his, given to him by his grandmother. The caretaker gave him the key. Rusty as it was, George guarded it as a treasure. Mother was obviously worried about something. She went to the storeroom, unlocked it, and began to empty it.

"Come and help me," she said to us. We carried out old beds, broken chairs, fishing lines. At the back, the storeroom made a turn and thus created a concealed corner. There we found a bulky object wrapped in cloth and paper.

"Thank God, it's there," Mother sighed. "Angelos, run quickly and tell Mr. Oikonomos to come. Tell him I have found the sarcophagus."

On the eve of the War, workers digging in Mother's vineyard had uncovered it. Before abandoning Skala, she had barely managed to wrap the pieces and put them in the hidden part of the store-room.

The archaeologist, George Oikonomos, had been assigned to undertake the excavations at Klazomenae, the hinterland, and the island of Anaxagoras. His face shone with joy when he saw the sarcophagus, and he began immediately to assemble it.

"It is a very rare piece," he said. "Only in the British Museum is there a similar one."

It was perfectly preserved. Lively representations of the battles between the Greeks and the Cimmerians covered the sides. Mother had suffered all these years over her responsibility for its safekeeping, and now she wanted it delivered as quickly as possible to the museum in Athens. Mr. Oikonomos undertook to transport it with utmost care. He handed it over to the Greek Commission in Smyrna, and the High Commissioner promised to send it with all possible speed to Athens.

Why did he not do so? Where is it now? It is the fate of things as well as of persons that our deepest concern for them may come to nothing.

This episode awakened a new world inside me. I remember the passion with which I followed the excavations that summer of 1921. Now and again we made a new find. Mr. Oikonomos, in spite of his great seriousness and his pointed beard, gave me courage with his kindly smile. And he was patient in his explanations.

On the island, the work was its own reward. Near the summit, we found the temple, on the shore, the villas. It was fun to take water from the sea to wet the mosaics. The colors lighted up, the images came to life.

A few years later at Rhamnous in Attica, Klazomenae came vividly back to my mind.

I wrote to George and waited for him. I thought about the great day when he would see the harbor under the Greek flag. He wrote back with intense longing:

I believe I'll be in Smyrna by the end of July . . .

George passed his examinations, but he did not come. I did not understand why. Was the money lacking? Did he have to study? By Father he sent me an ivory bracelet with some advice:

> Paris, 4 August 1919
> Take care of Mama and don't let her get tired. . . . I swear to you that it is not of my own will that I am staying in Paris . . . I would love to be near the sea . . . stretched out on the seaweed of one of our Skala islands, but it's not possible . . . Do what you can to entertain Mama. . . .

In the autumn we went back to Athens. We stayed at Old Phaleron. Once more the sea was spread out before my window. Father was waiting for us. He was preparing his lectures. It was to be the first year of his teaching at the University of Athens.

Meanwhile George was at loose ends in Paris. In his photographs we saw him as a thin young man with thick black hair. And he was very melancholy.

At that time he had the misfortune to become involved with

Suzanne, his landlady's daughter. She was good-looking, blonde, older than George, avaricious. The crafty kind of woman who gives the least possible to a man in order to suck him dry, who shatters his mind and soul so as to have him in her power. She would begin with the cliché: "I always tell you the truth." Then she would tell with whom she had slept the night before, and come forth with poisonous and groundless lies. If George had been an ordinary student, this story would have been just a usual affair, but he, as a poet, was defenseless. This woman's behavior was almost criminal.

A difficult period. An inexperienced young man, longing for love, sees the female suddenly enter his life, and submits to her charm, her hard calculation, and her underhanded deceit. With the warm faith in woman which he had from the memory of his mother, he wanted to believe in this woman, to put a soul into his beloved. But no soul found place in Suzanne, however hard he tried. She was good to him during the first days of the month. Together they squandered the little money Father sent him. Then she went off with the others, saying "I hate the penniless." There would be scenes and all connection would be severed. But it could never be conclusive, since they lived under the same roof. He needed to change his lodging. Then he might be able to wrestle with the problem. But in order to move, he needed money. He did not want to ask for it, or even to speak of it. At the time George considered me a child. Such a secret was not for me. Only later did I find out about it when we were together again.

His letters sent me into despair:

October 10, 1919:
Morally I am a mess, physically worse. Beside that, I'm only half of what you knew. I haven't the strength to lift a book. Last week I took a boat in the Bois. I tried to pull the oars, little fresh-water oars like the spoons of a doll — and it wore me out. Just think how, when I was younger than Angelos, I pulled the two oars of our caïque twenty-five times the size of these boats here . . .

I have so aged that I look with curiosity at the girls who aim to flirt with me. You ask about my poetry — let it go to the devil — not half a line came out of my head all summer. How could I write when I was so full of anxiety. . . . The day before yesterday, during a gloomy sunset, I was thinking about a girl I would have liked if I were still a boy, a rather pretty little face, somewhat melancholy. I thought about my own youth, which had committed suicide needlessly, out of sheer stupidity. Tears came to my eyes, and some verses to my heart — without effort, like a forgotten song,

> On the lazy horizon a sail disappears,
> In the heavens a bird's wing is drowned . . . .

On the 19th of October George wrote to me to make me laugh, so he said, a funny story which had happened to an acquaintance. It was his own story. On a page from a notebook he teased his friend with these humorous lines:

> I loved her, I unloved her, and now I love her again.
> I was befuddled, unbefuddled, and now I'm befuddled again.
> Who knows if my head will ever be free
> And my ravelled out pocket be sewed up again?

But then he became serious, with a translation of Keats' *La Belle Dame Sans Merci*:

> I saw pale kings, and princes too,
>   Pale warriors, death-pale were they all;
> They cried — La Belle Dame Sans Merci
>   Hath thee in thrall!
> I saw their starved lips in the gloam . . . .

He had long been accustomed to talk to me about his inner life. I lived it with him. But he found his present situation ugly, and for a while he avoided telling me about it.

Every so often this woman would come back, with all her power, to disturb him. Then his soul grew dark, and his thought dried up because of her infidelities. But his concern for art did not leave him. He was working on a translation of Theodore de Banville's *Aesop*. He had heard it performed at the Comédie with De Max. He thought the Greekness of the work might be good for him.

The 19th of October

I wrote to you yesterday, and I write again today to answer your last note. You see I do not delay. 'Answer' is a manner of speaking only, because frankly I haven't yet read it — I am stuck on the first page: 'Dear George: It is late evening. Today is the first stormy day, the first day of autumn — you know the kind of storm which shakes the whole house.' I don't know — is it the way you write, or the mauve color of your paper which brings so many memories of childhood to my mind. . . . And now I am alone in Paris, without desire, without love, nothing remains to show me that I have a heart except that sometimes I weep when I write to you. But not today . . . . Isn't that you sitting there in the chair opposite me? We are talking about many things. I am reading you my poetry. I am going to translate *Aesop*. It should be beautiful in Greek. Until now, no one has translated it. To be sure, it is difficult, but never mind. With patience it will come about.

He certainly wanted to write something original, but as he said to me later, he could not write in the old forms during a revolutionary era comparable to that of 1930. Work, study, inspiration were needed. This thought constantly gnawed at him.

During his melancholia, he would take refuge in the cemetery of Père Lachaise . . .

> When I came to the grave of Musset, I read the epitaph he had written in his youth for someone else, little knowing that they would one day carve it in stone for his own grave:
> 'Dear friends, when I am gone. . . .'

I believed that if I were near George, the two of us together would be strong. At that moment I was sure of it. Alone as he was, at the mercy of that harsh woman's savagery, he didn't know where to take shelter. He had lost his milieu. He looked back on our childhood years as if he were Methuselah. He remembered September in Skala when yellow leaves piled up around the wheel well. He remembered the prayer we said to the Virgin. He so much needed love.

But how could I help him, how could I give him a little warmth during that first winter of his stay abroad? I wrote to him as often as I could. In spite of all my efforts, there was a childish naiveté about my letters, as he suggests:

20 October 1918

You can't imagine with what pleasure I receive your letters. . . . Go on writing whatever comes to you, words out of the air, because often those words have greater depth. In Paris it is more and more wintry. Day before yesterday, all day fog. You couldn't see a man two meters from you; as for sun, let me not speak of that wreck, a parody of a sun. I recalled the poet's line:

Un soleil fichu comme un crachat d'estaminet.

29 October 1919

. . . but again, from time to time, there are some days not like the others, days that turn one's eyes to the soul and to the past. It is like being in a crowd where some noble faces force us to take notice of them. I don't know if other people feel this sentiment. I don't know whether you understand what I am trying to say when I write that. Look — the last days of October: the fog thickens; it snows leaves all day long. Now that my body begins to feel cold, my spirit also, in a kind of telepathy (if that word expresses what I mean), feels its loneliness, senses its chill, and I understand that it is looking for some fire of compassion, some fire of love, to warm me up lest I freeze stiff. Because let me tell you, however young a man is, however strong, he gets tired of being disillusioned. . . . In one of your last letters you write, 'If a stranger were to read your letter, he would find it hard to believe that you will soon be twenty, that you are handsome, and that you are in Paris.' This phrase of yours made me think . . . It's true, old chap — this girl is right to speak to me this way. Why am I not enjoying my youth? Now I see that it is impossible for me to enjoy it. What do you want me to say — . . . first of all, little sister, I am terribly tired, and this is due to my character, for I realize that I have always asked for too much. What I would like to have is just a little love without affectation and diplomacy, a little sweetness, a little kindness, but in this world this is so much that I shall never be able to attain it.

And now, after half a century, I reread these words with the old sorrow. The child whom we call poet wrote them to me. A plant uprooted from the warm earth, and tossed on the rocks.

Paris, November 16, 1919

A week ago today, little sister, I wrote you a letter in

French. I did this with the idea that it would be good practice for both of us if we were to correspond in French. Forget it. When I re-read it, I found it so cold that I tore it up. After all, I love our own dear language . . . and only to you can I write as I want to write. . . . It snows, snows without stopping, and these white clumps keep falling, regularly, one after the other, and you say to yourself they will never end. It is as if, up in the sky, they have gathered together all the shrouds of the dead, and they are dropping them, rag by rag, to make one huge shroud to enshroud the whole earth.

Monday — Thank you very much for your patience in writing me at such length and so beautifully. My only happy moments are when I receive your letters. . . .

Searching along the banks of the Seine, among thousands of dusty pamphlets, he found one with an interesting title: *Le Quartier Latin*. It contained a simple, artless poem which impressed him. He copied it out for me.

Sur les grands monts faisant cligner notre paupière
De fiers sculpteurs sculptent des coeurs qui sont en pierre.
Au souterrain du noir Satan, roi des enfers,
Des forgerons forgent des coeurs qui sont en fer.
Dans les forêts parmi les troncs faisant un choix
De forts tourneurs tournent des coeurs qui sont en bois.
Mais dans le ciel, dans le ciel pur, dans le ciel clair
Des anges blonds forment des coeurs qui sont en chair.
De tous ces coeurs Dieu fait un choix, puis il les place
A tout hasard, un par poitrine dans la masse.
Or, on dit, que par un destin peu généreux
Les coeurs en pierre, en bois, en fer sont seuls heureux.

It snowed and snowed in Paris.
Then came the holidays, the first holidays when we were separated. With difficulty he saved a little money and sent me the gift of a charming little beaded bag.

Paris, 8 December 1919
I am very happy that you liked the little bag I sent you. I am only sorry that there was nothing left so that I could send something to Papa. But I said: first children and then the grownups.

On Christmas Eve with a vague sadness he wrote me his good wishes. But I was taken by surprise when the postman brought me the picture of a small girl. It had hung on the wall of his room, and I had liked it. For some moments I stood, as if hypnotized, looking with brimming eyes at the picture.

1920

At that time I did not yet understand.
George was, by nature, a tragic person. This was his greatness. This was his strength. He was cruelly affected by the tragic dimension of events. Whether these events concerned his person, or his country, or mankind, he could not escape from the very heart of their suffering. He felt their most imperceptible vibrations. I saw him tossed in the whirlpool of his personal tragedy, and of the cosmic one. From one moment to the next, the vortex threatened to suck him down. There is a supreme point of sensitivity from which a man can be saved only by his own greatness. Otherwise, life is consumed by life. I think that if George had not lived under the law of poetic expression, he would have committed suicide or he would have been killed for an idea. In his letters, in his conversation, the phrase often occurred:
"Tell me — am I to blame?"
Often, when he was harried by time, by debt, by the specter of the dead fatherland, by injustice, I would see in him the figure of Orestes with his snakes. He was always going back to himself and digging up his personal responsibility.
"Tell me, little sister — am I to blame?"
But who is to blame when evil happens, since all of us are living the same moment of evil? This was the birth trauma which would never come to an end.

In so far as he could, George avoided taking part in politics and international problems. For him it was impossible to depend on any organization.
"I work only at what I can do," he said to me sadly. But deep within him, through his poetry, there operated a tragic sense of mutual responsibility.
I sensed this when, after the Liberation from the Germans,

some lines by George came back to me, turning the knife in the wound of our servitude.

> Now I cannot read further
> Because they tied you with chains
> Because they pierced you with the spear . . .

At one time I had believed that all those ghosts I saw on sleepless nights, all those suppressed tears, had made me invulnerable! Would every execution, every imprisonment remain forever branded on my flesh?

> Who is that behind who commands and kills us?
> Flowing blood,
> Words, texts, gramophones running down.

A profound awe with regard to this sense of the tragic prevented him from expressing it directly. His poetry continued along side of this feeling, but we see that it cast its heavy shadow.

> And if I speak to you in tales and parables,
> it is because it sounds sweeter to you,
> and the horror is not talked about because it is alive.

And one morning when we chanced on a ceremony at the Tomb of the Unknown Soldier:

> A moment of silence, is it the price of a life?

One noon in 1970, George and I were sitting in the National Garden watching the peacock opening and closing his wings. He spoke to me about his journal. I asked him:

"Perhaps you'd like me to give you your letters? They might be useful to you, to fill in gaps in your memory."

"No, you keep them," he answered. "You gave me the ones I wanted. These are your own. I wrote them for you. I lived them with you. Perhaps someday they will help you to convey that period."

Then he added sadly,

"Fruitful years those were because, as you know, when the first green sprouts, the whole work has been done."

How can I convey that period? And what became of my letters? This is the great loss which perplexes me. They would be so valuable to me. Now with effort I dig into memory.

I remember well my passion for poetry, and the faith I had in George. The matters which would prevent him from writing were things I could not understand. I was entirely of one mind — I wanted to help him. A desire stronger than the instinct of self-preservation. George himself reminded me of some of my phrases: "If now no one understands us, perhaps those who come after will understand us better" and "You have no patience with God; the hermit does not see the light immediately."

I was indeed a very young girl. But quickly, week by week, month by month, year by year, my faith in George matured as I matured. Our essential years are from twelve to twenty-two. That is when the spring within us rises. We are confident in our pride. Sidney Keyes, killed when he was twenty-one, said it to us in his fine poem, *The Wilderness*:

> So knowing my youth, which was yesterday,
> And my pride which shall be gone tomorrow.

Later the relentless need for conformity attacks us, at close range, insidious, sure. We react with less anger, we accept. Do we really know what we lose by this acceptance? If we gain anything, only God knows. The trees dry up in the North Wind. But the first form which Nature gave them determines their value.

Something else George found refreshing in me was my doubt. I would call it my innocence. I remember that he pointed it out to me then in various ways:

"A thought, an impression — the instant you question it, whatever is false and expedient brushes off like dust. We start again from the beginning."

And in later years he said one day,

"You are like the craftsman cleaning old Byzantine icons. The sweetest face emerges in the midst of living gold."

All events are in some measure a personal matter. To some they mean nothing, to others they mean death.

Paris, 4 February 1920
The holidays are over, dear little sister. . . . Now 'The leaves have turned yellow, and it's autumn in my heart.' Nothing, absolutely nothing arouses my interest. I don't know what evil eye is eyeing me. I am terribly melancholy,

terribly sad. Tears come without reason. Then too I have a mania for the old times when I am most in the present, and I whisper lines which I haven't the courage to complete — such as:

>When I remember doors that closed,
>and handkerchiefs that waved,
>the tears that were dried,
>and the boats that set out. . . .
>And my poor youth now turned into age.

The day before yesterday, last Sunday, pitch-like fog. At a corner of the street, a circle of people, where you couldn't distinguish man from woman — and in the middle, two violins playing a waltz. I watched with nose pressed to the windowpane and thought to myself:

>The violins are whining at the corner of the street
>In the fog in the darkness,
>And in their weeping there is something of mine
>Which the wind brought me with the cold . . .

This too passes, and I count the days until I see you all again, when you will tell me again how you love me. And I hope — I use the word without knowing what it means — and I dream of the hours I shall spend with you in our country, because I am tired of the hypocrisy of human beings, and of life abroad . . .

On my name day, St. John's, he wished me the quiet joy of contentment. And I wrote back

"George, what have you written?"

Like a musical refrain, with the simplicity of a child, in every letter I raised this appeal.

9 January 1920
You asked me to send you my poems. . . . I'm sending you two more . . . I'm not telling you that I have written poems which satisfy my aesthetic sense. It is so difficult, it requires such labor, and with my law studies it is impossible for me to do anything serious. But I see that you insist, and so I am explaining to you. When you left me, I was still under Suzanne's influence . . . I had lost the sense of the beautiful, naturally I mean the inner sense. Certainly I had always loved poetry, but I loathed feeling because feeling had tortured me. In that wretched life I was leading, all my powers of heart and soul were drugged . . . Perhaps I could write in French, but I don't want to do that because I

love Greece. In Greek it is impossible for me to say what I want to say. . . . Moreover, with poetry, with art in general, it is not enough just to write. You must create a tradition, and on this you must proceed. . . .
Art is a road plotted by artists. In Greece the artists are telegraph poles standing beside the road, each one alone. That is why each one must work at it from every aspect. That is what I count on doing if I live long enough. For the present it is enough for me to feel and to make notes. . . .

In spite of all his attempts to reassure himself, he was tortured by the attraction of writing in French. And it was natural. He was studying in a French university in the heart of France. He was studying, reading, enjoying French writers. He was going regularly to the matinées at the Comédie Française. When he left the theater, the excitement remained, and he continued reciting the lines in his little room. He attended the anniversary of the battle of *Hernani*, in connection with which he wrote: "Marvelous performance. Hall packed. Mad applause. Surely you know how much I wished you were beside me. . . ."

He knew the scene of the portraits by heart. He gave his own performance in the little salon of our house in Athens, pointing to the portraits of his grandfather, his father, and himself.

He criticized the works he was reading:
I enclose a poem by Henry Bataille for you. As an idea it has something, but I find its execution poor. Versified prose. . . .

He savored the French language as does the cultivated Frenchman. The French expression suited him, with its clarity, its infinitely original nuances as they appear in the great masterpieces. Only this expression could serve the Greek sense of measure which he carried inside him. Jean Moréas fascinated him. With such a foundation and such a model, the temptation to write in French was strong. To say nothing of his erotic disposition which always drew him to French women and to those who spoke French. Love easily becomes a country.

His only wholehearted exercise in our language was our

letters. And his yearning for Greece was even more vital than his yearning for poetry.

He wrote and tore up rather than be carried away. He was trying to find at last his own personal rhythms and means of expression. He had a vivid sense of what was living in our language and of what had died. He fought hard, disdaining the easy way.

He asked me to send him Katsimbalis' translation of *Omar Khayyam*, *The Scarabs* of Gryparis, *Language and Life* by Yannidis, *Altars* of Palamas, the work of Crystallis.

In imagination I followed him faithfully throughout his poetic peregrinations. I sent him whatever he asked of me, and whatever I heard of as being noteworthy at the moment. I passionately wanted him to write in Greek.

I expected that we would be together again soon. A justifiable hope, because Mother would never allow a year to pass without seeing her older son. And surely she would take me with her.

But I was troubled by his letter of March 14. The greater part was written in French. Then

. . . Today I received your letter. Thank you. How much good you did me. . . .

Since the Student Association had proposed that he give a lecture on Moréas, he added,

Tu sais ça m'embête de me prostituer de la sorte devant tant de monde. . . .

I would try to describe to him the Greece where I was living, the flowering trees, the open sails on the Bay of Phaleron. So, in spite of his youth, in spite of Paris, he was possessed by a longing to return, by a nostalgia for the years in Athens.

Paris, 20 March, 1920, Saturday
Little sister, thank you for making me see some Greek almond trees from your window. Here too spring is opening up. Here too the trees are in blossom, but I miss Greek almond trees. How well I remember past years in Athens. . . .

And in another letter a rather disturbing poem about the Virgin:

6 April 1920
O, Holy Virgin, when I pray to you
I see my mother
O, Holy Virgin, take pity on this pain
mad
hoarse
dense
this pain that eats my vitals.

O, Holy Virgin, You are kind,
toward You my sinful soul
turns and turns again for rest
but my timid eyes
are afraid, Blessed Lady,
to look at the majestic
the shining beauties of Heaven
they are afraid
and they waver.

Blessed Lady, take the form
the form I knew so well
silent
humble
On the altar-screen of the lonely chapel . . .

And at the end:
O, Holy Virgin,
let me die
let me be forgotten
— this is my plea, my only plea —
let me fade away
with my thrice-unworthy soul
at your holy knees,
compassionate, divine,
with my head on my mother's knee.

    The Fifteenth of August at Skala was there again in that poem — the great feast of the Virgin when miracles happened. Wave after wave of longing for his mother, for simple faith.
    From that moment I took courage and spoke to him comfortably about my religious concerns. Faith is like love: as it becomes deeper, it is entwined with a complex shyness.
    Later we spoke often about the sacred texts.

In 1961 I stayed a month with him at the Embassy in London. At that time he wanted to translate *Tobit*. We talked tirelessly about the Bible, about the redeeming value of the symbol. Later it was St. John who absorbed him. He approached every phrase of the *Apocalypse* with awe: "and in His mouth is found no guile" — "now was the wound of this death healed." Each one seemed the starting point for other writings. I try now to hear his voice again, but it escapes me.

It was during those days that I met Theodore Roethke, professor at the University of Washington. I liked his poems, and the question asked in the title of his volume *Where Do the Birds Die?* carried me to a winged end. Till then I had never thought that they too must die.

With sadness I left George and returned to Athens. The life of the Greek capital seemed to me like the galleys. Political battles were fierce. In a few months we were to have elections.

Almost all the letters which came from Paris in 1920 were addressed to me. Mother would ask:

"Is the boy well?" And when I would say to her, "Very well," she was happy. Father complained, however, that George did not write enough to him.

That year at Old Phaleron, Angelos was a great help. In the afternoon when we did not have lessons, we went walking together on the beaches nearby. The hour of sunset was beautiful. It gave us peace. I wrote to George about the beach at Skala, about the beach at Phaleron.

Now, at the hour of sunset, all the pains, all the nostalgia of those whom I have loved oppress me, torture me, more than they tortured them.

Dear God! How much I have still to say to my dead brother. How much devotion is left over!

But for him too:
> Tell me, little sister, talk to me about whatever was mine:
> The tiring climb up the old road,
> The boats, the fishing gear on the quiet beach.

Tell me, little sister, revive the old echoes;
The reeds, the wild-pistachio trees, the vineyards and the pines,
And the North Wind whistling at night against the windows,
Our laughter and songs on silvery evenings,
The prayer we said when we were small. . . .
Now above the reeds the crows are cawing,
Bad weather and dark nights press down
And the South winds break huge waves against the piers . . . .

Paris, 2 May 1920 — Sunday
A few days ago I answered Papa who grumbled because I didn't write to him: "What does it matter if you didn't receive a letter from me? Haven't you all been receiving letters? I have divided my correspondence with the family into three parts. To you I write about serious matters, to Mama about small questions, and to Ioanna, when I have nothing to write, I just fill the page." That's not quite true. To you I write seriously because I write the truth . . . Today is an important date for me — it's a year since you left. A year ago today I was watching the blood-red taillight of the train that was taking you away from me and disappearing into the darkness. It may be comical for me to write this to you, but it is serious because it is the truth. That parting from all of you caused a big reaction in me. . . . Sometime when I see you, I will explain to you how for a whole week I was distracted. Only later did I realize how tired I had been. A new period started in my life — perhaps it is closing now. From then on I experienced many sensations which I had not known before. From then on I understood what Mama meant to me, what my little sister meant, what my home meant, and, more important, how very much I love all of you. I write this to you because I think I am facing a critical situation which could have consequences. . . . You see, little one, man is not a machine. He needs a little love around him when he loves. . . . In July I take the examinations — whether or not I will succeed I don't yet know. With God's help I am studying as much as I can and doing all I can so as to be able to see all of you in summer . . . .

The past, that part of it which we love, has a living reality —

as if nailed into our being. One part leaves its sorrow, another its warmth. George was going through his most difficult days. And I with him. His law studies were a martyrdom for both of us.

> 15 May 1920
> You are very lenient in your criticism of the poems I sent you. I assure you I felt the one about Panaghia very deeply. I had had it in my mind ever since the Fifteenth of August last year. I succeeded in writing it on Great Wednesday from 1:30 to 3:30 a.m. It is full of mistakes. It is not as I want it, but to write it well would require study that I cannot afford now . . . .

Later, various hasty notes, on old scraps of paper, in the midst of his studying for the law examinations. Every night I prayed ardently that he should succeed in his examination, that we should somehow survive that terrible year.

The summer of 1920 came about as we expected. George passed his examinations successfully. Mother and I set out for Paris. Angelos stayed on with Uncle Socrates. They all loved him dearly, and he was happy with his cousins, Aleko, George, Stephen. As for me, in spite of the great expense of the journey, neither Mother nor Father ever considered depriving me of the joy of seeing George again.

But how thin and pale he was! Mother wept when she saw him.

He had everything ready for us. He had taken two rooms on the Boulevard St. Germain. For Mother, who did not go about easily, there was a room with a balcony on the street. Secretly George had taken a third room for himself. When we were settled, he took me aside, and said quickly:

"You must help me get away from Suzanne's pension. Otherwise that story will never come to an end. You can say that it will be better for me to be in the same house with you. With the reduction which they will make if there are three of us, the financial difference will be small."

I was flattered to be part of the plot. Everything went as we planned. Mother agreed immediately.

Years have passed but for me it is as if that moving were taking place now. We did not know how many times we covered the road between the two rooms. With every book, every picture frame, every trifle that we carried in our hands, I felt I was saving George from some terrible danger. And I was proud to feel heroic. He had taken me into his secret. He had asked me to help him.

His new room was larger, more agreeable than the old one. We decorated it together. I thought it was handsome, and furthermore, George seemed pleased.

I kept watching the joy in his eyes.

All his group gathered around us. Mother adopted them. She had it well organized. Every evening, late, after the theatre, she offered tea to the company. George was doubly happy to see that his friends felt the same reassuring warmth in her presence.

We were free from the obligation of studies, and again the two of us were together. We strolled on the banks of the Seine. We sat in the garden of Notre Dame de Paris. He told me the whole story of Suzanne — even worse than I had imagined it. I was speechless. How was it possible? It was all incomprehensible to me. He read me his poems, some finished, some unfinished. He talked to me about Paris, about the history of every corner. And I too learned to love this city, to know it.

In August the great heat began. Then the whole group left Paris and went to Normandy. There for a fortnight we explored the seashore, baked ourselves in the sun, and recited Rimbaud's *Bateau ivre*. George liked it so much that he copied it all out for me.

He always felt well near the sea. He enjoyed reliving the personal experiences of the past. The sea was his milieu.

When we returned to Paris the theatres had reopened. All the performances attracted us. Where should we go first? In order to get cheap seats, we stood in endless queues. But we didn't mind. The time passed quickly with our discussions, our jokes, our witticisms. Finally, outside the railing of the queue with our tickets in our hands, as nimble as deer, we scrambled up the six floors of the theatre to take over the gallery.

It was a good summer. Mother was happy. Little by little George became himself again. Suzanne no longer concerned him, at least, so it appeared. He never spoke of her. He read to me for hours. Sometimes Apollinaire, Lautréamont, Laforgue, and sometimes his own poems which he had written in the night.

The considerable effort to unlearn the romantic expression that had influenced us became a continuing inner struggle.

We all talked about the frugal form. But this is the most difficult rung on the unscalable ladder of Jacob. So unscalable that often you will lose hope. To achieve this frugality, you must stifle the passion in your feeling, you must work at it with effort, you must discipline it, and still it will tear you apart. Like Prometheus, you will struggle to bridle the wild horses and the winds. If you succeed, perhaps you will arrive at good art.

One day autumn came. These fruitful holidays came to an end. Again the "musts" began. Time to go back to Athens, to rejoin Angelos in our home, to begin our studies.

George seemed to me stronger.

And so there was again the parting. Love is a haunted place where at night frightening ghosts of separations move to and fro. Insuperable tragedy — this tearing apart of pulsing life. We are possessed and dominated by the absence of the one we love. This bitter experience first came to me when I was a small girl with George. It has followed me throughout my life.

George's friend Argyris concealed his poverty and his melancholy under uninterrupted joking. To dispel the dark mood of the farewell, he wrote to me, describing the last gathering of the group:

"The architect was studying the future position of his ego . . . Brother George dramatically recited many poems, all in one gulp, and everyone with closed mouth shouted bravo . . ."

And from George:

13 October 1920

Yesterday was the third time I received something from you, dear little one, and I answer only today . . . The evening you left, we made up two groups, in one Pittakos, Poniridis, and I — all the rest in the other. We sauntered the length of the Seine. Then the black hours began to dance around me again, the same dance they were dancing before you came . . .

He went on to write about Suzanne again, and in French. It hurt him to speak of her in Greek. He had met her in the bus. She greeted him, he raised his hat to her, and went with his friend to sit in second class. She, *fière comme une courtisane*, seated herself in first class. This encounter upset him. He despised this woman, but every time he met her, he was disturbed.

On the 14th of October, he was moved, as he often was, to describe our parting and give news of our group in some casual verse:
Thursday —
> When you went away, you left me alone
> in this deceiving world,
> in the cold of exile.
> Loneliness and boredom, like a dark beast,
> gnaw at my life, hour by hour,
> day by day. . . .

In Athens, one evening that autumn, Mother took me with her to the Hotel Minerva. She wanted to visit a sick friend. She left me in the salon and went upstairs. Sitting on a sofa in the corner, I looked idly out the window on to Stadium Street. I felt someone looking at me. He sat down opposite me and began to sketch. I thought for a moment that he was a painter. Presently Mother returned. The unknown gentleman greeted her, and she said:

"Ioanna, Mr. Philyras."

Romos Philyras came forward and politely gave me the paper he was holding in his hands.

"A poem for you," he said.

> To Miss Ioanna Seferiadis —
> In the autumn dusk, her little belt
> tight around her young body,
> she curls up on the sofa, not a sound
> escapes her soft velvet lips.
>
> Dark and piercing, round eyes
> look out at the street, abstracted,

> dreamily building palaces
> to enclose their own desire.
>
> One foot, lightly, magically
> extends its softness on the other,
> nor would the pomegranate, falling from the tree
> on to silk, strike more gently.
>
> She scarcely breathes, and only the hint of a sigh
> stirs the tranquil September afternoon,
> and a hand slowly raised to her eyes
> in a fleeting movement seeks to find
> what uneasiness is knocking at her heart.
>
> Of this You know nothing,
> but a magic breeze brings to the soul
> the peace of innocence.
> For me, pure magic. A vision. A holy moment.
>
> Romos Philyras

I read it. I was much flattered. It was the first poem written for me by a stranger. Naturally I sent it to George, who, in turn, responded in verse:

> I like Philyras' poem very much,
> good rhymes, fine lines, and overflowing feeling.
> Sometimes his words stand up like tapers,
> but other times his lines roll on without sense.
> I should like them more if they were worked over,
> more sensible, more closely knit.

Of course, neither George nor I took this doggerel seriously. It was a game, an exercise, perhaps an attempt to amuse me. And the verses did not at all represent what he really thought.

24 October 1920

Come for a little while to my room, little sister, you still have time. Sit down so that we can talk. Sit just there, with the light lowered. How did you like the concert? Wasn't it beautiful? That Beethoven *First* — wonderful! How small we are beside them — and they such giants! Strange, but I recall now something I read in a book: one time they asked Beethoven why he composed, and do you know what he answered — "I compose because what I have inside me must come out." He was certainly an unhappy man, but he was fortunate in being able to bring out what he had inside him. And do you know what is my misfortune? I cannot bring out what I have, and it gnaws at me. Never mind. Let us hope that some day it will come out as I want it to be. Are you cold? I'll close the window. . . . I must say that Poniridis is a great soul, a great worker, and really the only man I enjoy being with. We meet from time to time — we talk about art; we discuss the matter of honesty in feelings, and a whole heap of beautiful things. Then the others go away, and we remain alone. The hours pass quickly as we walk without knowing where we are going, two or three hours perhaps, and we can go on together till morning . . .

Father was preoccupied. His anxiety over the November elections was evident. He walked up and down in his study, silent, or perhaps saying to himself, "If Venizelos loses, from that moment we are sunk. Perhaps somehow we shall be able to avoid the reckoning." Then again a wave of optimism would come over him, and he would say to Mother: "After the elections we shall fortify the borders with firm guarantees from the Great Powers."

In November 1920, Venizelos lost the elections.

It was a day of great regret. But for Father it had endless consequences. I saw it in the depth of his eyes, chagrin for the people who had not understood, a feeling that the Greek cause had come to an impasse.

Informed people felt enormous anxiety in that historic hour. They knew well the fluctuating climate of European opinion. Deceitful powers, barbarous powers, were undermining Greece. After the elections, the rescue of Ionia through the Treaty of Sèvres was almost impossible.

I could not understand why Father, normally so active, sat motionless for hours, thinking fixedly, about what I could not imagine. Was he looking for a road out? The struggle to triumph over fate by logical arguments was a nightmare I could not conceive.

With his Venizelist colleagues he was driven from the University. It was not this that wounded him most. It is hard to be victimized, but it is even harder to feel a frightening responsibility. Father was certainly not responsible for the turn of events, but the damage could be irrevocable for millions of souls, and every man of his generation was obliged to feel some sense of responsibility. He abandoned Greece and established himself in Paris. Each time his own country wounded him, he took refuge in France. The university figures there esteemed him more highly than did those of his own country. And thus he could better help his own land. Angelos and I stayed with Mother in Athens to continue our studies.

In Paris, Father set himself to follow George's life closely. He realized beyond doubt that what occupied his son above all was literature and poetry. At eight in the morning he went to George's room to find him sleeping in a heavy odor of tobacco smoke. This was natural, since he had passed the night with thoughts and rhymes on the bridges of the Seine. The ashtrays were full of cigarette butts. Open law books were marked up with verses. Papers strewn about with poems scratched out, then rewritten.

Their first quarrels began. Father wanted his son to get up early. George wanted to sleep late:

"The stars of the night inspire me. The morning stars put me to sleep," he said in his defense.

Father never smoked, and he did not want his son to smoke.

As has happened often with fathers, from Ajax to those of the present day, he made his own life the model. When Father was studying at Aix, every year he passed his examinations with honors. He too wrote poetry, but only during his hours of leisure. George's passion for art frightened him. He was much worried about the future. Now, after the elections, he wanted above all to see George independent.

How could he understand that galloping impulse his son was struggling to discipline? How could he understand those intertwined circles — feeling, idea, imagination, technique, language — which George was supposed to sweep aside so that he could study judicial matters?

Understanding between them was impossible.

By its very nature, creativity requires concentration and patience. Harmony of opinion is difficult to achieve, among those who love us but do not understand us, as well as among strangers.

In the winter of 1920, when George was burdened with political and erotic disenchantment and with Father's demands, he was granted a respite of happy stability.

Deserted in wintry Paris, he became acquainted with a charming Norwegian girl, Kirsten. Six letters told me the whole story of their sentimental attachment. He sent me her photographs. She was very beautiful. She loved him. She suffered with him. She did not ask him for money, she did not ask him for marriage. "Before she came," he told me, "I was sad. Now I am certainly not merry, but when I am near her, I feel good."

They saw each other every day.

George's idyll filled me with joy. After so much gloom, a little sunshine. I was grateful to the girl. I wrote to her and sent her little gifts.

In spite of this, the depression which the November elections had left on our home was unrelieved.

25 December 1920, Sunday
I have time today to write to you, that is to say, time to send you a letter, because I am always writing to you, beloved little sister. I see that you are worried and pessimistic, and this worries me . . .

And then he returned to his *Aesop*. I had read it, and had been greatly disappointed that they had not played it during the summer when I was in Paris. George had translated many lines, but he had not managed to write them to me:

'Et la femme est bizarre et l'homme n'est pas beau.' Tell me how you feel about the play. I wish very much that you were here to see De Max, and especially when he pulls out the irons, you should hear him:
　'Enfin voici les fers, qui m'ont meurtri, les fers
　　dont la sinistre voix parle des maux soufferts.'
It was superb. He spoke the lines in a voice which had become iron and hit with his hands the chains that he had taken out of the chest:
　'A présent je suis libre et puissant sans les chaînes;
　　mais j'ai subi ces fers et j'ai porté ces chaines.'
How many times during hours of slavery and hours of freedom I have thought of those lines of Aesop!

I have given up my translation for the time being, due to the pressure of studies. I plan to take it up again when I am at Skala in summer . . .

Always the hope of returning to Skala. This repressed yearning would pursue him all his life.

Kirsten went home again.

2 January 1921
On the eve of her departure, we wept together all night long; next morning, a yellowish day; departure, funeral, and then the void, the pitiless void, unrelenting, possessing me wholly since that final moment. Little sister, beloved little sister, you understand the days which I have been passing through and am passing through now as I face a cold, frozen photograph — and hate it because it seems to mock me . . .

He found everything unbearable — the University, the pension because it reminded him of her, his friends.

How much I owe to my love for her! She took me back to poetry, to what I adore. Everything that the other blonde had been destroying for two years . . . with her goodness she built it again because she was good. I do not recall that she ever made me feel bitter. . . . She asked me to teach her Greek so that she could call me by the names you call me by, you who love me. . . . If only I had not before me the red gowns of the University, and my father's professorial chair . . . Why am I not a bastard? a foundling? And now:

    Alone with your picture —
    I have strewn flowers on our bed . . .
    miserable fate.

His despair was overwhelming.

1921

The despair of this parting did not last long. A brief tie was severed in the light of a yellow day. But George had come to believe again in the goodness of woman, to believe in himself. He felt free again, he regained his balance, and once more he could reconsecrate himself to his great passion, poetry.

> 4 January 1921
> Cold as ice, but I love you, and I warm myself through my memories of you. I write to you, and I feel somewhat better . . . Everything I see provides me with a subject, a sense of tragedy which I want to express. Unfortunately, I have only to put ideas on paper and I put them to sleep, perhaps never to be wakened. For an idea, once it has seen the light of day and quivered with life, has to be tied down, else it is lost forever. My drawer has become a cemetery. Every day I bury little bodies of babies who died when they had taken only two or three breaths of air . . .

Furthermore he began again to wrestle with his great affliction, self-distrust. He was always his own severest critic.

> When all is said and done, I haven't much talent, much merit. But what a curious type I am among men! From morning to night, I think of nothing except poetry. For me, everything else is marginal, even though I accomplish nothing, nothing, nothing — but if only you knew how I would write if I were a poet! . . . I never get past the halfway mark, even in my defects. I have neither a single real vice nor a single real virtue. How symbolic the date of my birth (February 29), that extra day in a bastard month . . . Don't laugh when you read this — I will hear you if you do . . .

He asked me to send him Heine's *Litany* as translated by Angelos Vlachos. Little by little he was building his own language. He searched his favorite Greek texts for words and syntax which he could make his own.

That winter it seemed that my letters were becoming more mature, and they were helpful to him. At least, that is what his letters to me indicate. I don't remember what I wrote to him. I remember more or less what I thought about things, from notes, from events.

I took to pencil and paper to relieve the chaos inside me.

What tortured me, less then, but later intensely, was the idea of Time. Surely God must have found it hard to conceive this complicated, fluid element of the human condition, so mysterious in its countless influences. The idea of time would not leave me alone. I felt my obligation to it all day long. Often I stood before it, empty, chilled, weak, begging it to go away. But if ever I wasted it, I was burdened with guilt. Some times I wanted to ignore it. Then again I would embrace it passionately, spurning trivial activities so as to make the most of it. Every interruption in this absolute relation between us was a rude awakening. But if grace was given to me to catch in words some moment of truth, then time accomplished its purpose. Recognition, glory were secondary matters to which I was indifferent.

I wrote to George, "Once the poet delivers himself of his work, it becomes a stranger to him. Fortunate he is if it enters into the great current to help sustain mankind. Its creator can then sleep the sleep of indifference."

At that time I first read *Erotokritos*, the great Cretan epic. The poetic rhythm of the tale gripped me. I remember that momentarily I was able to dispel George's complaining with Nena's lines:

> And was it for the throb of the lute
> and the sweetness of a song
> that you fettered and enslaved your beautiful youth?

14 January 1921

It is our New Year. Midnight, dear little sister. The best gift anyone could give me was the note from you. I read it until now I know it by heart . . . if we were together, you could tell me lots of things, you the only person who can speak to me and I can hear. . . .

Later he asked me for an article by some critic or other. "The poor fellow does not understand at all that a literary work is good quite apart from whether it kills or saves . . ."

Coming to terms with other people was hard for us — as though we were living within a glass bell. Also I was an odd sort of girl. My natural melancholy was increased by my secret, the terrible fear that George would commit suicide. From the time when he sent me *The Last Words of a Suicide*, this thought was always with me. How could I tell whether he had really taken that decision? Perhaps it was a theme he was working over in his poetry. That might give him some psychic relief. When he arrived at the ultimate point of taking leave of life, perhaps he would reconsider it with some affection. But there were moments when I was seized by panic. Would he do something mad in order to escape from mediocrity?

Now again he wanted to write *Variations sur le suicide*. He had not yet found a way to express this title in Greek:

". . . but it's got to be something first-rate. . . ."

At that time his friend, George Vaphiopoulos, was returning to Greece. They had had good times together, and George had been in love with one of Kirsten's friends. My brother said goodbye to him in a ballad warm with their common memories, with his own longing for home.

> You who go as a pilgrim
> to the fires of home,
> you who go back to the hearth
> to drink in love and life . . .
> Don't forget your old friends
> when you go home.
> When you hear the twilight song
> on the ridges of Old Morea,
> when the land is numbed
> at the hour of sunset,
> the branches of the trees will tell you
> of two girls whom you saw and I saw . . .
> Ask the North Wind about them
> when you go home.
> Envoi:
> Master George, cradle in your heart
> some of that radiance

> we saw together one evening . . .
> when you go home.
> If you were here, I would tell you a lot about all this, but at this moment the reaction is killing me. I have so much inside my head which no one understands . . . absolutely no one. You must know, little sister, how much I love you to be able to write all this. You are almost my child — more mine than are the children of all the fathers in the world . . . I am telling you all this so that someday you will know me. . . .

He wanted to give up his legal studies to devote himself only to poetry. His model at this time was Jean Moréas. He too had struggled on foreign soil to give form to his soul's fantasies.

I was frightened about George. I saw him being battered on the rocks. How sharply thought can cut!

> 22 January 1921
> Alone, all alone I am drenched in blood
> from the nails of pain . . .
> mankind is crushed by ice . . .

He wrote verse as he spoke, without effort. But they were lines he did not think well of, unpolished, romantic.

His tormented figure haunted me. Inexperienced as I was, I plunged myself wholly into his suffering and wrestled with his agony. At that very moment George might be finding release in some good lines, but distance prolonged our every sensation and continued to cast its gloom. As he wrote then:

> This longing for something which is not one's country or for a woman who is not a lover. . . . If I could open my heart, I think there would be written there on one side inevitable separation, on the other impossible love, and in between, unattainable beauty . . . .

And there were more verses: new petitions to the Virgin came to him.

> And all the days that have passed, mute,
> And all the days that are coming, filled
> with false suns,
> with tears I faced them.
> With tears I wait for the others.

You see, I opened my heart for your name day. I kiss you, and lock it up again.

His letters which I awaited so eagerly opened up a burning question inside me. Why was he so tormented, so warped? Without any external misfortune to serve as the cause, I felt that my own hold on life was slackening. I prayed before the old icon of the Virgin to which years of intense devotion had imparted much compassion and tenderness. But in the state I was in then, I was permeated with unbelief and even She had lost her divinity. I was alone, suspended in mid-air. No one shared my view of George. Not even Mother, though she adored him. At school we had studied Plato's *Apology*. A passage I had remembered and noted down concerned his idea of the poet: "Then I knew that, not by wisdom do poets write poetry, but by some genius and inspiration, like diviners and soothsayers." So why shouldn't George obey his nature? I remembered again his line, "Mediocrity freezes me."

He met briefly a beautiful girl from Athens.

She was good for me, but all these Ophelias wound me and sweetly bloody the stream of my soul.

I note this because of the Greek word γλυκοματώνω (to cause a sweet flow of blood).

That winter of 1921 we lived in Parnis Street. When father left the University and went to Paris, I moved my bed to the library. Then for the first time I sensed the great value of privacy. I enjoyed this fruitful freedom. No one knew when I turned off my light. I have always believed in night, the source of absolute silence. In this remote room of the sleeping house, I was writing, and reading aloud poems I loved. Those were the nights when I discovered Baudelaire. Fruitful emotions. For years I could not escape his fascination. All my books, even my law books later, were inscribed with his lines. I learned him by heart.

At that time I also read Moréas. If someone wanted to give me a present, it was often a small volume of verse from the Lilliputian Library. I still have Angelos' gift to me on my name day that year: *Les Destinées* by Alfred de Vigny. I very much wanted closer communication with Angelos, but Mother would not allow it.

"Don't distract him from finishing his school. You are, all three, daydreamers. You are a girl and will end up getting married, but the boys will have to work."

On my part, I felt that we did not have the right to be mediocre. To be sure, diplomas were indispensable so that we could earn our daily bread, but they were not the real substance of life. Beyond them lay the real values — beauty, truth, poetry, sacrifice.

George was being consumed by the flame of his sensibility. When this feeling is present in a man, he will either die or become great.

Some of his friends were publishing a periodical, *Vomos*. They insisted that they must publish something by George. What he had written seemed to him unfinished. Finally he gave in and let them have three pieces, all from '18 and '19.

> Old-fashioned and clumsy. . . . At least this can be said of me: I am not taken in by flattery. . . .

His pen name was George Skaliotis. He made up his mind that these would be the last. He did not want to begin with scattered publications. He always held to his dream of printing in modest format a minimum number of copies of such poems as had a certain musical utterance and true feeling.

> 27 January 1921
> I have so many things to tell you, all of them about myself, and all things which no one else understands. Thank you, little sister, for giving me some comfort. And even if my poetry is your only reason for writing to me as only you know how to write, that would really be sufficient consolation . . . It is because you understand much more than some so-called scholars and writers that I write to you as I do. . . .

And the letter continues with great tenderness.

Then he returned to his passion — the pursuit and the fascination of the word.

> . . . Yesterday reading Rodokanakis' book about Byzantium, I came on the word 'ἐρωτολογῶ (to speak about love). It set me dreaming. A single word can fascinate me as if it were a work of art. These lines came to me, and as usual, I am sending them to you:

> Bursts of love, words of love
> What echoes have stifled you?
> However shall I bring to an end
> The dirging dirge?
> If you only knew how much I have in my mind and how tormented I am in heart. And how much I love you . . . .

I am writing today at the end of May, 1973. In the darkness of night, the superfluous disappears. Heraclitus explains sleep wisely. It contributes to our fate, to our formation. A hush in an exotic forest where no bird sings. Of course anxieties may come knocking, but who will open the door? It was as if I had died. In the depths of a harbor, a half-sunken kingdom. A dim face looked at me, luminous, perhaps concealing a moon. Time had another aroma. In the mind, everything was blotted out, but in the soul — always that knot. Fine rain like light steps on the grass wakened me. It was you.

I felt grief watching beside me, that destined sorrow which life ends by accepting. Then silence again. I clung to it. It had the power of redemption. Such silence is rare, even in the deepest night. I listened to the silence. I let it bathe me as the sun of midday bathes the sea. Lest I lose even a moment of this gift. How long was it? The nightingale shook his wings. There was a quiver of joy in the feathered world. Then the noise of a cart tore harshly at my nerves. The bird of dawn began his words of love.

Ἐρωτολόγια. Love-words. The magic world of the word. I remember an evening in 1939 when George was seeing some friends in his home on Kydathineon Street. Henry Miller, Durrell, Katsimbalis were there. Once more they were discussing the burning subject: the word. Shyly, among those great men, I managed to say: "Bogus men debase words, and we who care for truth remain mute. If the world would just be silent for a while, what beautiful poems would be written afterward!" The discussion stopped. They had listened to me. And all agreed.

Few understood to what depths the word reverberated in George. He answered even ordinary questions slowly, rummaging in his head deliberately. Sometimes those around him thought he was faltering and made the great mistake of trying to help him. On one such occasion, when they were completing his sentences for him and explaining him, he leaned toward me and asked in a whisper:

"Arch or arc?"

This search for the genuine word that calls forth the truth, the choice that nails down the meaning — this was his everyday life.

To be able to work. To avoid false exaggeration. To remain what he was. To keep faith with himself. . . . He was afraid of influences, imitation. Great imagination, great desire, but he lacked time, quiet. He searched for solitude. He asked for information about Cleon Paraschos and Yiophyllis; for their writings.

. . . Write me again and tell me what lines of mine remind you of Laforgue, because I wasn't thinking of him at all when I wrote them, and I do not like to imitate . . . .

Along with our rational world lived other parallel worlds, struggling for expression. Unexplained intentions, feelings, longings, marvels, all entwined with logical thoughts. Without the saving power of his art, these other worlds would have strangled him.

9 February 1921

. . . I wish I could write to you in my heart's blood . . . This evening, "the man who committed suicide" as you call him, awakened again with me. He still wants to say things to the moon, to the evening, to the life which he holds in the hollow of his hand. He will die again without uttering anything but those dots of omission. . . . If I could, I would have a house without clocks, a place where there was the least possible difference between day and night. If it were possible, an eternal dusk or an eternal daybreak. A sea with little waves, all exactly alike, but opposite, a most beautiful island which I would never be able to reach. . . . I reflect on the difference there is in the effect on my heart of the glance of a woman who tells me that she loves me, and the glance of Salome at the head of John the Baptist . . . .

His first lover had left with him dregs of bitterness.
A wave of disillusionment swept over me. For whom would George write? Who were those who would understand him? As I walked in the streets, I studied the expression of the passers-by. Some flabby in their happiness, some so neutral that even their eyes were blank as if only a continuation of their flesh. Others were pushing ahead with a sly, satisfied look about them. Almost certainly they would cheat their neighbors. Few had any light in their faces.

Human beings seemed to me unbearable, without simplicity, without honesty, possessed by the monster of egoism. Was it just the inexperience of a young girl? George answered me.

. . . I suppose life is a burden only if intoxication is a burden. To write all his life long, to sing, to publish nothing, and, at the moment of death, to set fire to his songs with his right hand — there is the poet's greatest pride.

Again he was tormented by the Greek language. There was a poem that he wanted to write in Greek, but he could not. He had written it to Kirsten on the back of a cigarette box:

> Belle, svelte, hautaine
> Ainsi qu' un capitaine
> prêt au combat
> Je t'aime quant tu te pavanes
> dédaignant le profane qui
> te lèche les pas. . . .

This period in Paris went on and on, without interruption. Again I was sending him books and writing to him more often.

. . . Reflect on this and you will understand me. The years have passed when we wrote just in order to write, now we write in order to create something. That is why I am worried because I cannot devote myself wholly to what I want to do . . . I could write you a whole notebookful. And how I wish that you were beside me so that I could talk to you, and you could speak to me. When I am not working at law, I am preparing a lecture on Jean Moréas. It will take me about twenty days to finish it. . . .

On February 27 came a description of his room at 9, rue du Sommerard. Whenever he moved, I would ask him insistently to describe his new room. I wanted to see it in concrete detail so that I could imagine him getting up, taking a book from the shelf, and plunging into his papers again. He also sent me one of his book-plates which his friend George Ghoghos had made for him.

A good many days had passed and I had had no letter from him. I was not worried. I knew that he was preparing his lecture. In mid-March he was to speak in Greek about Moréas. The date was very much on my mind, George's first public appearance. Would he be able to convey what he felt? Would he be satisfied with what he would do?

Then came the first message.

> March 18, 1921, in bed, at midnight
> At nine tonight I read my lecture about Moréas to the Student Association. There were about a hundred people, including the Greek chargé d'affaires. I held their interest for an hour and a half, applause, congratulations, other nonsense. It is too bad you weren't there. The ambassador praised me. You know how hard it is to write Greek. Except for a few inevitably antagonistic ones, the rest were enthusiastic. Certain parts were really good, the parts I wrote as if I were writing to you. I am dedicating it to you. And I will send you the newspaper. But why aren't you here? What a headache I have! Good night . . .

At last the big envelope with the familiar handwriting: "Mlle. Jeanne Seferiadis, Parnis 18, Athens." Sixty-two small pages written in his own hand.

On the first page, like a cover:

JEAN MOREAS
Lecture
delivered in the hall of the
Association of Greek Students in Paris
March 18, 1921
Friday evening at nine

To my dear little sister
my first lecture
so that she may not complain
when I do not write to her.

I hurried to say good night so that I could shut myself up in my fortress, the library-bedroom. I sank into a deep armchair, whispering the familiar line:

"Mon berceau s'adossait à la bibliothèque."

and began to read slowly, carefully, noting with a pencil what especially impressed me.

Here, although he is well-known, let me give a brief account of Jean Moréas.

He was the grandson of Papadiamantopoulos, a squire of the Moréa who fell at the siege of Missolonghi. His mother was of the Tombasi family, descendant of Admiral Tombasi, the terror of the Turkish Armada. Jean was born 15 April, 1856, in Athens. From his family he inherited his good looks, his love of poetry, his pride. At the age of 16 he borrowed money and left Greece secretly to travel in various countries where he might learn about the literature of other civilized countries. He went to Germany, to Italy, and finally ended up in Paris. He mused by the Seine, felt its attraction. Then his father ordered him back to Greece and sent him his return ticket. In 1878 he published his first Greek poems, *Doves and Vipers*.

> Wherever I am, wherever I turn,
> Among people, or in solitude,
> Always and everywhere I shall see
> The image of your face . . . .

Later he settled permanently in Paris, and wrote in French. He called himself Jean Moréas.

His statements and his articles are celebrated. His first poems, *Syrtes* 1884, and *Cantilènes* 1886, established him as one of the leaders of symbolism. When in 1891 he published his *Pèlerin passionné*, this Athenian was considered one of the greatest living French poets. They called him the Ronsard of symbolism, but later he moved away from the symbolists.

But how much of Greece he had in him! And how much he longed for her!

In 1897, after a visit to his homeland, he produced *Iphigenia*, and in 1899, his greatest work, *Stances*. It expresses the mature poet's experience, both aesthetic and personal, as it was evoked by his view of the ruined Parthenon. Finally he achieved the ancient Greek virtues of restraint and measure.

George's speech, with his analysis of the era and its work, but also of the man himself, was made lively with anecdotes and episodes. It was full of warmth. It revealed all the grace and the tragedy of the young student who was George. He had not yet made it a law of his life to fight sentimentality of expression. Many points are self-revealing. They bring to light George's own personal sufferings. As I look now at the text, I am amazed at my pencil marks. They appear to mark the places where George identified himself with Moréas. His nostalgia, the darkness in which the poet finds himself, the slavery to learning, the conquest of art. We encounter thoughts like the following:

> His father sent him to Germany to study law, but after some months of cold legal study, he abandoned law and lawyers, and one day in 1880, he came to settle in Paris.

Further on, the poet's tragedy becomes George's tragedy.

> What was the reason for this sorrow we do not know. However much has been written about his life, it is veiled in mystery — not, of course, the life of the café, but the true life, one that has a familiar aspect for us when the door of our room is double-locked, or when, wrapped in darkness, we wander in the streets.

With the instinct of the craftsman, he knew how to evaluate Moréas' art.

> I wish I had time to explain with what experienced technique, with what strength, he handles free verse, rich rhyme, and, when he wishes, simple assonance.

His words are pervaded with emotion when he refers to the poet's Greek continuity. It reawakens his own longing for his country.

> His adoration and his pride in Greece, in his ancestry, which, through the centuries, instills the consciousness of beauty — these come forth everywhere. He dazzled men by showing them that the lode of the Golden Age of the Greeks had not been exhausted . . . . Moréas the

Greek, the classical Greek lost in today's civilized barbarity, made the Greeks of Kanaris join hands with the Greeks of Sophocles. . . .

Like archaeological strata, I seemed to see Greek civilizations, one after another, being uncovered in George's soul.
Further on, he brilliantly analyzed *Stances*. Measure — that was the miracle — wherever he found it. Measure — which excluded whatever was not beautiful.

Stances — the most Greek and the most lasting of Moréas' works. There the Greek spirit appears naked under the French language like a beautiful body under a transparent veil . . .

Again George came back to the need of the living language, as vital to the poet as the need for freedom. He came back to his passion for the word.

He had so instinctive a love for the music of words that sometimes he would repeat all day long a melodious word or a melodious line.

The lecture ended with the optimistic outcry which issued from the very depths of his conviction:

. . . the life and work of this glorious Athenian are an example for the workers, the craftsmen of poetry . . . He is the hope of all of us Greeks. The divine fire has not been quenched. We feel it in their song. Let me say that I believe that Greece, in the coming years, will be able, not only to give birth to the poet, but also to nurture him and rear him . . . .

I read the lecture, read it again. Once more I was on my winged white steed. How right I had been to believe in him! I still remember how excited I was.
George was aware of my emotion, and so he introduced me by letter to his friend, Peter Adam, secretary of the Student Association. And Peter Adam wrote to me:

In spite of my being unknown to you, I am a friend of our dear George. I am afraid that out of modesty he may not write to you what really ought to be said about his lecture. So I make bold to try to convey to you the impression he made. Before a select and cultivated audience, he spoke for an hour and a half about Moréas. His hair topsy-turvy, his eyes sparkling, they became more so as he got into his subject. His enthusiasm was soon passed on to his audience. At one moment when he was reciting a poem, they could not contain themselves and burst into applause. This interest was maintained throughout the lecture, so that at the end there was violent clapping and warm congratulations from both demoticists and non-demoticists.

At the restaurants frequented by Greek students, politics were shoved aside so that everyone could talk about the lecture. George appeared to have started an intellectual ferment among the students. As for his friends, their joy is beyond expression. After the lecture, they lifted him in their arms and carried him to the Boulevard St. Germain.

In a word, the lecture was an enormous success, and I congratulate you with all my heart.
Peter Adam
(Read and approved by another friend, Jason Demetriadis)

George spontaneously sent me his self-criticism.

"I am sending you the draft of my lecture so that you may have some idea of it. I made many corrections on the final copy, and therefore I ask you not to show this copy to anyone else. . . .

Some parts are good: the part on *Stances*, also the part on symbolism. The journeys and the description of Moréas. I wish you had heard it. . . ."

This first public literary success of George filled me, prematurely to be sure, with a wonderful sense of security and triumph. For me he was no longer the young boy riding the clouds. He had won public approval. Now my elders would not smile patronizingly when I spoke of my faith in him.

Only Father, more anxious than ever, continued to write to me: "Tell George to work at his law. His law studies must come first."

Forty years later in the autumn of 1963 a similar emotion was aroused in me. The final sentence of that first lecture came to mind, and it echoed in me like a prophecy: "I believe that Greece, in the coming years, will be able, not only to give birth to the poet, but to nurture him and rear him. . . ."

The eve of elections. I was receiving in my husband's political office. Endless queues, endless demands. The telephone rang. M. Clos of the French press was on the line. We had collaborated when André Malraux made his wonderful speech opposite the Parthenon, and my husband, Costakis, responded. "We are very hopeful," said M. Clos. "There is great probability that your brother will receive the Nobel Prize. They are asking for photographs."

For some time it had been whispered. Was it possible? I didn't dare believe it.

Next morning, again our friend, M. Clos: "Congratulations! Your brother is the Nobel Poet of 1963."

I stood up immediately. The voters discussing in front of me were just a blurred mass. What incomprehensible noise! Mute, dizzy, I went out into the street and fell into the first taxi, then up George's stairs, and in his arms. He had known of the rumors, but this was the first moment he knew for certain. An intoxicating tune went 'round and 'round in my head. The whole of his life, the rugged, tragic climb, unrolled before me, since "the man who committed suicide." Drop by drop, all those woes for the sake of poetry. And now the justification. Now a world-wide public would judge his work.

Back to the prison of the same law studies. Back to the despair over the time being lost:

Paris, 25 March 1921 Friday
Dear little sister: Spring. Sun. Blossoms on the trees. Children in the parks. I am not well today. I wish I could have just one day to enjoy the spring without pressing duties, without threat of the deceptive future. . . . The worst is that I can't relax. I just came back from the Louvre where I wrote you a card and promptly tore it up. I wish I were still the child I am in the photograph that I have before me. Or old, very old, without memory and sight. From Father I have a series of cards. He is in Geneva and is coming to Paris on the 9th of April. More troubles. *Concours* and nonsense . . . .

I too worried about Father's arrival in Paris. Would he understand George's fatigue? Would he be helpful to him? Or would they start their quarrels and differences again? I was not optimistic.

> I wish I had a house near the sea. The windows open, the wind blowing the curtains — and I stretched out in an armchair as if I were recovering from a serious illness, with people looking after me and walking on tiptoe around me. . . . Last Sunday I sent you my lecture. That draft is full of mistakes. I wanted to send you the fair copy, the one I read, but the rough draft may carry me nearer to you. . . .

I did not answer these words. I did not want to discuss in detail his moments of weakness lest I prolong them. What distressed me was that he was being held, as in a vise, by studies which he disliked.

> Paris 26 March 1921
> Dear little sister, It is impossible to tell you what your letter did for me. . . . You are such a wonderful girl. You say that I seem like a child as I confront life, but do you imagine that I show myself like that before others? When I am alone in my room and have double-locked the door, only then do I take off my mask to write to you, or to reflect, or to love. . . .

He knew that his letters caused me pain, but he also knew that I wanted the truth.

How I longed for us to be together at Skala! So that he could let himself go with confidence. So that he could soak himself in his own sea. He had been so long in that big city. Every so often a man must as far as possible merge his physical body with nature. By climbing mountains, by abandoning himself to the sea's embrace.

When I sought to comfort George, I went back to our childhood years, to the picture of our days at Skala. For example — the colorful pebbles which I liked to arrange in my special way on the little table beside my bed before I went to sleep. I might begin with the big red one. I would look at them, as if hypnotized, until my eyes closed. But George always woke up first. He would come in softly and shift them around in his own way. When I wakened, I couldn't imagine how they had changed places — we quarreled, we laughed.

The decision fell on me like a condemnation: we were not to go to Paris that summer. Nor would George come. He tried to conceal his disappointment in order to make the atmosphere less painful. To comfort ourselves, we began to plan for the coming year.

> Paris 30 March 1921 Wednesday
> Psychically I am a mess. I feel like an orphan, and I think that the feeling of being an orphan comes less from lack of protection than from the need of protecting oneself. I put it crudely, but I think I am right. I don't believe in logic anyway . . . I am glad, very glad, that you will be coming to me next year, my dears. We shall be so happy together, and you will see how I will look after you. I shall be well, too. I remember at my lecture — congratulations and more congratulations, applause, bravos, but when I was alone in my room, when I had locked my door, "Les ténèbres et rien de plus." It is terrible how many are the unhappy ones who see Edgar Allan Poe's raven enthroned on the brow of the marble Athena. I dream of next summer when I will lock my door, so as to be able to lean my head, stubborn as it is, against those beloved knees. . . .

But why was I not to be in Paris with him?

As the spring of 1921 advanced, a persistent fever kept me for days in bed. I was very weak, and I had no strength with which to resist George's unhappiness. It reduced me to tatters. I tried not to show it, because what if he stopped writing, even to me! In bed day after day, I re-read *Erotokritos* and folk poetry. Certain ones I liked very much:

> If the earth had steps and the sky had rings
> I'd walk on the steps and swing on the rings
> I'd climb to the sky and sit myself down
> Give a shake to the earth, and the clouds would be
>   gone . . .

There was another which we said over and over:

> for you I stood three watches.

I copied them out and sent them to George to change the atmosphere.

Paris 20 April 1921
I am reading Jules Laforgue's letters to his sister. At the top he writes, "for you alone, to read before you sleep. Tell our cousin that I'll pay for the light." Many things are tiring me out. Yesterday Father told me that you were ill. Something or other made me take up this book. How dearly Laforgue loved his sister! How dearly I love you! What a gloomy place that station was the night you and Mother left. . . . Your letter is sad, but now and then these separations, these sorrows are necessary if we are to preserve some of the childlike tenderness of heart. I will send you a little case in which you will put only my letters. Why am I so very sad this evening, little sister? Perhaps because it is night, or is it the pianola downstairs, grinding out the popular fox-trot?

    The night presses down — wake up and see
    how the stars are weeping in the zenith . . .

How much I miss you! How much I would have to say to you if you were sitting beside me — about the poems I want to write, the projects I have for work. You would understand me, in two words, without quibbling objections . . .

Feeling welled up inside him, but every day the lighting changed.

Examinations were drawing near, and Father began to be worried in earnest. The Greeks in Paris had praised his son's lecture, and he could not but be proud. But for him, failure in the examinations was the worst thing that could happen. He felt it his duty to be after George every day, pressing him constantly.

Adults feel very close to children, but for the young the old are far away.

22 April 1921
Hour after hour — and I don't know what to do to bring an end to this painful situation. Endless grumbling, monotonous grumbling. I have heard it all so often, and I am by nature so stubborn. Whatever will I do when the comb reaches the snarl? . . . . At least write to me, little one. Your letters are a relief.

The truth is that George was not as stubborn as he would

like to have been. The sense of obligation was deeply rooted in him. But what could he do? Poetry was the law of his life. He could not escape it.

> This evening I shall go to the Comédie where they will be reciting the poems of Baudelaire. Perhaps it will give me some relaxation, or will I then be even more tired? . . .

Now I was worried about Mother's health. She had dizzy spells, she was low-spirited. I did not express this anxiety to George. It was so essential that he finish his examinations. And to give him courage, I kept telling him that what is hard to do has its own fascination. On his name day, he wrote to me:

> 23 April 1921
> The greatest event of my life these days was the arrival of your letter which I received yesterday. If only you knew how it comforted me. . . . You write to me about Baudelaire. The important thing was that his poems were recited by De Max at the Comédie. Best of all, *A une Madone* — marvelous! His first word gripped me — He began loudly 'Je veux' — and then softly 'batir pour toi' . . .

and he explained to me all the nuances of the declamation.

> . . . I'm accustomed to walk in the evening — one thinks more easily then — and too in the evening one can remove the mask that one has to wear as long as the sun shines so that one can laugh at one man's stupidity or wince at the romantic sorrow of another. . . .

This was a passion which the two of us shared. We had to dig to the deepest essence of events, to start from their very beginning, and to follow them to their utmost limits. We sought to receive their slightest vibration. This was the psychic tension which later, when disasters multiplied, was almost too painful to be borne.

As for me, my friends were quite external to my life. They had other interests. I had mine. I felt alone. Communication with George did not solve the problem. Often it aggravated it. After his letters, which I so eagerly awaited, I was uneasy, and even more alone. Why did he have to be so far away?

The weather improved in Athens. In the afternoons when I had no classes, I climbed the Acropolis. I would take pencil and paper with me, and a book which I found in our library, *Le Parthénon* by Boutmy. I would sit on the steps of the temple and study the monuments scrupulously. Twilight there was unique. Quiet everywhere. Not a soul to be seen. The bazaar of tourism had not yet begun. Andreas Andreadis, father's friend, and later my professor at the university, had given me an anthology of ancient epigrams in the elegant English version of J. W. Mackail. I tried to translate certain ones into Demotic Greek, but I found it difficult. The ancient message, spare and tight, lost its tension.

> Paris, 3 May 1921
> A quiet evening alone, and I love you, so I write to you. It is terrible to find that this year I have accomplished nothing. I have spent most of the time examining my inner world. This fixation is like morphine. Can you imagine what glorious palaces I have built, but I am afraid to present them to the light lest they fall in ruins. But let us leave this and many other things until we can speak of them together someday. . . . At this moment the only person from whom I expect anything is you. The rest are either hostile or deaf. . . .

He had a plan, as soon as he finished his examinations, to withdraw to some corner of Paris where he could work on his own. He had made his program — he would study linguistics and traditional folk writings. His friend, Nikos Aronis, a scholar and a pupil of N. Politis, would provide me with a bibliography. What I could find I would send to him. The language of medieval Greece greatly interested him, as did the poems of the Acritic cycle. He was concerned with their rhythms, their syntax, their words, even with their psychic attitudes.

When we were together again, we talked of these things endlessly. He reminded me of one of my phrases: "under a pine tree with a bunch of grapes — Greece." In exile this picture captivated him.

He wanted me to send him all of Palamas' works so that he might be up-to-date on literary movements in Greece. He wanted to subscribe to the interesting literary periodicals.

But Father, in every one of these letters, was saying: "Tell George to study his law."

I did not obey Father. I looked into myself for pangs of remorse, but I did not feel them. I could not tell a great poet, as I believed George to be, that he should not write poetry. But in spite of that, since he was not studying literature, he must finish his law studies if ever he were to be able to give himself entirely to his own work. Entirely? Does one ever do that, entirely?

Days loaded with pressures. A charming girl comforted him for a while. Kirsten disappeared gradually into the mists of the North. Happiness ceased to interest him.

7 May 1921
. . . I have just come from the Comédie . . . I am writing to you before going again into the ice-chest of my books. The poems I heard are going round and round in my head, most of them of a rather common type which no longer arouses my enthusiasm . . . But one of them moved me, one you yourself recited from *Feuilles d'automne* by Hugo . . . "qui que vous soyez, jeune ou vieux." It was Pierrat who recited it . . . I no longer live. I only feel, and so excessively. Perhaps it is pathological to sense so deeply these dull trivialities which surround me. That is why, little sister, I find such difficulty with my law studies — a passing evil if it is common neurosis or fatigue, but a misfortune if I was born so, a misfortune for my family, that is. As for me, nothing is really misfortune any more except at night, when I walk alone, or almost always alone. Then I feel, piling up, all the bits of grief which my heart is dripping into my soul. On a scrap of paper I jot down a few words just as they come to me —
I weep for the woman I saw
caught in a ray of sun
on a night when I had no light. . . .
But isn't it comical, in this age of grocers, for a man to sit around and mull over raptures, loves, beauties. . . .

All of George's examinations were a great strain on me, but I cannot forget the ones of 1921. Father kept writing to me: "Tell him to study." His letters were full of his anxiety. George was going through a period of depression. Father was wearing him out. I could see them confronting each other, both of them wretched.

14 May 1921

From my bed at 3 a.m. It is a long time since I wrote to you. Actually, day before yesterday I wrote you a long letter full of stupidities, but since the stupidities of life are a bond between us, what could I do? . . . I am studying now for my examinations, but as you know, I haven't much strength to give to law. My whole soul belongs to another world, my own. . . .

He had not yet written anything significant, so he said, but he was certain that without poetry life would be impossible.

He felt he must not do what others wanted of him. His destiny was to be something different. If it failed, so much the worse.

"Am I really wayward?"

I wrote to him so that he should not feel himself alone as he coped with these dismal studies. It could not be otherwise since everything must pass through consciousness, poetic feeling as well as logical sequences of learning. What a curse to have to earn a living!

Our sensitivity was keenly sharpened. We were shaken by a simple graceful gesture which others would not even notice. A sadly spoken word was for us the echo of a secret drama. All that is beautiful is hidden. How can a human being drag about such a capacity for suffering?

For us, aesthetic form with its most sensitive nuances was of primary importance. On that point we agreed, naturally and immediately.

15 May 1921 Sunday

This evening I have beside me your two letters which I received yesterday. How many times I have read them! . . . I saw the Sunday crowd and it tired me out. I am remembering again the words of Bourget which you wrote down for me, and I find that he did not know 'combien le rêve de l'artiste était plus pénible que la réalité et combien plus inquiet, puisqu'il n'existe de vrai artiste qui ne souffre toutes les douleurs de toutes les réalités.'

The open wound gives you no peace, but makes you feel that you are part of the suffering world. This sad motif will come again and again, sometimes in meditative silence, sometimes in his letters and his poetry.

He understood my anxiety about him, and tried to relieve me. He changed the subject. He told me about his love-predicaments. Small infidelities to Kirsten. He continued to think of her, but he did not write to her often. It was good that neither of them was really unhappy.

At home in Athens the news was not rosy. Mother was ill and very worried. She wanted to sell her property in Ionia as quickly as possible, and for that reason she wanted to go to Smyrna. Father was increasingly certain that Asia Minor would be enslaved. After the fall of Venizelos a wave of pessimism swept the world. Foreign propaganda was literally seething. It bought all those who were for sale.

"Are we going to colonize Asia Minor?" so inquired some of the opposition papers, and created a widespread spirit of defeatism.

If I had been older, and if Mother had been stronger in health, I would have insisted on going to Paris for a short while to help George over this crisis. I would not have impeded his study. I was sure I could soften Father's attitude and make George himself feel less alone.

I wrote Father a long letter, telling him how proud he would eventually be of his son, begging him to treat him now with special care. Father replied that it was for the examinations to answer all this. He had not understood. And how could he? George revealed himself only to me. By a letter of 20 May, I was utterly unstrung:

> Little sister . . . I am so miserable these days — I have been for a long time. Aware of time passing, new days breaking, and so much inside me that belabors and pains me — and nobody, nobody to understand. And the world goes by laughing, and I laugh back, laugh because I am unable to weep. All my days and all my nights — prisons they are, dark prisons, and they frighten me. My soul is still that of a child, and life is so vulgar and so evil . . . Why should I reveal myself since they neither hear nor see? I have always taken literature seriously. But this is a different awareness. All day long I think of almost nothing else. I keep looking, looking, for the untrodden road, and I will find it because I must. And when I write, I shall be the best, but how much I shall bleed! . . . Tell me, little sis-

ter, I've given all my strength, all my resistance, all my will
— you know how I struggle — and I cannot manage to calm
myself. Tell me, little sister, how can I choose the first road
when the second says to me, '*I* am You, your life' — and
the first, tragic irony, is only a plate of lentils to fill my
belly . . . ? How much I long for rest . . . the quiet sea,
the endless horizons. If only I could be quiet, if only I
could lose myself for a little while in love — and then
begin again. . . . but before I pass through all those noonday suns, a little water, a little water in God's name.

This is one of the most tragic of the letters. Not only in what
it expressed. The syntax, the handwriting were a call for help
in a moment of great desperation. This time I roused myself. I
would leave. I would go and find him. But how? Mother —
would she help me? I went to her shyly. For the first time I
was proposing that she and I should be separated, that I
should go alone for a month to Paris.

"Don't do this, my child. Although I seem strong now, I
might die at any moment. Yesterday, as you know, my blood
pressure was twenty-four. Don't leave me."

I didn't answer. I shut myself in my room. Through the
cracks, I could hear her plaint. And I wept, wept with all my
heart. The pages from George lay scattered on the table. I
dared not touch them. As I read them again, all the old scenes
come to life.

I saw the impasse, and appealed immediately to Father.
George must go to the country. First his health, and then the
examinations. At last Father understood that George had
reached a point of exhaustion.

1 June 1921 Paris
Dear little sister. I am thinking about that clearing in the
woods I so long for, and so I write to you. Also it is a way of
experiencing a sort of liturgy and gaining some strength
which, weak as I am, I need today. Because, when I write
to you, it is as if I were going to the liturgy, and being
cleansed, and purging myself of a heap of filth which life
has strewn over me. . . . In my notebook I have been
arranging some poems, and plans for poems I shall write
later. . . .

> The day was sad
> like a day of parting . . .
> Go! I want to stand the death-watch
> 'Til the morning when the yellow candles
> are burned out. . . .

6 June 1921
As I wrote you, I have very little strength. I would so much like to go somewhere in the country. . . . I want to go also because I am bored with talking to myself. Quiet and tenderness and love . . . .

The famous examinations were set for October. George decided to shut himself up somewhere in the country so as to study in peace. The simplest and least expensive solution was to go to Sceaux on the upper Seine, a quiet place and not far away. This time with prayerful concern that I should not come in conflict with his personal worlds, instinctively vigilant lest I destroy his dream, I tried to bring him back to a mood of study. Since we had begun it, I urged that we finish at least this obligation so that we could again be ourselves. George listened to me because he felt that I was in agreement with his true self. He was sure that I too wanted him to pursue literature, that I was waiting, with more assurance than his own, for his poetry. He knew that the drama of his own life was unfolding within mine. Between us there was more than understanding — there was the great common ideal.

At one point, as a kind of intermission, he described to me the romance of a friend who was in love with a beautiful Athenian girl. He told me I should make her acquaintance and write to him. Affairs of the heart are always pitfalls.

9 June 1921 Paris
As I write to you, a little butterfly has come to kiss the paper which my pen is marking up. For some days now I have seen the same one. Who knows what she wants to say to me? She was 'born with her little wings' as you say. . . . All these logical things you wrote me I know well, and many times over. If I didn't know them so well, perhaps I would have made off some time ago . . . and how right you are about my pride . . . But I wrote to you because I need relief immediately . . . .

From the moment it was decided that we would not go to France, I felt very lonely. I felt deserted. In Athens, disunity, fanaticism. The very air we breathed was poisoned. The atmosphere was incomprehensible. How could our army be fighting with any confidence in the depths of Anatolia?

How could I cope with egoism, arrogance, avarice? I felt myself in a vacuum. There were moments when this futility was a nightmare. Depression everywhere. I was alone in sensing this thirst in a world which I passionately wanted to be just. Let me look for a drop of beauty which was surely waiting for me somewhere. It could not be otherwise.

17 June 1921 Notre Dame

As soon as I am somewhat calmer I shall write to you about some curiosities which will interest you, but just now I am à bout de force. It's terrible, little sister, to dream and be swept away by your dreaming. And to see all the suffering. . . . But is it for you, a young girl full of life, to sit weeping over the futility of life?

He took refuge in a church to find a little peace. Perhaps the prayers of the people there on their knees would help him. This happened sometimes when he could see no way out.

From Athens I sent George the books he wanted and some of his old papers. Meanwhile, he was preparing to go to Sceaux to study his law books seriously.

A few days before he left Paris, someone knocked timidly at the door of his room. It was Suzanne. She wanted to tell him that she loved only him. They saw each other a few times, then parted forever.

Sceaux July 1921 Saturday
Dear little sister. . . . I received the books you sent me as well as the packet from the old days. I locked the books in my trunk without looking at them — then spent the night with the papers, now buried in a drawer. . . .

Sceaux 5 August 1921
It is my good luck to have a fine view from my window. There is a little hill, and I can imagine that behind it are the sea and our house and Mother and you — and this is not caprice. In my character I know there is a tendency to play capriciously with serious things.

His letter was rather mysterious. He did not want to write more lest he make me unhappy. I suspected great tension between him and Father.

Mother had decided to spend two months in Smyrna. Before leaving Athens, I subscribed for George to the Report of the Educational Association.

It was a laborious undertaking to plumb the depths of Hellenism through all those rich centuries. And our time was short.

We started for Skala. Again Angelos stayed with his cousins at Uncle Socrates' house. They very much wanted him.

How can I explain? Skala had the power to reconcile me to myself.

I was alone among my elders, and I had their undivided affection. Mother had given me the lovely room above the sea. At night I buried myself in the huge bed to be wakened in the morning by the sound of the waves. I opened my windows and there were the boats going in all directions. I felt like a seabird in its nest. Whenever I wished, I jumped into the water, then dried off in the sun. I read. I wrote. I tore up what I had written. Neither then, nor for a long time after, did I dare show George the simplest of my poems. In mid-afternoon I went to the excavations which had now begun. This continuity of Hellenism in Ionia through the centuries filled me with optimism. It became customary for me to prepare tea for Prof. Oikonomos, and he would take time to explain the day's work to me and show me the ex-voto offerings from the graves. Nobody was in the least concerned about my recreation. I was always thirsting for time to myself.

I wrote to George about Skala. I wanted him to be living my impressions with me.

> Sceaux 9 August 1921
> . . . . With this letter I am sending you the plan of my room and also some ideas which have come to me here . . . Today the sky is calm . . . Do you know what it reminds me of? A Fifteenth of August, years ago in Skala, when the sea was calm, calm and broad and blue, like a freshly painted boat. I wish you were beside me now, anywhere, and I would tell you many, many things. About ourselves, about art, about women, and then I would recite for you

some new lines of verse that I like. Ever since I came here, I am haunted by Verlaine. . . .

> Une rythmique sabbat, rythmique
> extrêmement rythmique; Imaginez un
> jardin de Le Nôtre, correct, ridicule
> et charmant.

How I wish you could be here this coming winter! I would have so much to tell you which you would understand so much better than the so-called intellectuals with their learning . . .

At Sceaux he read *Diaboliques* and discovered Barbey d'Aurevilly. He marveled at his perfection of style. Again he was moved to grief over the poverty of our own language in its present state. He must work at it, work at Greek as a craftsman works. The most essential need of his life was time for his own work.

He sent me the book immediately: six true stories, so the author said, and some other imaginary ones, written in a style which carried one away. And George's dedication to me certainly revealed his chaotic state of mind at the time:

> A ma Jeanne ces histoires inquiètes comme malades, en souvenir de la vie confuse qui abdique en moi. De ma prison, Georges.

Sceaux, 11 August — Thursday evening
What a strange piece of luck! I left all my literary books in Paris, bringing with me only the *Iliad*, the *Gospels*, and Anacreon . . . so as not to be put on the spit by too many devils. . . . and I came upon *Diaboliques*! I picked it up to read for half an hour. Needless to say, I couldn't tear myself away from it. That evening I wept with rage, thinking to myself that, barring a miracle, no one at this moment will succeed in writing Greek with such perfection. . . . But, apart from that, there was something in those pages rather like what I am going through these days, when I am absolutely alone, and without anyone to help me. Not that I am expecting help from any human being, since there is only one thing that keeps me on my feet [he means poetry], and this I am obliged to conceal and hide deep inside me as if it were something evil. . . . You will read the book and I am sure you too will be enthusiastic.

All day long George studied his law books. Now and then he turned the pages of some Greek periodical I sent him. During a whole fortnight, he left his house only twice to meet a friend. There was complete absence of understanding with Father. George was full of protest. Why were they writing this way in Greece? They were forcing the language, not letting it develop naturally. He felt surrounded by deceit. Even Nature was lying to him! In his longing, he looked from his window into the deep valley, and saw the sea and the island of St. John and Monopetro. He thought he was in Skala. Anxiety turned into tedium, where everything was incoherent, unintelligible. Tedium like a swamp. He tossed words on to paper and never looked at them again. What was this crisis? Perhaps just the need to discover again his true self.

Sceaux — 22 August 1921
Here I am in Sceaux, studying law ten hours a day, and not a line worth reading — *Sale vie de goujat* — and the worst is that Papa is delighted now because he sees me glued to my chair. . . . You can see how sure I am of your love since I write you all this unpleasantness . . . But we Greeks can go on writing this way, and what are we contributing to literature by putting into verse the socialistic speeches of A or B? Shall we never get over sounding like Deputies? It is terrible to think so. . . .

I opened every one of his letters with a strange fear. And to whom could I speak? Mother's life hung by a thread.

One day as George was leafing through a pile of old engravings, his eye fell on a reproduction of the picture by Luminais entitled *Les Énervés de Jumièges*. The artist had painted a quiet, drowsy river on which there was a boat, or rather a floating bed. Two youths lay side by side, resting their heads on cushions. Their eyes showed their lives ebbing away, gasping, dying. Quiet all around them. They were the two sons of Clovis II who were said to have dishonored their mother. Their father had had them "denerved" (this is the meaning of the word *énervés*) — that is, he removed the main nerves from their extremities — hands and feet — and left them half-dead, on a raft, sending it into the current of the river to take them wherever it would. In the end a monk rescued them.

It was characteristic of this period in George's life that he should be fascinated by this legend. We discussed it at length in the summer of '22. He saw all its poetry. In other periods, the poet had been Prometheus, nailed to the crag in the Caucasus because he had given fire to mankind. Today, weary of soul, gasping, he was one denerved because he had been lacking in respect for the life-system.

Both of us had a good memory for whatever concerned poetry and verse. I wrote to him about the poems we had loved. He had no book of verse with him, but he wrote back from what he knew by heart. His handwriting got worse and worse line by line, and showed that he was exhausted. And he was tied to memories like an old man.

Sceaux 9 September 1921
Today I received your note, dear little sister. Strange that this very morning I felt the desire to write to you, but because such writing would be a diversion for me, I felt I had better study. Even now, though my heart is full of your letter, my pen plods along with difficulty as I try to throw off the torpor of my black mood. . . .

I long to talk to you about the past which you describe and to say to myself:
C'était, tu dois bien t'en souvenir,
C'était au plus beau temps de ton adolescence
or
Joël est dans sa tour assis,
sa tour et sa tourelle . . .
from Moréas. What beautiful prose when he speaks of memory, standing in his tower, as if all the past were a green valley spread out around him. . . Forgive me. I hardly know what I am writing — do I speak or do I rave? I am so tired. What a sad day it is, like the day you left.
The day was a sad one
like a day of departing.
Does any separation ever immunize us against the sadness of such a day? Everything must die like an unfinished song.

If only you knew how I long to talk to you, to have you talk to me — to such a point that I don't know how to write to you with the slightest hope of your hearing me. The paper on which a letter is written is really so cold! . . .

> The sea at Skala reminds me of a will I made one tedious evening two years ago. I wrote that when I died I would wish to be buried on Monopetro (the little island opposite Klazomenae) How the world has changed . . . and the times! . . . Little sister, you are the only friend I have ever had . . . And it's my turn to tell you how proud I am of you. Egoism on my part. I would like to write a beautiful poem, the most beautiful ever written, and then die. I have such extravagantly high ideals that they frighten me and make me despise all the rest. . . . I never thought of myself as a student of jurisprudence, and it is just this contradiction which causes all my quarrels with Father . . . .

We were nearing the end. George had gone through all his material and must now review it once more. The examinations would be taken in a month. He was not to write to me again until they were over, and again he spoke with great bitterness about his studies.

> Sceaux La Vigie 21 September 1921. 1, rue du Lycée
> I need fresh air. My life is a womb which wants to produce a child, and is prevented by all kinds of drugs and treatments. . . . My life has to be otherwise . . . I was not born to be a notary, so I give the impression of being a man with the camel's bell around his neck.
>
> I want to tell you everything because this is the last letter I shall write to you until after my examinations, and you must know everything, absolutely everything, because no one knows what will happen afterward . . . I am assuming you will be strong enough to hear and understand whatever I write to you, and that you will still help me with your love. That way I shall know you are close to me. . . .

I did not answer for fear of distracting him. Neither the sea, nor the sun, nor the excavations any longer gave me joy. Every morning in the Church of Saint Nicholas I prayed for him.

At last, addressed to Mother, came the magic telegram: "Success". George had taken his diploma (*licence*). Relief for him, and a great joy for his parents. Father calmed down, and even took a kind of pride in his son's stubbornness. He still had two years to go before his doctorate, but we had rounded the cape.

Sceaux 31 October 1921
. . . I've finished my examinations, thank God. So much for that. Better to say no more about these disgusting matters. . . . I am eager to talk to you again. You remember you once quoted to me somebody's line: "Mon âme est née avec sa plaie" and I had already begun a ballade in honor of a hunchback who was born with his hump; . . . So, as for myself, I dare say that, when I was born, God took the soul of some recently dead Methuselah and forced it into my body before there was time for it to be washed in the waters of some Pool of Siloam — they must have such a pool there in Heaven so that souls can be washed and renewed. . . . A week before the exams I broke off and went to hear poems at the Comédie. The temptation was just too strong. . . . Homo sum . . ."

What with law and the lack of time, my God, what a nightmare those years were! I kept thinking how happy George would be working at literature, and it tore my heart. Once or twice I tried to talk to Father about it, but it only made him angry.

"You are only a child. You know nothing of life. A man can't live on literature."

George experienced a kind of torture for many years. It was not easy to be a diplomat, a wage earner, and a poet.

Even in September 1953, he was to write to me from Beirut:

. . . Every night I lie down with the feeling that forty per cent of my work has remained undone. . . . Thank you for being concerned about me. It is a comfort — and I need it . . .

And from London where George was living in an atmosphere of change and struggle, Father's words found their justification.

30 December 1951
Dear Ioanna. . . . Unfortunately today earning your bread with your pen is greater slavery than following a profession. At least I now feel myself entirely independent on intellectual matters, but every night when I go home, I begrudge the fact that I cannot even open a book. . .

George returned to Paris from Sceaux and tried to find a place to live. He had given up his old room.

I was easier about him now. Peace for a while. But for George tragedy was inborn. External events could aggravate it, but they did not create it.

We returned to Athens. Mother wanted us to move. Parnis Street seemed too far out. Then we found the apartment in Cybele Street by the Museum Garden. There we lived for twelve whole years, until we moved to our own house in Kydathineon Street. Naturally the work of the move fell on Angelos and me. Mother supervised and gave us instructions, but we saw to it that she did not tire herself.

The circumstances of my life had greatly matured me. I felt responsible for George because only I really knew him. There was also my responsibility for Mother's health. And although I had little talent for housekeeping, I had to deal with those problems. Father, dismissed from the university and settled in Paris, had his own life. "Write to him often and tell him about home," George advised me.

16 November 1921 — Paris
Always I feel the same wilderness around me and inside me, and I am always out of step. . . . I've been two or three times to the Comédie and you will know how much I missed you. . . . Now I've begun my work for the doctorate, and as I get nearer the end, practical life frightens me more than study . . . What will I be doing? Will I perhaps find some time for my own work, or will I die "lawyerizing"? Sometimes I think I will just buy a field and cultivate it without having to worry about material things. . . .
There is something strange about my ideas concerning the poetry of our epoch, so different from that of the others, and how I despise popularity. . . . If I could, I'd spend my life saying my poems to myself, not even bothering to write them down. I think I understand Baudelaire's hatred of print, and I still remember a letter from that 'friend of mine', Laforgue — "*poems* — what a strange word, something which one writes down to escape from tedium, and to reassure certain friends . . ."

Verse and more verse, the complaint of the King of Thule. There followed a period of composure, one might call it. He cleared his mind of the confusion of study, found a room at 160, rue St. Jacques. He saw his old friends again — even Suzanne, who no longer meant anything to him. He had passing love-affairs. He worried about Angelos who was about to begin his studies. He wanted very much to help him. He asked me again for many books. He had not received his copies of the periodical *Noumas* since last September. Would I go and find out what had happened to his subscription?

I felt that he was returning from his intensive legal studies like an exile. Since from now on he should have some peace of mind, he must find the atmosphere which suited him so that he could work again at literature.

4 December 1921
. . . If God wills and I find the strength to write something I have in mind, I'll tell you all about it . . .

But his melancholia was not over. In the midst of his course at the Law School, he wrote to me:

6 December 1921
. . . . Exactly at noon today I received your letter. If you only knew how much good it did me! Because I must tell you that I am terribly depressed here now. I have hours, sometimes of boredom, sometimes of anxiety, which make me wonder if I am after all really ill, physically or morally. . . . Nothing interests me, although, in all sincerity, I do not want to appear 'blasé.' I never liked poses. Man is so vain, and so much of life is vanity. Sometimes I wonder if it is worth while to try to learn all this rubbish which the so-called reorganizers of human society have worked out . . .

How much we need to recognize essential value in work assigned if we are to accept the discipline of study!

His professor, Mr. Goudis, was astonished when he heard that George's lecture on Moréas had been given in Demotic Greek. Had his good student become a *malliaros* (extreme Demoticist)? — the one to whom he had taught the best Katharevousa? Whenever he met Mother, Professor Goudis would ask her how this dreadful thing had come about.

Tell Mother that if Goudis asks her again when I became *malliaros*, she is to tell him that I was born that way.

Always, whatever he was doing, whether he was preparing for examinations or had already passed them, whether his love affairs were lucky or unlucky, George was dissatisfied. This is the black chasm in the soul of the artist. Dissatisfaction and uncertainty about himself as he faces the emotion he feels when he touches the truth of poetry.

21 December 1921

. . . . Dear Little Sister, I think there must be a world inside me, one which revolts against my will and disobeys my mind, a world which is galvanized by a chord — call it what you will — a line of poetry, a word, a woman's glance, even a popular song played on a violin which is out of tune. I am ashamed to write you all this rubbish, but this uncertainty is my worst suffering. Have I something within me? Have I something beautiful to say, but it gets away from me like "the foam from a sailor's fingers?" Will I ever be able to catch it? And if I succeed, will it be really beautiful since beauty is unattainable? Or is it just some cheap copy in plaster, stroked by the dirty hands of a peddler for the eyes of the patrons in some coffee shop? Tell me, little sister. . . . In his madness, Nietzsche seemed to be singing a dirge: "I love you, Ariadne." Was she only the woman he loved, or, by some coincidence of fate, was she the hand that held the thread of rescue, leading to the exit from the terrible labyrinth, the thread which disintegrates into ashes the moment we grasp it? . . .

Men who depend only on their five senses will find it hard to understand these writings. This overmastering nostalgia, when it is unfulfilled, leads to despair. There were times when George had fun. He had love affairs. Often he saw the world around him with humor. But when he was alone, the same old demon of tragedy seized him. His visions, tossing about in his unbridled imagination, took on monstrous dimensions. His world was strangling him.

The suffocating inner life, that fortress of his selfhood where he took refuge in order to escape from the prison of reality, was not without value. Poets are not always equal to their work. Some are greater than their poetry, some are less. During this period, although he had not yet produced anything important, George was great — he was gathering into his soul the poetic substance of his whole life.

His letters to me from the 20th to the 30th of December 1921 were certainly not festive. He himself felt this.

> . . . When I see myself these days in the window panes of the big shops, on the outside of these places wherein people are laughing, I feel a sort of beggar. . . . I think that the sense of tragedy is to be found, is created, only in great souls. Think of Andromache, Hector, Astyanax. Certainly the sorrow of all three was profound, but remove the human in them . . . I wonder would there not still exist something that transcends crude pain . . .
>
> 30 December 1921
> . . . Today as always I am grumbling and life as always is still terrible. I am suffering from longing and from "the unattainable" if one can put it that way . . . Always I shall be wanting something far away, always I shall be reaching for something I can't grasp. . . . When I am reborn in metempsychosis, perhaps I'll be better off . . . I believe that my birth was a trial shot which will either go very far or fall very short. Who knows? Is there such a thing as metempsychosis?

At the turn of the year, I saw him before me, reaching out his hands. What gave me courage was my certainty that he was great.

1922

Christmas. The New Year of 1922. St. John's Day. Gloom in Athens. Mother had no spirit. I had some joy in studying Taine's *Philosophy of Art* in the evening. His account of the Italian Renaissance was as entertaining as a novel. There I found answers to many of my questions. I was still uninitiated in the theory of art, and it was a revelation. When I read "every impression of the artist is uniquely his own," I thought of George. How could I doubt that he was a poet? So different! I wrote to him about all these ideas, important to me at the time.

Alone. But after all, what is loneliness? It seems to me it is just the rise and fall of our soul.

I was searching for someone to share my eagerness as I tried to understand many problems. And for me there was only one such person. The margins of the Taine volume are full of my lines:

> I leave off thinking
> It tires me
> I fly to you — always far away.

From then on I ceased to care for rhyme. Why sacrifice the vital poetic word, the poetic meaning, for the sake of a rhyme? Even in my idolized Baudelaire, sometimes rhyme spoiled the atmosphere of the poem for me.

In the margins of my book I would write ideas meant for George: "Evils exist so that the heart may play all kinds of tunes." And with the question mark underlined: "What dies within us when it does not take form? What is nourished by silence and time?" And further: "We must be clear. We must be brave."

8 January 1922 — Paris
Here is a poem I wrote one night recently. I was full of feeling when I wrote it, but this one, like the others, is now cold as the hail. What a nerve I must have to write all this trash and not feel sick! Never mind. I send it to you only for its historic value. If I did not have so many distractions, I would write better. But why all these excuses? Perhaps it is true that I do not have a great penchant for poetry, and one of these days I must burn all my papers, cut my hair, and devote myself to the study of law. . . .

Nocturne

Steady, steadily, always steadily
incessant and effortless
without repining
the hail pelts down.
Laugh! it's youth's day to love!
Laugh! it's youth's day to be merry!
And if the hail rages
does youth change? It does not.
And the old road, which carries on its back
thousands of weary footsteps,
is now like a bridal bed,
with fresh-ironed sheets,
a bed made for laughing,
the revels of lovers,
soft raining of kisses . . . .

So it went on. It was a very long poem, and it had its weaknesses. Bored, burdened with legal concepts, he could not concentrate. Duty tormented him.

He was always making fun of himself, of his thick black hair. He wanted to be two people at the same time: one of them Aristophanes, mocking the other.

Today is Sunday. I am bored. Now it is Sunday evening and I am twice as bored . . . Yesterday I went to the Comédie. Those are the only evenings I really enjoy, and De Max is the only one who knows how to recite poetry.

At the end of his final school year in Smyrna, he had burned his books in the small courtyard of our house. That fire had impressed me. We had both suffered from standardized learning-by-rote. Now again he wanted to burn all his papers.

Nights he wondered through the dark streets of Paris. He

walked alone for hours on end, and everything appeared to him as a phantasmagoria.

> 13 February 1922 Tuesday evening — Paris
> I can't go on. That is why I am writing to you — in order to forget — to forget what? If I remember nothing, nothing bothers me. I assure you I am not exaggerating . . . I am suffering. . . . I shall choke to death . . . If I could only breathe the sea . . . I seem to live continually in the middle of a comedy, and I hear the laughter of the audience. I long for light, and everything inside me is dark. I long for quiet, and I feel as if five hundred automobiles were passing over my head. . . . Perhaps my brain is affected . . . I went to the Jardin des Plantes. Lots of birds, golden peacocks and other feathered creatures, some with red wings, some with black. All of them croaking inside me. When I tell you I can't go on, I can't. . . .

This sensation of choking is referred to again and again. And that phrase 'if only I could breathe the sea' — I thought about it as a poetic subject for George. If he could just have a summer at home in Skala . . . if he could only hear the waves under his window.

I no longer knew what to think. I feared for his health, I feared for his poetry — that he would give it up. That would be his final catastrophe. I wanted somehow to give him faith in himself. Certainly the productive days would come. A man only happy or unhappy, one or the other, would be against God's order, God's equilibrium. Some change must come about. Then why all this suffering? Was it perhaps the road to truth? I wrote him an encouraging letter about *Nocturne*.

> 20 February 1922 — night
> At last today came your letter. After such agony, again some hope. . . . We are happy when we write something which satisfies us — agreed. But what of the time when we write something and it does not satisfy us? That is unhappiness. On the other hand, the true artist is never satisfied. . . . I am really thinking about publishing a book which I have not yet written, but little by little it is maturing in my mind. It's understood that I won't do anything without having you read beforehand whatever I intend to print. You see I have a weakness for you. I respect your opinion more than

that of all the critics in the world. That's why we must get together again. . . . I'm thinking about a series of poems to be called *Nocturnes* . . . Beautifully printed, only a few copies, just to make the effort you might say . . . I may include some ballades and sonnets . . . For these ballades I would want to study our popular language of the Middle Ages. But I am still considering the question of rhyme. . . .

He was gaining confidence, his dream was becoming clearer, more certain. But there was always the loneliness, the fatigue.

The dialogue with himself was lasting too long. He had so many things to say, but he could not find his own way of saying them. Memories of the countryside, animals hurrying along dirt roads. And he was homesick for the house at Skala which he owned. Perhaps it would be sold. A prophetic fear took hold of him. Perhaps he would never see it again as its owner.

2 March 1922 — Paris
Whole liturgies waken in me at the word 'never'. . . . Liturgies. Does the word seem strange? Don't you sometimes imagine that you have a whole church inside you where prayers are being said? . . . especially that moment when we go to our knees. As for me, chiefly in hours of unhappiness, this picture comes to my mind. We must talk about this when we are together . . .

His prayer took various forms. It could be song, seclusion, genuflection. Above all, no one must be aware of it for fear of arousing pity.

Mother was again suffering from dizzy spells, from worry.

15 March 1922 — 10 a.m. — Paris
. . . take great care that Mother should lack nothing, that she should not be worried . . . and you, poor child, so young, and with so much to worry you . . . I do miss you so much, little sister, if only you knew, if only you knew. . . . my visions turn into tears without you . . . only stagnant water around me. . . . All the girls I see who may resemble you seem premonitions of you, and these meaningless imitations are the waves which will produce the big wave. . . . I am bored with my solitary babblings and

discussions. . . . They are choking my spirit, these endless futilities. . . .

I write now on Pentecost, 17 July 1973.
In church, on my knees, I listened to the prayers. I prayed with the others for those who had gone. I prayed for George, that no bitterness about earthly things, his or ours, should trouble him. I felt alive inside me a cell of love, wrought from the bitterness of life, but undamaged, all-powerful. How could we soil it with sighs, or with forgetting?
That night I saw him in my sleep. We were walking on a hill which reminded me of Kalamakia at Skala. For the first time I saw opposite, in the middle of the sea, an island with towers, orchards, cypresses.
"George, see how beautiful it is! How is it we never saw it before?"
He held my hand tightly, his eyes widened, and I heard his quiet voice: "But it was always there."

20 March 1922
Little sister, today came your letter, and quickened my blood . . . I am in such a contradictory mood that I see everything upside down, but that does not mean that I see them wrongly: "My dawns are twilight, my springs are autumn." . . . So it is with everything. What terrible scenes a man's soul has the power to make for his own eyes! . . . . Unfortunately the farther I go the more I see how vast and how unattainable art is. The whole problem is in what you say, lest you repeat yourself. And the manner, the form must be your own, in a style unknown to others. And our language is so poor, corroded. . . You are right about *The Altar*, childish . . .

Now it amuses me to hear the word 'childish' on the lips of two children. But at that time we felt our great responsibilities and also our claims. We believed that the world was material at our disposal so that we could build something unique. The idea of futility had not yet begun to penetrate our thinking.
The tightrope of sensibility is no easy matter.

26 March 1922
Dear little sister, it is terrible. I know nothing,

> nothing . . . and I believe that a poem which does not make you shiver should be burned. Consequently I find shameful and unbearable what I have written up to now. . . . My *Nocturnes* are constantly stewing in my head. I fear that the title does not make them sufficiently my own. . . . One is *Nocturne for the Moon's Suicide*. Don't laugh. You will weep when you read it. You'll see.

He wanted his book printed in the same type as were the poems of Malakassis in the *Revue Critique*.

That was when he sent me *The Crucified Christ*, a copy of Carrière's original in the Luxembourg. A Christ almost bodiless. For years it hung above my bed. Along with it came the following letter of March 25:

> Dear little sister, Here I am writing to you because I have your photograph beside me recently dressed up in a new frame, and because I am reflecting on life. Life always brings me to you. Are you not the heart of my life? . . . I remember when I first came here what a great impulse I had for writing and what a lot I wrote in two months. Then one morning, I took a notebook, and wrote on it: 'From today I shall bury my poetry here.' Think what a martyrdom I've been through!

Great trunks obstructed our road — doubts, insecurity, examinations, difficult love affairs, and again doubts. But beyond those black trunks there was something great.

Then he began again: he asked me for information about intellectual developments in Greece. This he needed after so many years of absence from his country. He wanted me to write to him regularly a couple of pages about Greek literature without cutting down on my letters. Criticism concerning both Greek and foreign books interested him.

He wanted a list of the works of Palamas. He wanted all of his poems as well as the second volume of his lectures on Greek poets, the Maraslis edition — also the songs of Rabagas. He wanted Solomos too.

That Easter Angelos and I went for the first time to Mycenae. We studied weeks to prepare for this expedition. The weather was cloudy. In Old Corinth there broke out such a storm that we could not continue. We waited there for the downpour to stop. Only in the afternoon could we move on to the Lions' Gate. But what a moment that was, what a unique moment! Was I influenced by the *Oresteia* which I had just recently read? Was it the overcast day? Surely only in that place could Orestes kill his own soul.

The mountain of Sara which protected the palace of the dead king was sunk in a black cloud. We went ahead with some difficulty over the wet soil, looking at the earth which had been excavated.

"His blood" the guard suddenly said in a loud voice, pointing to something black. I shuddered, sure that the murder of Agamemnon had taken place within that very hour.

On how many levels does the spirit of the Greek move when he really relives his history?

Time haunted George as it also haunted me. Time for himself, his inner time. Uninterrupted concentration on his aspirations.

> Paris 22 April 1922
> You ask me how many hours a day I can devote to poetry. All and none — that is to say, I seek and I do not find. Nevertheless, I feel that I am making a little progress and that finally I shall come out with something, a series of perhaps thirty poems . . . Later some ballades which I want, and also something which, for the moment I cannot describe to you. The title may be in French — *Variations sur la Suicide*. . . . Unfortunately, just now, when I am so full of ideas, there is no possibility of carrying them out. I must waste all my time preparing for examinations. . . . You know, little sister, how unhappy I am, how all this falseness bores me, and how troubled I am by this life of mine. . . . Art requires work — and more work — and a heart unconfined by stays. Will I ever bring all this to reality? Maybe in my old age when my brain will have been scattered to the four winds? . . .

I remember that I was always writing to him, again and again in a thousand ways: "George, go on being yourself. Don't give up and lose the poetry you have inside you."

Our home with Mother ill had little joy. The political situation was beyond understanding. The expedition to Sangario was dragging on. We had heavy losses. It was difficult to provision our forces. The Greek soldier went on, exhausted, hungry, almost barefoot. The men who fought there still remember the same meal every day — macaroni with cotton-seed oil. But worst of all was the erosion of their spirit.

Printed matter about the uselessness of the war circulated among the soldiers. The leading articles in the Government papers of Athens cultivated the spirit of defeatism. How could those boys lost in the depths of Anatolia support a sacrifice which they thought unreasonable?

Often in the evening when we were alone Angelos would say to me and to himself, "Where will this all lead us?" But I did not write of these things to George.

With classes and study, time passed. But the sadness crept into my letters. George would write back the same day to encourage me.

> 22 April 1922 Tuesday 11 p.m. Paris
> I foresee happiness for us in times which must be coming. I too feel life sometimes unbearably heavy, so heavy that I think the wings of my heart will be broken. But so far, they bear me up . . .

He was fortunate in getting on so well with his friend, Poniridis. They had fruitful discussions. Poniridis tried out his new compositions on George, and George put some of his ideas on paper.

He took the marriage of his best friend, Nikos Aronis, rather skeptically:

> . . . I wish him happiness, a happiness which I never wish for myself because art is my love, and she is the most wretched of females. . . . I want only to be left in quiet, and where in the devil is that to be found?

A little peace in solitude. Once he had said to me: "Even prison would not be so bad if they gave me my books. You would come to see me, and would ask me 'What have you to say to me?' and I would answer 'Verses, my lady.'" (Rostand, *La Princesse Lointaine*)

He went to see a sick friend whose mother and sister were looking after him, speaking tenderly to him.

The First Day of May 1922 — Paris
I feel like a poor little child with his nose stuck to the showcase of forbidden toys. Let me tell you that if ever I get home again, I plan to be sick for some time just to experience that special warmth of love . . . Now, in the state I'm in, to have to try to talk, to explain to others. . . . I want just you. . . . We would run on all day and harvest our impressions . . . If you were here — just you — imagine our endless conversations. . . .

He was giving much thought to Angelos who would be starting his studies, and he was thinking too about our scattered family. That winter he had little contact with Father. It seemed that he too wanted his freedom.

Now the plans for our journey became more definite. Father wanted us to spend the summer in Germany so that we should know the country and become familiar with the language. As soon as Angelos and I finished our examinations, we would set out for some German city where Father would be waiting for us.

In the fall, Angelos would go to Paris to take up his studies there. Father wanted me to do the same. Thus we hoped that we three children would be together in Paris. With a little money this could be managed, and we had some money because Smyrna was still Greek. All we had hoped for was coming true.

18 May 1922 — Paris
Dear little sister, Two letters from you this week. Surely we shall see each other very soon, somewhere or other. The principal thing is that we should see each other. Imagine, after two years! I am choosing the poems I shall read to you, lots of new things I shall tell you about. . . . How ideal it will be for us both to be living in Paris! I have so many new things to show you. That's why we must make the impossible possible so that we can spend the winter together.

Where would we meet? George was to go on ahead and wait for us at some point about halfway to Dresden. He was happy because he thought we would not be separated again. He had made up his mind. If we did not all remain in Paris, he would return to Greece.

At that time he translated *The Waters of Damascus* by the Countess de Noailles. Kostas Katsimbalis, Father's friend, was in love with her, and he had asked George to make the translation.

In the Katsimbalis home at Trianemi, the beautiful hand of the countess in marble, on the mantle, always reminded me of *The Waters of Damascus*.

Worlds submerged.

Time after time in Paris, and later in London, when it rained and the sky was dark with clouds, longing for our sun, we murmured that line:

"Que de bonheur perdu, loin de vous, beaux climats!"

3 June 1922 — Paris

I have written one or two more little pieces of my own — just musings. I'll read them to you when you come. I rather like a ballade about Kirsten. I'll read that to you also. This is its l'envoi:

> My lady, my soul withers
> like an exotic flower in a cold wind.
> Come back and revive it again
> with the sweet warmth of the greenhouse.

So much for now, little sister. When you come, I shall be king. Don't forget the books I asked of you because they are much needed.

The *Ballade in Her Arms* (about Kirsten) he gave me later in Paris. It began:

> You opened your arms to me one day!
> I remember those open arms. . .
> was it today? was it yesterday?
> The time doesn't matter.
> You opened your arms to me one evening.
> In terror I saw you standing before me
> and I trembled, feeling possessed
> by a warm sweetness,
> like that of a greenhouse.

As I recall those years now, I see Mother before me. Sick, high blood pressure, traveling much in wartime in order to see her elder son, always fighting for the education of her children. She felt that her hold on life was uncertain, and she longed to see us settled. I never remember her really carefree. She longed to have the joy of seeing George independent. She bent her head sadly: "Before I die, I want my son to bring me violets which he will have paid for with his own first earnings."

Now as we started for Germany, it was agreed that we should stay for a week in Venice. Angelos and I begged this favor of her. We so much wanted it. Angelos, always self-contained and of few words, opened up. I saw him discovering the beauties of art for the first time, and with such gratitude.

He was truly a wonderful companion. He too was a poet, and he knew how to find poetry in the old churches, in the narrow streets, in the Renaissance paintings. For nine days we lived in every corner of Venice. We lay on the floor of the Ducal Palace to study the painted ceilings. We forgot our hunger at lunch-time. Mother left us alone. She must not tire herself. She knew her children's manias and did not bother them. So we wandered among the palaces, the monasteries, and it all came to a climax in the miraculous Byzantine Virgin of Saint Mark's. When we were exhausted, as we often were, we sat down on the curbstones, and watched the canals. In the evening we sank into bed, stiff with fatigue.

George went on to Dresden earlier and waited there for us. The days were rainy. He went every day to the picture gallery. He stood for hours before the paintings of Boecklin for whom he had great fondness. It was his way with musuems. On his second visit, he would go directly to what he cared most about, and there he spent his time. The city of Dresden, with its houses all alike, left him indifferent.

The attitude of the people was hostile, and naturally so. With the local currency so depressed, foreigners lived luxuriously, even with little money, and they bought whatever they wanted. The local inhabitants were extremely poor, they were hungry. His privileges weighed heavily on George. Everything was dead, long-suffering. How could he live out the holidays he had dreamed of in such an atmosphere? Paris it had to be — Paris again.

Leaving a note for us at his hotel, he returned to Paris. He wanted to make it a *fait accompli*. So the idea of our sojourn in Germany was abandoned. Father raised no objections.

Every human program successfully carried out is a gift from God.

The great joy which George and I felt in seeing each other again affected those around us. Mother forgot her health, and was sure that she would improve. We were amused by Angelos' jokes, his funny verses.

George, though always struggling with the black wings of his imagination, found again the sweetness of life near his mother, in the familiar embrace which he could trust. He looked after her devotedly every moment, as if she were a little child.

With great emotion, I rediscovered Paris. And it was as if it had ripened inside me, as if it had come into flower. Perhaps it was because I now knew more about French art. Every corner I had known and loved now had a greater significance for me.

There are cities which open up one's senses, like the petals of a rose. In every little street, at every bridge, behind the statues in the grassy parks, in Paris there sprang up a picture, a verse, a human drama. Here the well-known painter, there the great writer. Ideas were dancing all around us. Even when we traveled by the underground, we recognized the advertisements. In their swift passing, they tossed us a sudden thought, a joke.

That summer, 1922, unknowingly we were living our last carefree days. As evening came on, George would read me his poems. The poor old Queens of France around the Luxembourg again heard his lines with me. And those endless discussions about rhyme, about the silence of the word, about frugality of expression, about avoiding adjectives. There were other subjects too: why must everything be defined? why must it be judged? We always ended with the great problem — how could there be peace without universal well-being?

At night, on the bridges of the Seine, question and thought and answer came freely. We had also the dialogue of silence.

We were together — all was well.

We stayed in the Latin Quarter with George. Father lived in the center. His clients were shipowners, and his law office must be accessible to them. He often called me to take lunch with him. One day after we had eaten, he took me to the big stores. He bought me various small things I wanted, and also a very beautiful and very expensive hat.

"I won't be wearing it, Papa. Why did you waste your money on it?"

"This evening we are having tea at the Ritz, and I should like you to wear it. Telephone to your mother that she should not expect you before seven."

All this seemed very strange.

At five we appeared at the Ritz. There we met an older lady and a rather fat young man who appeared to be her son. Tea was served. The others talked. I had no idea what to say; I was lost, and I felt stupid. The big pearl on the young man's red necktie annoyed me. It annoyed me so much that I could see nothing else. I was bored to death. What was I doing there? I couldn't imagine. What they talked about was quite foreign to me — autos, rides, toilettes. The lady asked me two or three questions. I answered in monosyllables. At last the elders stood up. Without saying anything to me, Father put me in a cab and sent me to our hotel. He was not pleased with me.

When I saw Mother, all my supressed boredom burst forth. George came in, red with anger.

"I saw you. I was outside the Ritz, that bride-bazaar. What was Father thinking of?" Angelos arrived too. He examined my hat with great seriousness. Very elegant — the quality of the velvet, the color of the ribbon. It was all very comical. I laughed and laughed, and the tears ran down my cheeks. We never again spoke of that occasion. It was unique.

That evening during our usual walk on the banks of the Seine, we heard a distant bell. And George began to recite to me — I remember it vividly — *The Bells* by Edgar Allan Poe in Emile Blémont's French translation. Together we heard De Max recite it at the French Theatre.

> Ecoutez les traîneaux à cloches,
> cloches d'argent!
> Quel monde de gaieté leur melodie annonce. . . .

I heard every word, round, like a pebble falling into water. The first night of Creation must have been luminous like that. Then George said to me:

"I remember when you were little, I used to take books down from the high shelves to show you the pictures. Look now at this one before us — the silhouette of Paris at night."

The wind was blowing briskly. The trees, ruffled by the breeze, bent over among the reflections of the lights on the banks. The wind made waves on the water.

From George came the plaint:

"Something which could be written on my tombstone:
> Oisive jeunesse à tout asservie
> Par délicatesse j'ai gâché ma vie."

How certain memories, certain pictures, are fixed in us, above the current of daily impressions!

Valiant, fruitful summers. For many years, the days of summer provided us with a way out of despair and deprivation. The earth, the sea, the river, time to ourselves. And dreams. We wakened on the edge of the abyss. The terrible future was lying in wait.

Why was Mother in such a hurry to return? Why did she want to go back to Smyrna before winter began? Perhaps Father was insisting. Certainly I could not leave her alone. So I went back with her, and, through no fault of hers, my great hope of studying in Paris was ruined. After August 15th, we began preparations for our return. Angelos was to remain and was looking for a room.

We were much out of sorts. We tried to talk of other things — to live each moment as if it were forever. But the days, the hours, grew fewer. The bitterness of parting roots itself like ivy in the heart — it does not pass. And as often as we relive it, the deeper it becomes. The train pulled out slowly. Through the glass, misted with my tears, I singled out George, pale, motionless. Nothing more. A chasm opened. Emptiness. Thirst.

It was our last complete moment. Then we were plunged into the titanic wave of the general disaster.

III
1922–1928

THE DOOM OF IONIA

The news from the front was not good. On August 26, Kemal made his great assault. The Greek lines had broken. Our soldiers drew back, but none of us thought that Smyrna itself was in danger, that its peaceful inhabitants would be annihilated. For many centuries they had lived with the Turks, for good or ill.

We had scarcely arrived in Athens when Mother sent me to buy two tickets. She wanted to reach her brothers and sisters in Smyrna as quickly as possible.

The old clerk looked at me sympathetically and smiled in a melancholy way.

"Where are you going, child? What will you do there? Better wait for two or three days. You won't lose your places. The boats leave empty and return full."

I went home having done nothing, and told Mother what the good man had said. She consulted friends and they advised her to wait. They were hopeful. Nurredin, the Turkish commandant of Smyrna, stood guarantee for the safety of the inhabitants. Indeed he asked that the consular guards be disbanded.

National despair was annihilating us. We had surrendered Greek soil, become fugitives. Greece shrank, shrank, crumpled. The leap toward the fulfillment of The Great Idea, the daily impulse toward a great country — these had been lost. As the boats returned, there were silent plunges into the sea. Our officers were jumping overboard and being drowned. They could not survive the shame.

And George wrote to me:

> . . . Why was I not killed with the others who were exterminated on the fields of shame through the stupidities of egotistical imbeciles? All our eyes are full of tears, but is it

possible that Smyrna will again fall into the hands of the Turks? . . . As I write, perhaps the crescent flag is flying over the city hall, and the sun is setting quietly as always. . . . Dear sister, I am distraught. . . .

and he went on to write of Father's despair and that of Angelos.

But even more than nations, men themselves were being crucified. Now we began to get details of the terror. The Turks invaded the area. What unbelievable horrors! Terrible death for every Christian. Unburied, the slain filled the streets. Boys were made prisoners of war and sent to the interior by forced march. Girls were violated, slaughtered. Whole neighborhoods were unapproachable because of the heavy stench of putrefaction. And the Holy Bishop Chrysostom, who would not be separated from his parishioners, was torn to pieces by the Turkish mob. He was one of the great churchmen of enslaved Greece, accountable before God and history for the souls of his flock. Bishop Gregory of Cydonia they buried alive.

The mind of man cannot take it all in. These atrocities took place before the eyes of Christian officers and crews of battleships belonging to the great European powers, lying at anchor in the harbor of Smyrna.

"Happy he who was not born in our generation," wrote the historian Frantzis at the Fall of Constantinople in 1453. "Happy he who was not born in our generation" we too should say when the thought of 1922 tortures us. We too were bearing the fate of our age-long tragedy.

All those who survived to bear in their blood the death of a country, let them read on.

It was a morning in mid-September when I felt a black hole open in the midst of the heavens, spread out, and cover the earth with darkness. Smyrna was in flames. Christians were jumping into the sea to save their lives. They were hiding in cemeteries. Skeletons were keeping company with children lest they cry out, and be heard.

The words of the Apocalypse were coming true.

Boat after boat arrived in Piraeus full of miserable bodies.

They had left their souls behind, in the warm embrace of the Ionian earth.

On the sidewalks of Athens, rich and poor spread out rags and overcoats to sit on. Exhausted children fell asleep on the stones.

The doctor came to see Mother. He took a blood specimen and kept her in bed. She wept softly, not understanding. Her tears frightened me. I sensed that she was weak, helpless, facing the incomprehensible. She kept asking about her own people — her brothers and sisters. But who are 'our own'? Who are 'strangers'? One slain in his vineyard, another killed at Kalamakia. Dead, all dead, like an Attic tragedy. And those who survived, uprooted.

"Oh God," I prayed, "make me strong enough to bear the fate You are sending me."

When Mother began to go about again, I would often miss her. She would come back late. Every day household furniture, clothing, kitchen utensils were disappearing into the refugee encampment. Often I would hear her at night. She could not sleep. One morning she called a taxi to carry away with her her bed and mattress. I ran after her:

"Mother, where are you going?"

"Old Mrs. Riga and her daughter have taken shelter in a shed," she answered. "They sleep on the ground. I am taking her my bed. We have at least a roof and a floor," she added to herself.

I had grown up here in Athens, had put down my roots. This was my country. Here I had my home, my teachers, my school, my best friends. Its every stone, every marble, they were completely mine. I was bound to them. But now my whole soul was a refugee on the sidewalk.

I hated the houses. I hated the well-established people, the refined, the complacent, the charitable, heartless all of them. And the others, the miserable ones, whether singing dirges or suffering in silence, the apathetic, the indifferent — all drove nails into my skull. The order of the world had been overturned.

There was a gentle lady in a torn, bloodspattered silk dress, sitting silent at a street corner. Convulsively she moved her hand, stroking the blood spots on the clothing over her breast. Mutely she was asking for help. Not for food, not for a bed. She was asking us to take away from her eyes a terrible vision. I kept going back to her. I asked her softly:

"Did you leave some one of your own back there?"

"Yes. My daughter." And she added to herself, "I must wash her face."

An old woman nearby told me that before the mother's eyes they had violated and slaughtered her daughter, Anna.

"Only time will bring healing," she murmured.

Truly, but we are still here, in this hour. And how can we survive it?

When she became a little used to me, I took her by the hand and led her home.

Our poor house was spilling over with relatives, friends, and strangers . . . People were sleeping in the hall, even in the kitchen. Every night the whole place was an encampment where they turned over and over as they tried to sleep. Even with the windows open there never seemed to be enough air. I slept with Mother in my little room. At night she found it hard to breathe. She would go to the balcony, picking her way among the sleepers on the floor. I wept in my sleep, and it was not a dream.

The soul of man has come a long way to be able to survive so many deaths.

And now George's letters seemed to me uncertain, as if he were whispering in dizziness.

>20 September 1922
>
>Dear little sister, Yesterday I wrote to Mother, today a few words to you. I am terribly anxious about the situation. We learn of the atrocities from the English and Italian papers — the French cynically write nothing. And you must know of other horrors. We sent you a telegram. I cannot stand this anxiety. If you can possibly do so, write me a few words each day with the main news. I beg you as I never did before to write to me, and to look after Mother . . . Now our only refuge cinders and ashes.

Where could we look for a little hope? What should I write to him? I had lost him too, as I had lost myself. And how I grieved for him! We were staring at each other in the darkness, and only our love enabled us to perceive one another.

All these people wounded me deeply. Men with eyes like those of animals in a storm, full of fear and hunger. How could I help them? How could I loosen the iron band pressing on my own forehead?

I fell into bed with a temperature of forty degrees. Possibly meningitis, the doctor said, but it was not meningitis. The fever did not go down. My older friend, Sophie Charitakis, came to see Mother.

"You must take Ioanna to Kifissia, the sooner the better. She must have a change of environment. I have the use of the house of a friend who is away. I shall be nearer too."

Mother accepted this, but not immediately. She was anxious about me, but even more anxious about her sister, Aunt Maria. We had had no news of them — neither of her nor of her husband, Uncle Socrates. All those days when Smyrna was burning, with their two children — what had they done? Where did they hide? Were they alive?

I remember the first day I got up from my bed — as if it were now. The bell rang loudly. With difficulty I got myself to the door to open it.

There was Uncle Socrates, that strong, severe man who used to scare us — there on his knees, weeping. A door of refuge had opened to him after the nightmarish pursuit. His wife, pale and thin, stood by as if turned to stone.

"Mother!" I cried, and sank down on the nearest chair. My legs would not hold me up.

How they escaped, what they went through — why tell all that? The world is full of such tales of sadism.

We had been plunged into a barbarism which was unprecedented. Human beings would be born, they would be taught to read and write. They would use and misuse words. But who would fight the gigantic beast of injustice? As long as injustice exists, humanity will continue to destroy the spirit. Why is the world not obliterated so as to put an end to this problem? A sense of insuperable futility choked me like thick foul air. And there was George, waiting for my letters. Under the weight of the sorrows of the period, all that I loved became remote, inaccessible.

30 September 1922, 5 rue Bréa, Paris
After almost a month of silence, yesterday Father received your letter. . . . I wish you would write to me. . . . How many dreams had their wings burned in the flames of ravaged Smyrna, sold by the piece. . . .

And like prophecy —
. . . I suppose the new European War which bellows from time to time and is on its way will not spoil things for them . . . But never you mind — the West will pay for its indifference, its cowardice, its blunders. The slaughter of women and children at Smyrna will be avenged . . . . Anyway, I am glad you were born so that I can write to you things that no one else would understand.

16 October 1922
Now other days have come. . . . Such storms, such whirlwinds, that one tries to find a moment of tranquility, a moment of remission, so that one can look within oneself . . . The external world destroyed everything — and this disaster passes through us like water through a filter . . . Mankind is miserably base — some souls are satanic, some are angelic, and some are neither the one nor the other — I mean they are nonexistent — and life is something like a performance of Karagözis, taking place between an entrance which we call birth and an exit which we call death. Dreams and lies . . .

Way off there in Paris, George was not yet as totally engulfed by the Asia Minor tragedy as I had been. His absence abroad both troubled and protected him. But the evil, though more slowly, was penetrating the fibres of his soul.

Mother and I left for Kifissia.
I felt lifeless, without strength. I could not swallow solid food. I wanted the windows wide open. I drank in the air of Penteli, it was a balm. Thrust into the corner of my bed to be out of the draft, I experienced the fleeting peace of utter exhaustion. My sleep was more calm, without nightmares. I remembered the phrase of Nietzsche: "To be compassionate is to have your soul crucified, but who can survive the crucifixion of his soul?"

Somewhere there must be a tree still green, a wing still flying in the air.

And life is as inevitable as death.

I could not forget, but I wanted to live. My flesh said "yes" and my flesh knew. I set up my defenses. October in Kifissia was mild. I dug into myself, and once again — silence. I remained motionless for hours without thinking. How had the cruel North Wind so suddenly subsided? Was I recovering? I had a number of books with me. On other occasions they had filled my time. Now? What place had books in a savage world?

The dark roses in the night were unbearable. They reminded me of blood, spilt and now drying.

This goodness of nature in autumn, this quiet death of the year after the dance of the mad Furies, had its own wisdom for me. It helped toward a kind of reconciliation. But the bitter taste of the irrevocable did not leave me. The same thought came back in a thousand forms. The land of Niobe was lost to the Greeks. Perhaps that weeping mother who had never ceased to lament was now mourning this hour. Never again would the Ionians inhabit Ionia. And this "never again," sealed by the evacuation and the fire, was not to be endured.

Sophia called on me often. She was a beautiful woman of great personality. She satisfied the aesthetic values I held for human beings. She was more or less happy with her husband and her little son, but she had gone through hard times. She lost her mother when she was small. Her father, General Smolenski, was old-fashioned and very severe. An older daughter could not endure his tyranny and little Sophia saw her sister dead upon their mother's grave. She had killed herself.

In spite of the difference of age, a deep friendship developed between us. At her house in Kefalari, I always found warm affection. She had a big garden. Her little boy, Constantine, was a beautiful, lively creature. Together we ran after Azar, his big dog. At sundown they would take Constantine away for his bath.

"You come too, and you'll see I am not all clothes," he said, dragging me by the hand.

That autumn Sophia stood by me with all the experience she had gathered during her difficult life. She understood the psychic tumult which had almost destroyed me. Without many words, Sophia would appear frequently and take me away for the evening. (Mother went early to bed.) On her terrace I came to know Zacharias Papantoniou, Miltiadis Malakasis, Constantine Demertzis. Each one in his own way gave me strength. One with a new idea, another with a line of verse.

Little by little our house emptied itself of the refugees. Uncle Socrates and Uncle Koko (Mother's brother) rented some accommodations and established themselves in Athens. Most of the others found their own people.

St. Demetrius' Summer, the Greek Indian Summer, passed too.

"We should be back in Athens before the first cold weather," Mother said anxiously.

So we returned to Cybele Street, such as it was. What was left there was our books. We lacked almost everything, but we had a coal stove burning night and day. That luxury was on my account. I was still weak, and I took cold easily.

The catastrophe had many unexpected consequences, and back once more in the city, every day I heard unbelievable things. In the face of this desolation, I felt worthless. I could scarcely utter a word, nor could I put anything in writing. It sounded false, out of place. With difficulty, in telegraphic style, I managed to send our news to Father. Nothing else. As soon as I began to forget myself in some household activity — putting things in order, sewing — I would feel a presence in the corner, a sharp instrument in his hands, aimed at my heart.

Paris 27 October 1922
Little sister, for days now I have had it in mind to take up my pen and write to you. Throughout my absence abroad, these are days when I am thinking of you especially. I am in such despair as I never imagined, such turmoil in a human heart. Things which at another time might have given me rest — perhaps a work of art, things which at another time might calm me down — perhaps a song, all these seem to me now insipid, like sugar in water. Little sister, why have you left me? Why do you still leave me so alone? . . . We have wintered in strange places, always strange. This must be my own song. Who knows whether it comes from birth or from habit — this homesickness which is being kneaded inside me. . . . What I love of humanity is you. How can I help it if I am clumsy? I am so alone. . . .

"Why do you still leave me so alone?" This sentence would not leave me in peace.

"Why do you still leave me so alone?"

With trembling spirit I seized my pen and wrote to him as I always had, the whole truth, the unspeakable tragedy. I wrote with dry eyes that had within them all the tears of the earth. I remember how my bitterness poured forth — I had seen so much death. . . . I wish I could read that letter again!

Paris 2 November 1922 Thursday
. . . Little sister, today your letter came and plunged me into the truth. It was a break in the cycle of pain which revolves around me. I located a point, and now it begins to turn again. I am on my knees before your spirit, my true sister. And I take a certain pride because no one has been aware of this genuflection, no one senses it. Here am I, disabled, weak, even my parents take me for a mediocrity — but I am able to feel my love for you within me. . . . Smyrna, Greece, treachery, slaughter, dishonor, the shame and scorn of the civilized world — all this has stripped me naked, torn from my soul its last pretense, and now for the first time, I really look at my soul. . . . I see it for what it is, because I have measured it, measured the strength of the last nerve, as if I had a compass in my hands, and I tell myself I am worthless. I have been wallowing about this autumn without finding any answer, and feeling — only two fingers away — nothingness. Just now I am not speaking of art, little sister. There is something above art, the unhappiness that is our birthmark, the sound of the world's heartbeat which will not let us rest. To be an artist means that you have a position in the world, but this other thing is something higher. If you call it art, you debase it because you put into it all the interests and self-pride of the others, of those who are not like us. . . . There is a relentless pain which claims its tears. . . . And I have heard inside me the terrible "why?", the word which every precipice cries out to you when you find yourself on the edge and your ears are ringing from the height . . . And now that I am writing to you this way, and hearing your words inside me, I feel some serenity and your image comes back to me. I see you a sick little girl, weak and so alone. . . There is no way for our life to change since our star is as it is, and our stars are the same. . . . And now that I've written it, forget all this . . .

And for the first time since the Asia Minor catastrophe he went back to poetry and wrote it down:

Nocturne

Now in the distance I see
the cypresses, bending to
the breeze in the grey sky,
and I seem to see open graves
there below. . . .

Answering my letter of 28 October 1922, he sent me the following from Paris on 22 November:

Hush, little sister, the ruined chapels are still, no psalming,
the candles burned down, the lamps dry and thirsty;
Hush, little sister, let us hear the voices of the cypresses.
Look, in the clouds, the nights, choking nights, make their lairs,
Ah! how well I know them, the nights lurking in clouds,
Ah! how well I know them, the nights roosting in my heart!
Ah! how well I know them, they said to me, knocking at my window,
that the slender cypresses, their tops bent
to our grieving, to our sadness,
will speak and remind us of cures long forgotten.
Hush, little sister, gently, don't speak, the silence is waxen,
And if our hot breath encircles and drips on it,
it will melt, and burn your porcelain fingers.
Are the stars perhaps drowsy, do they hesitate?
They too know fear and must hide it
lest a tear or even a ray of light
slide suddenly onto the strange silken night.
Night, but what of that, hunger is night for the soul;
blind and trembling, it searches, famished, dwindling,
finally reduced to what you can give it. And then
What to do? Where to take it? What does it expect? Why does it not die?
Oh to wake some morning and see the funeral of one's soul!

> Since hope wastes away, why does the soul not waste away?
> Hush, little sister, it is the Fates, angry, and close behind.
> You are shivering, take care, you'll catch cold, cover up for my sake;
> Alone at the crossroad, I shall hear you coughing,
> Alone at the crossroad, what shall I do
> if even close to me, you turn into ice?
> See, a full wind is blowing through the slender cypresses.
> Hush, little sister. . . . listen, listen, listen . . . listen
>
> What did they say?
> Something about damp graves open below. . . .

He worked this poem over and sent it to me again from London two years later on November 25, 1924, saying:

> I began it two years ago, and though I tried often to finish it, I could not. One evening I finished it all of a piece. I'm sending it to you because it is yours and I cannot keep it any longer. It weighs on me. . . .

Throughout this period, Angelos was not writing. God loved him. Over and above expression, He gave him the gift of silence. Later, during the years of the Axis Occupation when I lived every moment with him, I understood that he was ready to die, with that imperceptible smile, without a word.

Now the immediate problem was Mother's health. She suffered greatly. Her head ached. Her arm was numb. The doctor made a monthly blood test. I used to smile when I would hear him say to her again, "Madame Seferiadis, if your house is to burn, let it burn. Don't worry." Meaningless words! Given her nature and her anxieties, surrounded by people without work, naked, starving, she too was wasting away. Every day she went to the refugee camp. What could she do? The money Father sent was not much. It barely sufficed for the two of us. She could no longer help anyone, not even her children. But she kept going to the unfortunate people just to be near them, so that they should not feel themselves abandoned. I tried always to go with her lest she suddenly be taken with vertigo.

Her sons were her other worry. She said to herself, "I wonder if they are eating properly?" It was very cold in Paris. Their overcoats were old — would they be warm enough?

And in every letter George would write: "Take care of Mother."

George threw himself into his studies. He was in a hurry to take his diploma so as to begin to work and to help the family.

His intentions were the best. But what to do? In addition to the reverses of those difficult years, in addition to the problems of art, there now entered into our blood the death of an entire nation. And even more, the death of The Great Idea. An event of incalculable consequences for our whole life, and far beyond.

In the Great Church, we had lighted our candles, our souls. Suddenly the black sexton passed by and extinguished them all. We trembled under the dark dome, our spirits in suspension. Long before we were born, at our very core was rooted our responsibility for the Great Idea, for the liberation of Hellenism. Now we saw this sacred responsibility lying in a heap at our feet, but we had to go on. How? The awful turmoil started from the depths of our being. Like Kierkegaard (*Journal* 1945) George saw the bird in the storm:

> I saw snakes crossed with adders
> entwined in the loathed generation of our fate.

How were we to exist, without foundations? We were going from nothing toward nothing. And I, young girl that I was, decided for the first and only time that I would die. I could achieve nothing. I was indifferent to faith, to love. I wanted to die. I searched for injections of morphine for the purpose of suicide. Violent death frightened me. With the prescription from the doctor, I had obtained two doses for Mother. I guarded them like a treasure until I should get others.

Later, much later, I tried to express something of this experience:

> The houses bent double in fear
> And the trees
> The ocean grew dark
> Death
> The sky fell in a heap on the earth
> Under the broad-leafed poplar-tree

> Leaning alone against its trunk
> We watch in wonder the hand
> That quietly gathers the pieces together
> To weld once again the steep dome.

At that moment, the steep dome was still bits and pieces at our feet.

How were we to find a new rule of life for our country, for ourselves? This psychic claim, so fundamental to us, was almost impossible to satisfy. We carried the great lesson of the ancient world within us. The smile of the archaic *kore*, the harmony of the temple had opened a deep furrow of aesthetic emotion. But we were surrounded by broken marbles; they abolished time, and flung our plight straight in our face. The mind was befogged, unable to cling to the vision.

We do not leave the past behind. It leaves burning signs on the earth and in our blood. I understood this much better in later years. The surge I felt within me when the conquerors of 1941 stepped on our soil came from far back. And the passion to drive them out, with all the deaths of children and friends, and our own death, was a responsibility built up over many years. As a young girl, I could not grasp it, but now, as a grown woman, it was a condition of my life to discharge this obligation fully. At the time of the first group executions, together with lost companions, whole legions of those unjustly slain descended on me at night.

We do not leave the past behind. Both in George and in me the things we had gone through left an unalterable bitterness. The mystical command of their bitter presence would return again and again. Often the poison of resignation turned into indignant revolt. . . . Enough of that! Stop hitting at that trunk. Let it breathe freely! But so many dead in one generation! And our dreams — bits and pieces!

This had its own value, because it came forth again in George's best poetry. These elements may seem unrelated, but, with a little care, one finds their direct connection. The painful experience is there, lighted up from unexpected angles, impregnated with an unadorned sorrow which he was never able to overcome. In every respite, in the emotions of every day, love affairs, desires, disappointments, there always remains in the soul a place for that pain.

In me personally his lines arouse a heartfelt memory of those days of destruction.

> swimming in the waters of this sea
> and of that sea
> without the sense of touch
> without men
> in a country that is no longer ours
> nor yours. (p. 21)

Again in *Mythistorema*:
> We set out again with our broken oars. (p. 31)

And in *Santorini* (weighed down by personal sorrow):
> Here we found ourselves naked, holding
> the scales that tipped towards
> injustice. . . . (p. 63)
> when you can't any longer choose
> even the death you wanted as your own — (p. 65)

I am reminded of his letter which asked why he was not killed at the front in Asia Minor.
> hearing a cry,
> even the wolf's cry,
> your due: (p. 65)

But where *Mr. Stratis Thalassinos Describes a Man*, there most of all George speaks his own truth — the parallel presence throughout our life:

> Sometimes that obstacle seems to me like a teardrop wedged into some articulation of the orchestra, keeping it silent until it's been dissolved. And I have an unbearable feeling that all the rest of my life won't be sufficient to dissolve this drop within my soul. (pp. 147, 149)

Later on, in *A Word for Summer*,
> . . . . even though I was born
> close to the sea that I unwind and wind on my
>   fingers
> when I'm tired — I no longer know where I was
>   born. (p. 169)

Still later, in *Narration*, there are some lines which could be a compelling symbol, without bombast, of the Great Idea:
> Some have heard him speak

>   to himself as he passed by
>   about mirrors broken years ago
>   about broken forms in the mirrors
>   that no one can ever put together again. (p. 243)

May God keep me from explaining poetry, and above all George's. A good line detached from its starting point becomes from then on an aesthetic phenomenon and travels with the reader on its own road.

But I see before me his spirit, transparent, a watery surface in whose depths swims a black monster. It is the sorrow of our nation. Sometimes we see its shadow, sometimes its wings, sometimes under the quivering of the water, whirlpools, hollows, curves, sometimes other signs.

In the well-known *The King of Asine*, every line is permeated with the burden of life, the ancient monuments, and the contemporary tragedy together with his longing for the now-lost homeland:

>   . . . . and his ships
>   anchored in a vanished port: (p. 261)

and further on:

>   while the yellow current slowly carries down
>   rushes uprooted in the mud
>   image of a form that the sentence to everlasting
>   bitterness has turned to marble:
>   the poet a void. (p. 263)

Is it a picture of Asine? Is it a picture of Skala with the rushes so strangely reduced? Vanished harbors and so many boats tugging at our hearts.

In *Last Stop* the whole monster rises to the surface of the water,

>   our mind's a virgin forest of murdered friends.
>   (p. 309)

George bore on his shoulders all the woe of Hellenism. The wounds of his country were his own most grievous personal wounds. He felt them one upon the other, past and present. And he lay awake foreseeing those of the future.

With the passion for the concrete which possessed him, his anxiety and his bitterness and his nostalgia always took a tangible form. Sometimes it was Lost Ionia, sometimes the Patriarchate, sometimes the language.

There were those who considered the Greek element dead, whether ancient or medieval or contemporary, but George could never find it in himself to let it die. It always had a powerful hold on him.

I remember the fear I felt in July 1950 when I received his manuscript of *Another World*. How could he go to Skala again? Could he bear it? Thirty-six years had passed since he left the harbor, blossoming with Greek masts, among the boats his own with the brass fittings. There he had left the kind, cheerful fishermen, his warm friends. Thirty-six years! And not only the uprooting — the slaughter.

> . . . My God, what am I going to do? I am the participant, engrossed in a magic ceremony which I do not understand. I know I did something to provoke the dead, violated the nature of things, committed a shameful act.

Did I understand him? I don't know. Perhaps I would do the same. When you have so bitter a feeling about this so-called end, and when, embedded in it, is this longing to return, there's nothing worse to fear. So I say. . . . But thirty-six years of such painful history. It could be centuries. Who would I be if I were to go there? on what planet? A ghost. No, I couldn't do it.

> . . . There on the beach, near the lighthouse, I abruptly turned my back on the houses which were looking at me like sick animals. It was as if only from me came the little life still remaining to them. . . . I looked at our islands. . . .

These words shook me. He deserved to see again that Promised Land which he had adored since childhood. But not like this, in God's name!

"It's a private matter," he said when we met. "A matter which concerns only you and me. No matter what I write, who else will ever sense this lump in my throat?"

So nothing dies as long as man's soul holds it in embrace.

A letter ten years later describes the ceremony at Cambridge University when they conferred on him the honorary Doctor of Letters.

> 11 June 1960
> Dear Ioanna . . . I am truly sorry you were not there . . . The Savvidis' will give you the particulars. I will tell you about two or three things which moved me. One was the love shown for me by various of the Cambridge people. (One international scholar asked me if I were related to Prof. Seferiadis — that would have pleased Father.) Another was the enthusiasm of my good friend, E. M. Forster. Last year we celebrated his eightieth birthday. He enjoyed my affair like a small boy. For the first time in the annals of the University the citation was spoken in Greek rather than in Latin. And finally, when I was standing there in that red gown, in that solemn atmosphere, as I listened I did not for one moment think that they were honoring me, but that all this was an offering to a world I have loved . . . This feeling reached a climax in me when I heard them speak of "tales heard in boyhood from fishermen and peasants at Smyrna or Klazomenae." Skala had come to Cambridge. That touched me most of all.

Always Skala, always the Greek language.

But genuine Hellenism, rooted in Cyprus since the time of Homer, did it not engage George completely? He was to become one with the island in its new awakening.

His heart was stirred and began to sing. Again we were speaking in verse.

> For us the war for the Christian faith was
> another thing —
> Also for the soul of man, seated on the knees
> of the Virgin, Leader in Battle,
> With the sorrows of Hellenism in her mosaic eyes.

On 29 October, 1953, when he left for Cyprus:

> Don't stop writing to me. I'll find a way for your letters to reach me. . . .

In '54 and '55 he returned again to Cyprus in the autumn.

> Beirut 25 October 1954
> Dear Ioanna, . . . For me surely the best thing about this post is its nearness to the island: an hour by plane, over-

night by boat . . . I have fallen in love with that place. Perhaps because I find still alive there old things that have been lost in the rest of Greece. . . . Also because I feel that these people need all our love and all our help. Loyal people, stubbornly and benignly firm. Just think how many conquerors have crossed the island: Crusaders, Venetians, Turks, English — for nine hundred years. It is hard to imagine how true to themselves the Cypriotes have remained, how little the various masters have changed their color. Now they write on the walls of their villages: "We want our Greece even if we have to eat stones." I wish our young people would go to Cyprus. From there they would have a broader view of our land. I'm afraid I'm getting sentimental. . . .

On another occasion, that of his first visit to Constantinople, he gave expression to his emotion with a line from an ode: "Rich earth, where the corn grows, uncultivated."

The holy places of St. Sophia, the City walls, the Monastery of Chora. And in my turn, when I went there in 1952, I wrote immediately to George, fascinated as I was by the magic of the tradition, by the mystery of Christianity. He answered:

What a pity we were not able to see those places together.

The heat is unbearable. The birds come down low to find a little shade. The garden is full of countless fleeting presences.

I am writing these lines on 11 July 1972.

It is the period of tourism, of spiritual leveling. All ideas, all sensibilities crushed by the tanks, or on television.

On such days last year George's terrible illness began. An endless procession of painful images follows me. But neither bitterness nor death can tear up the deep roots.

A month ago a friend spoke with regret about Chalkis. New laws by the Turks had made the famous school useless. That haven of study and of Orthodoxy was slowly being liquidated. I saw before me the forested hill of the island with the School on the summit. I saw too the revered figure of the Patriarch Athenagoras . . . I knew how he was suffering. I wanted to tell him so.

I felt I must go to Constantinople. A way would be found. Some friends were going there, and I arranged to go with them.

Early on the first evening I went to St. Sophia — with beating heart. The Virgin glowed in her niche, in the grandeur and poetry of perfect spatial proportion. I genuflected and made the sign of the Cross. I felt myself a castaway who had at last found a way to sail the roaring waves. Tourists around me chatted relentlessly. Their guide intoned a series of dates. I gazed at the Virgin in deep devotion. She shone in the familiar atmosphere of prayer.

Man cannot contain all that God gives him. My personal grief was softened in the presence of the immense sorrow which each of us in our turn, throughout the centuries, must bear.

The Patriarch received me.

"Most Holy One, I came only for you. I bring you my faith, the faith of all of us here below."

"Holy water dries up without faith. Man is great, my child. He can touch God."

His eyes had a mystical light.

"The Christians in the City grow fewer," I whispered.

"They are countless."

I did not understand. He bent his head and added softly:

"I am guarding their bones."

I wept, unaware of my tears.

After two days, I went again to say goodbye.

"It is I who am coming to you, Ioanna. Sit down. Let us look at each other."

He talked to me about Chalkis, about the Dark Virgin in his church.

"I sit beside her there at Vespers."

As I was leaving, when I kissed his hand, he whispered softly the first line of my *Elegy*:

The parting took place within the wave.

But when had he read it? On the stairs of the Patriarchate I thought that I must find George and tell him. Only he would understand.

The bells are tolling mournfully. Today, at this moment, they are burying the Archbishop.

The dictatorship of 1967 was the last national blow George would receive. In the beginning he believed with many others that it was temporary, an inevitable situation. But as the months passed, then a year, and another year, he could not be quiet.

I can see him in the armchair in our living room. It was early March in 1969. He did not come often to our home. One of his legs troubled him and the stairs were difficult.

I always went to him and often we walked together in the National Garden. That morning he had come with his wife, who left us alone while she did some errands.

He was depressed, with the expression of the seafarer who smells a coming storm.

"I can't sleep. How shall we escape this slavery? Disaster is threatening this country. But is it only threatening? Day by day, whatever is true, whatever is alive, is being strangled."

In his sad eyes, in every wrinkle of his face, I saw concentrated our old and our present suffering. At that moment I saw beyond George refugees stretched on sidewalks, armies being wiped out, and on that very day, there were martyrs in prison. I was overcome with sadness.

"You are crying?"

I could not contain myself, and said softly:

"We live our lives with death in order that our country may be free, and now we shall die as slaves."

"I cannot remain silent."

I did not answer immediately. He was disabled, tired. My love made me tremble. Any rough handling would kill him. But on the summit where he stood, he had a great responsibility for all of us. He had raised this ancient land on his shoulders. Under its weight he had rooted himself in the soil like a cedar.

"You must speak out. It cannot be otherwise," I whispered.

On March 17 he telephoned. We agreed to meet by the statue of Karaiskakis. We went a little way into the garden, loitering idly by the bust of Moréas.

"What a pity he has no throat at this time!" I said in order to say something. George listened without hearing.

"Let's go home. I want to read something to you."

There in his study, in a low voice, he read me the first draft of his statement against the dictatorship.

Then he made changes — more changes. It must not be long.

"Now I am considering three dates. The first is March 28th, as soon as I return from Delphi. The second . . ." I broke in.

"Never mind about the second. Release it on the first date, the earliest. If you had not promised to go to Delphi, I would say even earlier. Postponement is fatal. The secret gets out."

He agreed with me.

"All right. It shall be March 28th. You know best. You lived through the occupation."

On Sunday, the 23rd, he went to Delphi. From there he sent me a cryptic card. It showed one of Ulysses' companions escaping from Polyphemus under a ram. And on the back:

"Wednesday. A magical image. We return this evening. Kisses. George"

As soon as I received it, I telephoned. He was back.

I gathered that things would happen as we planned. The day had come.

On March 29 I telephoned to him in the morning. He could not speak freely, but he knew I was anxious.

"I'll be over to see you soon," he said.

This calmed me. Around noon with effort he climbed our stairs. He wanted to tell me what had happened that morning. A member of the Bureau of Police Security had called on him.

"You are receiving many foreign journalists?" he inquired politely.

"Naturally I receive them, but of what importance is that? A short while ago I was in America. Everyone asked me what I thought of the situation in Greece. To them all I said, 'Away from my country, I have nothing to say. When I step on its soil, I shall speak.'"

They did not bother him further.

That evening I went by his house and we sat a little together. He had the uncertain feelings of a man on trial. The pro-dictatorship papers continued their attacks. I said as a joke: "Neophytus the Prisoner."

He smiled and asked, "What are you doing tomorrow?"

"I'll come back here." I sensed that he wanted it.

The next day was Sunday, and after church I was again with him. He was remembering Mother sadly. I proposed that we go the following day to Kokkinara for a change of air. He agreed.

Monday morning we set out for Kifissia. We left the car in front of our house on Koundouriotis Street, and continued on foot to the small chapel of St. George. He leaned on my arm. The chapel was opened. With a lighted candle, we searched the wall:
> the paintings of the damned being tortured with fire and brimstone . . . (p. 75)

The words of Mathios Paskalis were all around us.

"A whole life," he said sadly.

This deep surge of spirit disturbed me. I whispered: "Perhaps we shall have something to show at the Last Judgment?"

George always approached the antiquities with great tenderness. I remember him gently caressing the "little bear", a votive offering to Artemis, found at Vravrona. And he had an inner affinity with the ancient texts. He studied them with delight, and was always trying to integrate them with the places of which they spoke, trying to feel the ancient moment.

The autumn of 1922 Plastiras' revolution was in power. It had a heavy task, a difficult one — to rebuild the army, to provide for the refugees, to conclude the treaty with Turkey. Plastiras worked with good intentions, so Father felt, but every government involves some malicious men. Every day in the Old Parliament buildings a Special Military Court met to try the politicians who were governing at the time of the disaster. They were considered responsible for the national catastrophe. Mother, with the fear of God in her heart, was saying, "Let us not call down on ourselves further curses . . ." At that time I was not politically minded, but I sensed that other irreparable wrongs were in the making. In mid-November we heard the overwhelming news that six leading political figures had been condemned and shot.

When is Nemesis appeased? Where does vengeance begin?

I envied the indifference of the people around me once they

were assured of their own safety. They were like children who close their eyes tightly so as not to see what frightens them. Only George would understand, and he was so far away.

> 28 November 1922
> This evening, little sister, I am so full of sorrow that you could cut it with a knife like a thick fog. . . . I keep thinking what I might be able to do, keep thinking that my hands are tied, that no one except you loves me, and I have so much to say, so very much; and the world is so strange, so grotesque, that there is no one whom I can approach and to whom I can speak. And then, they want everything explained, weighed, proved, cleaned, polished like copper pots. Can one speak of proving what one feels? . . . Have you ever noticed, little sister, what emotion is concealed by hoarse voices? I so want to be able to speak lines which are like the drops which spill from an overflowing heart . . .
>
> Day before yesterday I reread your letters . . . time stolen from study, and I had no right to do it.

And always he was discouraged by the weight of his obligation to study law. A disabling slavery. He felt like the blindfolded mule going round and round the wheel-well. He complained about Father. Two men who greatly loved each other could not agree. And with the chagrin of an innocent child, George wrote:

> And it is I who have understood his verses as has no one else! Tell me, do you know how much love is required to understand other people's poetry?

Mother no longer went out. It was cold. She worried about me if I followed her. In Paris, Angelos had finally succeeded in finding a room so that he was now separated from George, for the better perhaps. The despair oppressing his older brother might rub off on him. Each one had to find his own way.

> Paris 9 December 1922
> . . . I have courage for nothing, absolutely nothing. I am only stagnant water. . . . It is true that everything has come to an end, and has turned out to be incurable, absolutely incurable. At least, little sister, tell me — is it my fault? Have I done wrong? . . . Am I to spend my whole

life, watching the yellow water of the cistern evaporate until one day it becomes dry? I have appetite for nothing, nothing. If only I could sleep for months, without hearing, or seeing, or reading. I write all this to you because you still have the innocence and the love to believe me. The rest explain my condition — some as laziness, others as the result of strange literary influences from the North . . . I am poisoned. . . . Little sister, why are you so far away? Why am I so far away from you? . . . I re-read your letters, all of them, to be lifted up a little, and then the same terrible disillusionment comes back again . . . They have taken everything away from us. Before, we had at least a corner of our own, a sea, a house. . . . And I think of you, dear little sister, again and always, and I am frightened because you are like me. . . .

Father came then to Athens. I think he came on account of me. What I owe Father I feel very deeply, but for his presence at that moment I shall always be especially grateful. A man of experience, prudent, loved, took me firmly by the hand and drew me to the light. Surely he must have understood how, on the edge of so many precipices, it would be hard for me to keep my balance. With love, with confidence, with firmness, he explained to me that I too must study. And as I could not be separated from Mother in her condition of health, I must study in Athens.

"Now all that remains for you children," he said sadly, "is study and your personal honor."

Those first holidays after the Asia Minor catastrophe were unbearable, awkward, false. And impoverished. George and Angelos fasted in order to save enough to go a little to the theater, to buy a book or two.

28 December 1922
The picture of my life — a frozen Sahara.

As for the idea of art which had so tormented us, George had to start all over from the beginning. The groans coming from all sides had to fade away. Then we had to look at ourselves again to see what had remained. At the point where we stood then, whatever did not touch on man's tragedy said nothing.

1923

Father went away again. He left me a little light, rather uncertain light, and he left me some hope of the unexpected. But this hope quite often turned into fear.

I also greatly missed Angelos. His quiet presence had taken on importance for me. I thought of him in those difficult hours, for the first time far from home, of few words, trying to make jokes. My poor brothers! It is not easy to begin life, despising money, often being without food in the evening. And moreover, wreckage and death still around. The fate of thousands of souls in our civilized century.

I listened patiently, complacently, to the political discussions going on around me. Something essential was missing. All these older people in charge of the destiny of our country seemed indifferent to the only matter of importance in my view: Man. Man who was plunged into the cyclone of evil and fear and want. In their golden mantles of virtue, they talked pompously. I found all their sermons unbearable.

21 January 1923

Beloved little sister . . . Well, these days of formalities, these holidays, have passed, your name day too. . . . Now our poverty seems less because the rest of the world is less festive. I'm glad the holidays are over, less for myself than for Angelos. He is such a good fellow, the best I've ever known, and I love him. It is a comedy to see us, pencils in hand, figure how we will get through the month, and whether we will eat in the evening . . .

You know about all these unsatisfied dreams, which have something in common with the purple of the sunset. Unfortunately, Angelos is of the same race as you and I. Atavism or original sin — take your pick . . . You remember the dirge of the poor young man:

Quand les croque-morts vinrent le chercher,

Quand les croque-morts vinrent le chercher,
Ils virent que c'était une belle âme
Comme on n'en fait plus aujourd'hui. . . .

Letter after letter continues this tone of despair, of isolation, of the consciousness that life is an impasse. Many times I asked myself what was this loneliness? Lack of being understood? One or two people near him more or less understood him. Lack of love? There would always be some woman near him, steady or temporary. It was certainly not the lack of company. Company can be an escape from self, and we never wanted to escape from self, however tormented it might be.

George's loneliness went much deeper. He was himself the night. The night that works and prepares for the dawn, despairing that it will never come. For a moment we believed that something was beginning to light up. Then again we relapsed into darkness.

Together we felt more secure. The darkness was familiar to both of us. What one said went straight to the heart of the other, starting processions of worlds which were indubitably true for us. We felt open, productive. Because productivity, like acceptance, is a feeling that every seed goes down deep. Whether it will bear fruit is another matter. There was also between us our love — it always gave without ever asking. Mine at least, ready and whole, like a mother's love, and with that bond that unites the young of the same generation. This feeling between us endured throughout his difficult life, in spite of activity and success, in spite of frustration and endless separations. Even in the summer of 1961, he was to write to me:

30 June 1961
Dear Ioanna . . . and something else: now that my arrival appears really to be on the horizon, I want to tell you how much I am counting on you. I mean to say that I want small, quiet company. However good and sympathetic many people around me might be, I feel the need of someone really close to me. . . .

4 February 1923
Dear little sister. . . . You see, I have no one but you in the world. Sometimes I think about the trains that have borne us apart — every face that I loved there in the pale

light of the railroad car, almost lost, as in a portrait by Carrière — then a push, a grinding of iron that had in it something of the grinding of bones . . . And nothing more, nothing. How is it possible for a man to be so alone, so inside the night? This is the way we have parted three times. . . . Little sister, I can't go on . . . I've lost the courage to live. I've lost my ideals. I've lost everything — my talent, if I ever had any — buried now, and chanted over. I cannot write two words, one after the other, nor put two ideas together, nor conceive a poetic image . . . You remember one time you reminded me of what Lamennais said, "My soul was born with its hump." . . . I am the deep-sea diver. My apparatus takes me down to the ocean floor where I find unutterably precious stones from the lost Atlantis — rubies, diamonds, pearls. If I return to the surface, the world will consider them pebbles from the beach. So I cut the line that holds me — also the breathing pipe, and I stay with them down below. And let me tell you — nobody, nobody among the other divers will reach me without returning half dead and with blood in his ears. . . . Little sister, I know I am right. . . .

His poverty wounded his pride. His clothes were worn and shiny. He had no money to buy new ones. If he had to attend a social event, he was ill at ease, embarrassed.

Paris 13 February 1923
Little sister, Today I arranged my drawer . . . The letters I have written to you are my whole life. If by chance some day I read them again, drop by drop the moments of my life will pass before me. I am reading your letters now — I have put them all in order, beloved pages that make me forget how hard life is, and also make me hold on to it. . . .

After that he wrote about his lack of funds, and his hours of privation.

. . . Day before yesterday, the very day I wrote to you in my latest letter that I could not go on, I took to the streets and walked all evening. The rain soaked me through. I wrote the poem which I am sending you . . . Write me sincerely — what do you think of it?

Rain, rain, your ashen pellets,
nails and hatchets, barbed hooks.

> Rain, rain, lancet of boredom,
> tears of fate, beating the wind.
>
> Rain, rain, reeds at the windowpanes
> thirst, hunger, death . . .

and it goes on like this for many more lines.

George brought me much sorrow. Not because he wanted to grieve me but because I suffered from his fate more than from my own. I sensed the dregs of his bitterness, the nervous fatigue which he was scarcely aware of, or never expressed. When he wrote to me, "I can't put pen to paper these days," I knew that he could find comfort nowhere. Though he was far away, I saw his anxiety and unhappiness in his manner of writing, even in the character of his penmanship.

But he also gave me my greatest joys: to him I owe my sense of humanity and of mutual understanding. As for his poems, I loved them more than he did, and more constantly. I felt that I traveled with him in his wanderings.

His journey to Cappadocia was a revelation to him. I came to know its churches as if I had been there with him. I followed him mentally to Cyprus, and in the spring of '57 to the United Nations where he went in support of that great island. In 1960 he went to Louth where Kalvos died and undertook to move the bones of the poet so that they could rest in Greek soil. He made an expedition to Scotland to Rex Warner's home. The house was built above a lake, with little green islands and quiet water. Through his eyes I saw the pheasant promenading on the lawn before his window.

Later to the island where Steven Runciman lives. It touched us both to think that here Runciman was preparing the history of the Orthodox Church after the fall of Constantinople.

"I am finding Byzantium on a lonely Scotch island," he wrote.

His description of each displacement made up for my apprehension about it. I followed him even to Amorgos where he rode a mule in company with his local friend, Lemonis.

The misery of that winter! The snow turned my heart to wood — how to help Mother who woke up every day weeping, how to help her friends who were in mourning. I went regularly to the refugee settlements — to New Ionia, New

Philadelphia, Polygono. Everywhere unemployment, sickness, cold. And that cough, and the unbearable boredom like mold which comes from the acceptance of fate's absurdity. Men crouching silent in corners. Mothers trying to light a small fire to heat some soup. And there was I, inefficient, inadequate. I would come home shaking, haunted by their misery. The empty walls of our house looked luxurious. At least they had no cracks. I stayed near our lighted stove to get some warmth for my own body, and was ashamed of that warmth. My nerves were frayed. This tempest of disaster to human beings was not to be borne. My only courage was my silence, above all, to George. I felt that he was terribly disturbed, and I wanted to make him feel my abiding confidence in him. George was a poet. In a world of deception, this at least for me was true. But eventually my despair penetrated into my letters.

17 February 1923
Little sister, you know that if anything holds me to life, it is the love I have for you, and the hope that one day you will be able to warm your fingers on my forehead, but the other day your letter showed you so unhappy that I lost my way like some drunkard at a crossroad. A heart like yours does not fall sick. To have broad wings does not mean that one is a cripple . . . how much broader they seem, those folded wings, when suddenly they open out . . . Write to me — I miss you so much, and it grafts life on to me whenever I hear from you. . . . Little sister, I, whom you know so well, am desperately unhappy. The stupidity of it all torments me, I am pricked by impulsive ideas. I who suffer so from my own incapacities. I who have you wholly in my heart, I tell you, I beg you, keep your courage at all costs, though I know how life can reduce us to tatters. Little sister, you must be proud to have such a soul.

We were both fighting ourselves, made wretched by our sensitivity. How could I explain this to him? How could we overcome the distance so that one could support the other? Only George could help me, by his own attitude, his courage.

George continued on his hard road. One could say that all his poetry would be paid for in blood and tears, as may be true of every work of art.

Then, in the spring of 1923, he met the girl whom he would truly love; he met the great passion. With all his heart he wanted to marry her. But how could he? A poor, impoverished student, without any income of his own, what had he to offer her?

For at least eleven years, in spite of all their separations and his relations with other women, Jacqueline — for that was her name — remained his dominant concern. The greater part of his love poetry was for her. *Erotikos Logos* is their tragedy, "the rose of destiny, the dark shivering in the roots, the desire, deep like the shade of a walnut tree." And his "waiting on the stone of patience" would end in the merciless solution of resignation.

> Won't there be a navigable river for us?
> Won't there be a sky to drop dew . . . ? (p. 433)

This poem, with its persistent wandering around the subject until it hits the target, with its free poetic imagery, with its substratum of profound feeling, is one of his finest love poems. I am expressing my own opinion, and I try always to keep separate my personal emotions and my aesthetic judgments.

What can a third person understand? To write a poem like *Erotikos Logos*, a soul has to have followed the dramatic march to the very death of love.

In the absolute of love, everything lies heavy. There is our immeasurable longing. There is life, the great inevitable. After that, one either rebels totally, or one accepts and resigns himself. Resignation! What despair is in this word!

> who will calculate for us the cost
> of our decision to forget? (p. 19)

Seated beside the lighted stove in Cybele Street, I listened as he read to me in his deep voice the *Erotikos Logos*, for the first time in its entirety. It was the winter of 1930. Couched in the wonderful 15-syllable lines, the story I heard was the one I had suffered through for many years. Thought traveled back . . . I saw Jacqueline for the last time one day in her home in Paris. She had seated herself at the piano and was playing a French song:

> Moi je n'aime plus rien,

> ni un homme, ni une femme,
> ni mon corps, ni mon âme,
> pas même mon vieux chien. . . .

Tears fell on her fingers.

The aesthetic charm of George's poetic structure was revealed only on second reading. These young lovers faced great obstacles — the severity of Jacqueline's father who had great dreams for his daughter, and George's pride.

In many of his poems I saw his erotic desire for her:

> Great and immaculate love, serenity!
> In the lively fever one night
> you bent humbly, naked curve, . . . (p. 433)

And in *Mythistorema*:

> Star of dawn, when you lowered your eyes
> our hours were sweeter than oil
> on a wound, more joyful than cold water
> to the palate, more peaceful than a swan's wings. . . . (p. 17)

> at night if we remain in front of the white wall,
>   your voice approaches us like the hope of fire;
> (p. 17)

> you breathed like a tree in the quiet light
> in the limpid spring I watched your face: . . .
> (p. 37)

Again in Spetsai in 1934. George was enjoying the sun, the sea. Suddenly one morning he drew me out on to the balcony. "Sit down. I want to read something to you." It was *Description*.

> She draws near with her clouded eyes,
>   that sculptured hand . . .
>   everything threatens her silence. . . . (p. 101)

And I had thought he was beginning to forget! I said softly: "Dear George, no matter what road you take, there is no escape for you except a good poem. Let us accept that."

Jacqueline was very much a woman, and she was also a very special human being. She was beautiful, with a certain depth in her expression. She spoke little, but with every one of her words, she shared her soul, and when the poet heard her speaking, he was involuntarily transported to worlds without frontiers.

In the winter of 1923, Father chanced to meet again old Parisian friends, among them Jacqueline's mother, Marie Louise. They renewed their acquaintance. She was a cultivated and open-hearted woman, and she asked to meet George and Angelos. She invited them to her home. Jacqueline played the piano well. They talked about music, about poetry. George felt himself in a congenial atmosphere. He opened out to these friends. He read to them from poets he loved. Theirs was a warm and pleasant atmosphere. Marie Louise began to invite the boys regularly, every week. And this warm-hearted home became an oasis for my brothers.

Paris 17 February 1923
. . . . I am sending you some photographs. The faces you do not recognize are those of Marie Louise and her daughter, Jacqueline. You can't imagine how kind they are to all of us, especially to Angelos and me. Today at noon we ate at their house, and talked a lot about you. Jacqueline wants to know you. I told her I would write you to ask that you send her a few words. She is a girl of eighteen, warm-spirited and she loves beautiful things. She plays the piano . . .

George began to love and feel attached, but without joy. There are women who from the moment of first meeting will count seriously in a man's life. Jacqueline was such a woman. But all George's dreams were unfulfilled, even the flowers he wanted to give her.

That critical winter, life was a problem for all of us. Our financial situation was a matter of deep concern to Father. His wife was ill. He had three children all at that crucial age on which their whole future depended. His nerves were on edge, and he would lash out, even at me. He grumbled about small things. I had not listed his books. My letters were abrupt. And there was always the indomitable pride which was characteristic of the whole family. Our deep concern was that we should never be pitied by the outside world. Agla, Mother's sister, would never come to Greece after the Asia Minor catastrophe lest someone should wish to aid her in her poverty.

She gave piano lessons in Paris, living in isolation with meager means, and eventually she died there.

I sensed that George, moment by moment, was plunging deeper into the great love of his life. A love beyond desire, beyond happiness, beyond separation.

I opened my window softly, very softly, so as not to disturb the nightingale nesting outside, so as not to interrupt the sweet voice, for there was awakening in me the first essence of life. Whoever, without egoism, has suffered the pain of love, will understand.

Now George was writing his poems in French. In every letter he spoke to me of Jacqueline: "All this is absolutely between us." He was afraid of what might be said; he wanted strangers not even to touch her name.

At first George did not wish to admit even to himself that he was in love. His life was always dominated by a great sense of responsibility. Her family trusted him. He tried to conceal his weakness for her under the guise of a great esteem.

Paris 27 March 1923 Tuesday
Dear little sister. . . . You know how much I miss you. . . . Yesterday Marie Louise and her daughter left for Nice. In the evening I went to their home to say goodby. Their departure was painful for me. Recently they have become so much my own people. . . . Your letter came a half hour before I went to take leave of them. You can't imagine how it pleased them both. Jacqueline was delighted. She resembles you. That is one reason I find her sympathetic — she too has her inborn wound. . . . Little sister, I long for you, long for you. If you were here, I would have much to say to you, and your presence would relax me after the tedious and distasteful work I am doing. . . . I read only law. . . . I can't go on. I want courage, I need courage, and life gives me little . . . But in the end, I am grateful that I have you. Just imagine what my life would be, what pandemonium, if it were not for you. You see, I am suffering because no one understands me. I have so many plans in my head, so many plans for serious work, but until now, I have written only sketches, mere shavings, of my ideas. . . . Today I'm really not concerned to tell you how unhappy I am. I am so accustomed to my distress that it no longer makes any impression on me. It has become

my natural condition. Heredity, art, life, what you will — can one root them out of oneself? No . . .

And after these words, like a cool daybreak, words of his genuine love, and they brought my tears.

. . . today . . . I would like to write you a letter, simple, relaxed, child-like, calm, pure, like one's first love letter. I long for these sentiments now that it is spring, sentiments that seem like the convalescence of the spirit, but where shall I find them? . . . . There comes to mind the beginning of a song:
To the last branch
all has become night —
The night was choking me. I haven't been trying even to play with verse. The conditions of my life prohibit it. But what could I do? . . . I might be able to give some direction to poetry in Greece. . . . We'll see. I kiss you, little sister. Goodnight.

A difficult period of adjustment — 1923. Futility everywhere. I found no way to give him courage. I could do no more.

George threw himself into his studies. Whatever it cost, he wanted to acquire his independence.

Paris, Tuesday, 22 May 1923 11 p.m.
Little sister, I feel darkness around me, and this means that for a long time I have not seen you on a sheet of white paper. Our letters have become fewer recently. Somehow within us the precipices have become so deep that we are afraid to face them any more . . . So stupidities that are called realities will always be tearing us apart. . . . So much the worse, there will always be a new wound to make us howl like the dog that senses death and goes mad. Our hearts were born hydrocephalous . . . Little sister, my unique little sister, I keep thinking about the hours and days I have spent here so far away from you. How have I been able to stand it? Happily no one knew what I was going through. My door locks from the inside. Fortunately. Otherwise they would take me for a lunatic or a simpleton . . . Bah, everything in life is tragic if you have eyes and ears. There are some human beings who can see and hear; the rest are either rascals or gluttons. Rascality is not intelligence, nor is gluttony desire. I know you share my

> opinion. . . . I am very tired. . . . Perhaps I work from a sort of moral *élègance*.

He was more than just tired. He simply could not take any more. Four months without respite from his law books had dried out his spirit. It was the life of a convict. In ten days the examinations would finally be over. He was disenchanted, indifferent to everything. Without emotion, without confidence in himself.

He inquired about Jacqueline, but avoided her. Thus his loneliness was the greater. He needed quiet. He needed the stable love which knows how to give without being asked.

> Little sister, . . . a city where nobody knows us, and where there are plenty of narrow streets where we can walk alone without a care to bother us. A sky, a sea, a clinical city . . . All this will happen some day, won't it? Since we both want it, surely it must come about.

George succeeded in his examinations, the first toward his doctorate. One more year and he would reach the end. Angelos passed his first year of medical school. For Mother these were the first good moments since the Asia Minor catastrophe. And Father felt relieved. He had been reinstated as full professor at the University, and now he would return to live with us in Athens.

As for me, along with the others, I was happy that we had escaped the rub of failure, but I found little joy anywhere. And I continued to feel George's many-sided drama keenly. His love now rose like the tide. He suffered over the fate of the girl he loved. I longed to help him, but how? I had corresponded with Jacqueline. We had become good friends. I loved her because she loved George and understood him, because she was kind and gentle with him. In their first meetings after the examinations, I hoped that some happiness would brighten up his spirit. But if this miracle occurred, it would be only temporary. He avoided talking about his love. He avoided talking about his unhappiness. Our letters became fewer. Perhaps he was afraid his despair would deepen my own.

> Paris 23 July 1923
> Little sister, if you knew the feeling I have for you, you would weep. . . . If my life is silent now, it is because my

> pain, my wound — I don't know where it came from — has come between us. Now see how, after months of silence, I am starting a letter to you. It's a pity, isn't it? I'd like to give you joy, much joy, but I feel incapable of it. Why then should I poison your life? I am very unhappy and this story will not change. Why should it? It's common enough. It is a powerful grief, and wide as the world, if the world were an ocean. Little sister, whatever happens, I say whatever happens, you will always be to me my first, my great tenderness, deep like faith. I am stamped by fate, but I do not suffer alone. I look at all the people I know, and even those whom I find laughing, are, in my company, overtaken by sadness, that sadness which we know so well.

He was thinking now of Jacqueline, and this tortured him, both then and later.

> As I write to you, I feel some remorse — bitter remorse . . . Who knows whether it is not my influence on you which I have seen as you were growing up, whether I am not to blame for this lagoon of melancholy which you have within you. . . . Even so, how much I want you near me. And now it is too late to change . . . because I feel that at this time only I have what is required in order to be your companion . . . But why do you want life to change? . . . I believe that he who does not give even his life for freedom does not deserve freedom.
> Little sister, you see what I've come to. I'd rather not write to you, but I cannot do otherwise. . . .

George and Angelos had grown thin and pale. That summer the heat of Paris was unbearable. Poor Father thought of sending them to Brittany for a fortnight. It was a good idea. For us in Athens, no move was possible. Mother had suffered a partial stroke and lay motionless in bed. She barely survived the catastrophe. The doctor was not pessimistic. He took her blood and told her again not to worry — that she would get well. I took care of her as best I could, and waited anxiously for Father. The heat of Athens was at its worst, but her big room was cool. Mine was an oven. The house was almost empty so I slept in the dining room on the big table with all the windows and doors open. Only there some cool breeze might sweeten the sleep of early morning. I was then writing for the first time:

I wonder do I hear the sea
in my eagle's nest,
boundless, without horizon,
so that it becomes the sky,

The rocking of my mother, the sea,
the sound of my dream,
the sound of my love,
and now a sheltering embrace.

Landward, sickness and death groan on,
men are wild and lawless like wolves,
with you, my own sea,
I am far from the ugliness.

The sea gulls on the white waves
are guiding me.

I put these forgotten verses on paper as in a dream one August dawn in the dining room on Cybele Street. What breath had carried me in sleep to the big bedroom at Skala so that I could hear the sea lapping below the open windows? I never showed these lines to George.

That was a bitter year.

Paris, 25 August 1923 Night
Little sister, this evening your letter came. Everything that gave me joy has gone away and left me alone. If you only knew how I miss you! . . . I was in Brittany. . . . In the evening, coming back from my walk, I passed little houses which reminded me of our house in Skala — whitewashed walls, the wooden bed at the back, on the table a loaf of bread with a knife beside it. . . . I remembered the days when the meltemi came and we all gathered around the teapot. . . . Now I begin to feel the autumn here . . . Voici que les corbeaux hivernaux . . .

I might feel better now if I were not thinking so much about Mother. Take good care of her, little sister. Please do. . . . Soon Father will be returning to Athens to give his lectures again and you should have a better winter . . . I am sending you a seal which Jacqueline found for you — in the style of Louis XVI, really old . . .

My connections with the refugee world continued to be close. Mother was still immobilized, but she wanted their news. Their re-establishment was going very slowly. They were starting their second winter, still in their wooden huts, still hungry.

And now, even before the weeping and lamentations of these homeless people had subsided, Corfu was bombarded on August 31st by the Italians. They might as well be Turks. But the "civilized" Mussolini wanted to show his power by striking a small country in its death throes. Everyone knew that Corfu was unfortified, and above all they knew that refugees were encamped in the citadel. Even now I cannot forget my indignation when I heard that Mussolini's fleet was bombarding the fortress.

Where should they go? Where could they stay? These persecuted children of God? Fifteen were killed, among them a young girl. Her murder aroused all Corfu. Disregarding martial law, they followed her funeral. Byron's *Curse of Minerva* buzzed in my brain:

> Next prowls the wolf, the filthy jackal last;
> Flesh, limbs, and blood the former make their own,
> The last poor brute securely gnaws the bone.

That bombardment wakened my political conscience. The past year had taught me many things. I had matured through misfortune, not just from the passage of time.

When Father came in October I admitted to him that I was discouraged: "Is there no justice? Is there no League of Nations?"

Father answered sadly: "The balance of power is difficult, and the League of Nations is achieving something. See to it that you are strong, with few needs, and a good education."

From then on I was never indifferent to politics. They too are part of the human drama. Human weakness, human egoism, and, on rare occasions, human greatness. I followed events and made judgments about them. I saw jealousy, even hate among the army officers, the creation of cliques round Plastiras; plots by other generals. At a given moment, we did not know who would be governing us tomorrow. Had we perhaps come to the end? Was it possible that, surrounded by enemies as we were, half our army would be fighting the other half? Finally Plastiras succeeded in getting the upper hand. It must have been the end of October, 1923. But things were no better. Every day the prestige of some famous officer was reduced to bits by his egomania.

Venizelos did not return. His advice was not followed.

In the gloom of that era, who would be worthy to take up the cross of our suffering people?

Actually I never wrote to George about my political anxieties. He too avoided this barren subject which made him so unhappy.

> 15 rue Bréa Paris VI, 1 October 1923
> Little sister, do you remember that song of Laforgue? . . . 'tous les ans, tous les ans j'essaierai en coeur d'en donner la note'? So with me, this time of year always brings to mind your departures. It's my season, you know. It always makes me suffer — perhaps that's why I love it. . . . I think from time to time how we are bound by the same fate, even though we are far apart, and even though we differ on certain matters. We are in the same key, and that is rare. . . . But then who knows? Perhaps heaven will open up for us at last, why not? Perhaps one day we shall feel ourselves on the summit of some acropolis that we ourselves have fashioned. Then we shall take a deep breath and feel again the pure spirit of song. There will come a day, it must come. You must say this too, little sister. Sometimes I feel a little spark in my heart. But something strange! at this moment, as I write to you, a shadow passed across my wall, like a frail, sorrowing woman. Of course these are all fantasies, but somehow, so real . . .

With our imagination we built ourselves bridges.

To me that year of our separation seemed endless. Daily events were so important that it made the time seem much longer. And George had been very slow writing to me. I was uneasy. What should I say to Mother who was always asking?

George had fallen ill. They had taken him to the hospital. Actually, it was not serious, and Angelos was with him, but Mother must know nothing about it. Even I learned about it only later when he returned to his new room. Marie Louise and Jacqueline had stood by him.

> 16 November 1923
> How much I would like to hear your voice a little . . . to

hear your steps in the room. . . . In the clinic I remember the all-white room, the all-white furniture, and the pale light which came through the pale curtains. . . . It was as if I were traveling alone on a calm ocean of oblivion. And I was unhappy, not so much in body as in soul; I was seized by a vertigo that made everything go round and round, and I was just a black speck in the middle of this white chaos. And those I loved were passing me by, their eyes fixed on what was not I. I was bored and I was lonely. Little sister, how I longed for you those evenings. . . .

I remembered that letter and I re-read it many times during his final illness. He could not speak, and I struggled to enter into his pain, his thought.

Sleepless at night, I spent the days at the hospital. After the first hemorrhage, through the open door of his room, he heard my steps, and asked anxiously: "Is it Ioanna?" His wife, to avoid exciting him, stood in front of me.

"No, it is Savvidis."

I waited a little and then went near him. He squeezed my hand.

"Let me explain about the blood — I really must explain to you . . ."

Distressed, I stroked his hand. "Later, dear George, when you have recovered your strength. There is so much more we have to say."

They took him to the intensive care ward and performed a tracheotomy so that he might breathe more easily. This cut off his speech. Then the second surgery took place.

His great patience had come to an end. His body could take no more. That look of the wounded animal, speechless — how can I forget it? The following day, he held on to me with his old tenderness.

"Try, George dear, try to cough." He gave a little cough.

In grave illness one rejects all one has acquired in life. The man becomes a little child again, looking for his mother in the dark. George smiled when I smoothed a wrinkle which registered his pain. We looked again in each other's eyes, his grown larger. He stretched his bound hand toward my neck and drew me to him.

Two sturdy legs in white stockings came and went, a nurse. The doctors too in their smocks. Some hope perhaps? To look at each other again! He had always been looking at me, even before I came to the earth. His tenderness sweeter than my mother's.

I had abandoned reason, and was roaming in a world of miracle. He would live. It could not be otherwise. No matter what they said to me, he would live.

But the difficulty of his breathing haunted me, choked me. The fresh air of Penteli — let me gather it and take it to him. This air — I felt it at night, and hated it because it came to me and not to him.

My God, how does a man die? This infinite yearning — what becomes of it? Late at night, perched in the corner of the dimly lit waiting room of the Evangelismos Hospital, close to the intensive care ward, I listened to the clock, the tears of time. Then came the hour of the great return.

No, the hour has not come. The secret song of solitude is still ours. Our love still lives, indestructible. George, you still have so much to say! The earth binds your heart with its strongest tentacles.

Grief mounted in me. Everything was so hard for him. The road to poetry had been hard, and hard now was the road to death.

This moment of life — how infinite!

Quiet now, he looked at me again with the little smile he had as a child. Time stopped.

For two days I watched with George in the Church of the Holy Saviour. In this neighborhood church, so familiar that it seemed almost the chapel of our father's house, it was as if he were a little alive and I were a little dead. Nothing separated us. We spoke again of the sorrows of our life, and they passed before my eyes, one by one, even those of which we had never spoken to each other though we knew them well.

As on the ancient grave steles, the young people, boys and girls, bowed before him. One would leave a piece of laurel, another a cyclamen. What touched me most was the tears in their eyes.

Newspapers, articles, photographs, words upon words, the

story of your life, your fame. That is to say, you have become a dead man. But how is that possible? Where are you?

In the street one man would say to another, "He was a great poet." And the answer might be, "And what is it to him now to have been a great poet?"

Your funeral procession with your own songs diffused into the vast crowd the yearning for the absolute. I followed you hypnotized. You were tenderly showing me the road to the other world. Under that September sun, death, kindly and simply, found its place within me. I felt that you were beside me and that I was beside you on a blinding march.

With what powerful attraction the depths of the earth were drawing me on! Surely, wherever you are, you know that with the earth that covered you there is forever the very essence of my love.

For months I was sunk in a pit of darkness. I could no longer see. A white light which did not shine came and went. I groped for a rope. If only someone would throw me a rope!

In the autumn of 1923 George was writing all his poetry in French. I began to be frightened again. He had so compelling a need to communicate with the woman he loved.

Father returned to Athens and began his lectures. Mother was better. She had left her bed, and was walking freely. Of course she never went out alone. Life at home gave some promise of serenity. I tried to please Father. There was some awkwardness with the boys, but he certainly had great responsibilities. I tried to help by copying his lectures about international law on the typewriter. Meanwhile, I had enrolled in the first year of Law School.

Father received his friends and colleagues regularly, and he also received his students. Our house began to liven up, not with disasters and illness, but with work.

On Sundays I went regularly to the orchestra concerts. Evenings, before sleeping, to change my train of thought, I read Plutarch's *Lives*.

December 22 1923
Little sister, you remember the caïque we wanted to name Vanna, how prophetic, your name, for the caïque I liked so much? . . . And an even greater coincidence that last

Sunday I too was hearing *Scheherazade* and it made a great impression on me . . . You remember the second part, you must have felt it too, when Prince Kalader entered Bagdad. There came back to me all the Arabian tales of Halima, the winter evenings in Smyrna, when we sat cross-legged around a burning brazier. . . .

We were the sea-going Sinbads, traveling toward new seas, searching for sapphires, till one day we found ahead of us the magnetic mountain which drew all the rivets out of our boat and left us with detached boards, just enough to get us back to the beach, drenched and ridiculous. That's the way we pass our lives — on an armful of boards which began as a beautiful boat.

He needed to feel himself again a child. The memory of his boyhood years provided him with a refuge. Logical conformity to the rules of a system was hard for him. It is good that we are able to transcend the rational limits of the world through our imagination.

1924–1925

George's years in Paris laid the foundation for his attitude toward life.

In the beginning, in the cthonian power of his loneliness, he unearthed his tragic self, discovered his personal law, poetry.

Later he was engulfed by the loss of Ionia, a loss which he never accepted. Throughout his life, drop by drop, he sipped the poison of the national calamity, whatever form it might take.

And it was in those years that he confronted the blind alley of love.

So this last year in France was not easy. Besides poetry and poverty and law studies, he was tormented by the coming separation from Jacqueline. He was exhausted by his effort to make bearable, in some way or other, this terrible eventuality, life without her. Hour after hour they wandered without speaking over the bridges and through the parks of Paris.

This was a great weight on his heart, as he told me later. He could not sleep.

"If at least she had not loved me — but it was her sorrow as well as mine."

I was completely upset. Why? Why? Had George no right to a little joy, a little laughter? We were so young!

But real love, in its hours of crisis, is more death than life. One is no longer just one's self, one is the other person as well. And when we lose the other one, we feel genuinely annihilated. In the despair of love, the spirit is quenched at the very moment of its struggle to reach the pinnacle of life.

The most wonderful things are the most terrifying.

In February 1924, George sent me the following poem, written in haste:

To Her Whose Eyes Are Closed
(perhaps after a portrait by Da Vinci)
Who am I? You chose me with closed eyes.
I? Your closed eyes entreated me.
Your thirst took me in a close embrace. . .
Come drink, come so that I may drink!
Forget so that I may forget
The vows, the prayers, the tedium, the twilights.
At the bottom of our glass we shall find the blue sky.
Run, dare, the dawn says to us:
Unhappiness is cowardice.

In the summer of 1924, George passed his final examinations for the doctorate. Now he would definitely abandon Paris. I thought a great deal about that terrible moment. I wrote to him cautiously lest I touch a wound. He answered me from England.

Hove 14 August 1924 — Wednesday evening

Dear little sister, before leaving Paris I had your letter. . . . Today I am about as I was before. I really don't change, you know. . . . Never mind . . . It's nothing.

Always when something really worried him and he sensed that I shared his anxiety, he would whisper the phrase: "Never mind. It's nothing."

Now there is a fine rain, the sky is dark. The time of year when one is reminded of Baudelaire's lines on autumn. If one or two such men were to be taken away from the world, it's a question whether anything would remain to redeem humanity.
Tout bas comme d'un coeur qui saigne
Il s'est mis à pleuvoir.
In January I hope to be in Athens. I fear this return as if it were a departure in spite of my longing to embrace all of you. It is unfortunate that one must go through things on the deepest level while one is going through them on the surface.

He was somewhat relieved by the thought that Father was near us and teaching at the University. He believed this made Mother happier.

That stay in England in 1924–25, so fruitful for George's poetry, was a period of tremendous psychological struggle.

The two lovers still had some hope. They wrote to each other, but correspondence can squeeze us like forceps with its dubious comfort: "Christ, tell me what to say to her."

He had suffered the change which we all know well, when the blind alley turns out to be a permanent condition. The tree of bitterness roots itself in silence;

> And life's cold as a fish —
> Is that how you live? — Yes, how else? (p. 409)

Some time later, we talked for hours and he told me all about it. During that period, we were not communicating often. Our correspondence, turned sharply inward, had exhausted us. The tension that breaks the bow. The thought of futility had become feeling. He sent me scattered lines on scraps of paper. In spite of all this, for the moment, life seemed to me to have its proper rhythm. We had the necessary time at our disposition and our hearts were open to full awareness of the dramatic events around us. We knew that this close coexistence with our destiny was the only right road to poetry. But it was difficult and oppressive! How was it we did not try to escape through movement and action? We kept coming back to it because it was our best self.

I was often frightened about George — sensing that he was desperate there in the fog. His letters to Father were infrequent. They were like telegrams, brief accounts of his studies, of his finances.

At the end of 1924 a note from him gave me joy: he asked for some books: *The Social Significance of the Greek Revolution* by I. K. Kordatos and *Our Social Problem* by G. Skliros. But most of all he wanted *Our Orthography* by Manolis Triantaphylidis. He needed it urgently.

London, 25 November 1924

Dear little sister. . . . I am desperately alone here. . . . The distance is always the same, and we do not feel the breath, sometimes weaker, sometimes stronger, of what life gives us, which is perhaps life itself . . .

I am beginning to love English. I read it many hours a day.

Angelos abandoned medicine. He had passed his examinations brilliantly the first year, but in the second he could not cope with anatomy. He too would study law in Greece. His warm presence nearby would be a comfort to me.

1924–25–26–27, the study of law for both Angelos and me. In the atmosphere of the family. With parental supervision. I too passed my first-year examinations successfully. Father was pleased. He was beginning to respect me in a new way. He gave me more freedom without petty restrictions. I was not away from home a great deal. Mother's image was always before me. But I was ambitious to carry out all my obligations as a student. So, with great satisfaction, I took part in my first rebellion. Pangalos, then dictator, retroactively sentenced two thieves to death. Since we had just been studying the "nulla poena sine lege", we felt enlightened about justice and considered it our first duty to protest. We made demonstrations in the street, demanding that the law be applied. At that time we women students were few. I remember that there were only young men around me. After we had carried out our political duty, we were hungry, so we took some buns and sat down on the sidewalk to wait for the next class. I was discouraged and said to a boy beside me:

"The authorities despise us, or they would try to disperse us."

He was optimistic. "Our voices will get through to them."

A futile hope. The condemned were hanged.

My participation in the demonstration brought me closer to the young people. I got rid of my odious identity as the professor's daughter, and made many friends, many boys and a few girls. The male mind suited me, not lost in trivialities. The jealousy and hypocrisy of the female sex surprised me, humiliated me. . . . But in Father's presence, I could never speak to anyone, even a classmate or friend, in the singular. He considered it a mark of unacceptable intimacy.

"But, Papa, you are influenced by the French language. In Greek the singular is more natural. Remember the Platonic dialogues."

He could not be persuaded.

Every evening I continued with him another serious discussion. He wanted to publish his translation of Byron's *Songs of Greece*, but under a pseudonym. I objected seriously.

"But why under a pseudonym? It is as if you were ashamed of your beautiful work. I don't understand you."

"You know very well that in Greece a poet is not considered a serious person."

I was dumbfounded.

"All the more reason why you should not give in to so great a stupidity." At the time I did not persuade him, perhaps because he was absorbed in his classes, and was not really paying attention to me. But in 1930, he brought out under his own name the collection of his poems *From My Drawer*. How happy he was when the aged Palamas sent him this quatrain:

> *To Stelios Seferiadis*
> In a drawer you tossed them lightly
> as unworthy of much care;
> I have read your lines with their old-time grace
> and with their fragrant flair.

Another good sign: that year I found again my old refuge. Evenings, alone in my little room, I began to read poetry again. There in my law books I discover lines I had jotted down — like confidences:

> Vainement ma raison voulait prendre la barre;
> La tempête en jouant déroutait mes efforts. . . .

Once more poetry assumed its dominant place in my life. I welcomed it, and see it now as a sign of my progress toward health after the shock of the Asia Minor catastrophe.

IV
1926–1931

OUR EXILE RETURNED

At last, on Christmas Eve 1925, the great event occurred. Our exile returned. I longed for the hour, but I was also fearful. He had been away from Greece for seven years, years of enormous change. And now he was coming back to this country staggered by the defeat in Asia Minor, to this house staggered by Mother's illness. I marveled at his composure. All he expressed was joy in his return. Mother embraced him:

"Now that you are here, my boy, I shall get well quickly." She was putting on an act, and I was grateful to her.

I tried to make him comfortable. I had prepared his room: his desk, his bookcase, his armchair, some familiar pictures on the wall. Beside his bed I put his silver bowl, his silver aspergillum. All this pleased him.

We sat down at the table. Angelos tried to break the atmosphere of emotional tension by making fun of their old privations:

"You may have a second helping of meat, George. Here they don't count the portions."

"We'll lick the platter clean," George answered.

After dinner I helped Mother to bed. George kissed her and said goodnight.

"God bless you, my boy, for coming," and she stroked his hair.

Back in the parlor, he whispered gravely, "What a wreck it has made of her!"

When we were alone, he pressed my hand:

"We have so much to say, and how much I need you! You have had time to get used to it. For me it is a great blow. And now I'll ask you a favor — my letters from Jacqueline — as far as possible, let the others not see them."

"Don't worry about it, George."

At sunset next day we went to the Theseion. The Acropolis was spread out before us. The only spot where we were untouched by the "earthly stain". There in a little café, he talked to me about his love. On his way home, he had passed through Paris and they had seen each other.

"But why, why these separations?"

I did not know what to say to him. His bitterness was more than I could bear. I tried to understand. But after all, how is man, this microscopic speck in the vast chaos, to endure this thirst, this ache? Does there perhaps exist some justification in time?

I remember well those days of his return, his slow adaptation. The state of the country, the refugees — all this tortured him. Abroad he had suffered for humanity in general, but it was not like this. He had not identified with each suffering individual as he did in Greece. Here the disillusion of every day was insupportable.

Competition for posts in the Ministry of Foreign Affairs had been announced for the first months of 1926. George wanted to take part. While Mother still lived, he wanted to give her that joy. Again he threw himself into study. So books and correspondence filled those first months. Evenings we tried to take walks. Since we lived beside the Museum, we would go toward Omonia and then up Aiolou Street. It was deserted at that hour. On winter nights when there was a moon, the Acropolis looked brand-new.

Before George submitted his papers for the competition at the Ministry, Father insisted on testing him. As Professor of International Law, he always examined the candidate for the Foreign Office, and therefore he knew well what was expected. But the demands he made of his own children were always prodigious. He did not find his son perfect, as he required him to be, and therefore he forbade him to become a candidate at that time.

The life of study continued more intensely than ever. The next competition would be in the autumn.

"So this is what is to become of my youth! I can't stand it."

Evenings, to clear his brain of law and Katharevousa, he read Makriyannis: "As for now, there is no other cure."

He would also murmur French poetry.

"I would write well if I were writing in French," he kept saying to me. Other times he took refuge in Solomos. And always he was thinking of Jacqueline. When he became self-supporting after entering the Ministry, he would make a flying trip to Paris to see her again.

At that time, I too was in love. I spoke of it to George because I did not want to conceal it from him. He said nothing. He did not know the man in question.

We were both in agony over Mother's life.

"She is so young," said George, "barely fifty-two. It is unjust that she should not go on living."

Summer drew near. Father was about to leave for Paris. I proposed to him that we take a small house in the country nearby, especially for Mother's sake, so that she might sleep well. Actually we found such a house in the village of Kifissia. Two rooms, a dining room, and the necessary facilities. There was also a courtyard with a jasmine vine in full bloom. Mother could barely stand on her feet, but we took her to see it and she loved it. So we moved her there. Over her bed I hung the silver Virgin from which she was never parted. Angelos would go to Paros with one of his fellow students so that they could study together. This allowed George to have a room to himself so that he could concentrate on his studies. I proposed that he too go to an island for a while. The expense would be small, and he adored the sea. But he did not want me to be alone, even for a short while.

So, hand-in-hand, like two convicts, we passed those difficult months together. Mother no longer left her bed. I could not study since I dared not light the lamp.

I was trying always to protect George, to help him: "You, George, are the one who must study now. You must not miss the next competition." He had reached the final step in his preparation for the examinations.

"Study, George, I beg you." He kissed my hand.

"That's what I am doing."

We decided to call into consultation for Mother Dr. Kavvadias, a specialist of great standing both in England and in Greece. After his visit to Mother, he said he would wish to see us privately in his office. I insisted on going alone. "If you stay home, George, you can study. Don't lose any time." So I went alone.

I shall not forget that morning. I was very slender. In my dark blue linen skirt, my long hair tied back, I looked like a child. The doctor asked me kindly, "To whom can I speak? Where is your father?"

"You may speak to me, Doctor. My father is in Paris now, and Mother wants my brother near her. He gives her great support. You may speak freely to me. I am brave."

At least, so I thought. And I asked shyly,

"Doctor, she *will* get well?"

Dr. Kavvadias looked at me again, hesitating.

"My child, you must write to your father that your mother is very seriously ill. Her kidneys are affected."

"Is there any hope?" I asked again softly.

"If she survives for two months, it will be something to report in the medical journals. There is nothing to be done." I thanked him and started to go.

"I will take you. I have my car," he said with genuine sympathy.

"No, thank you very much, Doctor. I am not going home." And I left in haste. I barely reached the street before my tears began to flow uncontrollably. I walked as fast as I could to Canningos Square, ignoring the other pedestrians. I didn't even feel the burning midday sun. It must have been two o'clock when I finally got into an empty bus. I sat down back of the driver. There, unconstrained by the presence of others, I wept my heart out. This outburst in the isolation of the noonday ride helped me. As we neared the end, I dried my eyes and fixed myself up. Mother was waiting for me.

"Why are you so late? I lost my wedding ring. I've been looking for it ever since you left."

"But you gave it to me to keep for you," and I kissed her.

"God bless you, my child."

By then it must have been about three o'clock. George heard me, opened his door, and drew me into his room. He saw immediately that I had been crying, and spoke in an agonized whisper.

"What is the news? Is there any hope?"

"As long as she is alive, there is hope, but her condition is very serious." How could I tell him the death sentence I had just heard? "Doctors," I thought to myself, "are not gods."

George stayed near her like a lost child. He was seeking that warmth he had so richly known, the warmth he had longed for all the years of his absence abroad. With the most tender masculine awkwardness, he tried to look after her, to give her a little lemonade, to pull up the covers. I no longer told him to go and study.

One evening, when we were sitting, George and I, in the door to the jasmine courtyard listening to her breathing, he said very softly:

"We must tell Angelos to come home."

I also wrote to Father to report what the doctor had said. It would be very hard for him to come before mid-September. No one imagined the end would come so soon.

On September 9, Angelos arrived.

"I am so glad you have come, my boy," and Mother smiled at him.

She looked at her sons, one on either side, and dropped off to sleep. The doctor was there and he whispered: "Perhaps she will survive this time too."

Angelos, more rested now after his island stay, asked to spend the night beside her. I lay down in my clothes, as did George. I was exhausted, and fell asleep immediately. In the middle of my sleep, I heard my two brothers murmuring.

"Shall we waken her?" I jumped to my feet.

"Is it the end?" I asked.

Angelos whispered brokenly:

"Look" and pointed to the silver Virgin. In Her eyes — truly — there shone two tears.

A face of overwhelming love.

What power love acquires in time of trouble! How does man become so strong? George took full charge. He took his dead mother and started for Athens.

"Take Angelos with you."

"No, I want him to stay with you. I shall go alone with her."

"Perhaps he still has something he wants to say to her," I thought to myself.

It was getting late. He must not delay. The meltemi had come. A cold northern wind was whistling through the cracks of the lightly-constructed house. George was traveling, through the night and the wind, with Mother. All the lights were on, but it still seemed dark. I was trembling all over.

"Angelos, where are you?" He came and sat near me. What time was it? I was not living in time.

Was that knocking at the door? Was it the North Wind? We opened the door. It was George, pale, back again, and with Mother.

"The army stopped us and sent us back. Kondilis has made a *coup* against Pangalos."

So we buried her in Kifissia. We stayed on a few days near the cemetery. And Father came.

George was waiting for something. Finally it arrived — the warm-hearted letter from Jacqueline. He was comforted.

> And all this is an old story that no longer interests anyone;
> we've hardened our hearts and grown up. (p. 207)

When you love the poet, and know him almost as if you had given him birth, it is both painful and sweet to read in his verse the substratum of his heart, the upward climb to his tragic world.

I caress these golden pages rustling in my hands.

In the long run, what have we to give to others except our unquenchable love?

On that our fateful day, September 9, 1926, Athens was in revolt.

Friends who came to console us told us what had happened. The people, exasperated with the revolutionary movements, had risen on their own. They armed themselves with boards from buildings being built for the Stock Exchange, and beat up the police and the gendarmes. All without program, without plan, without leadership.

For the first time I heard George utter his famous phrase: "We are not a serious people."

We abandoned Kifissia. Then I truly understood what it was to be an orphan.

How Mother's advice had helped me! Now the three men, Father and my two brothers, wandered around me, lost. My responsibility for their peace of mind concerned me more and more.

Most difficult were the clashes between Father and George. They would begin with simple discussion. From that moment I was on my guard to lessen the tension which was almost sure to develop. Later I would go to Father's study and appeal to him:

"Be careful with George, Father. He is very worried and is doing more than he can. You'll be proud of him." Father really listened to me. For some weeks he was an angel.

At last came the day of the diplomatic competition. To all appearances we were calm, but I couldn't sleep, and turned over and over in my bed until dawn. I was afraid of the storm which would follow a failure. Father's extreme anxiety affected us all. A competition where there are many candidates and only three places involves also an element of luck.

In the life of the past now unwinding before me, there are certain crucial times when those I loved were threatened or actually stricken. These never pass. They are yesterday, today, and tomorrow. I write about them with the certainty of now.

On the morning of the competition, I watched George from the balcony of the house on Cybele Street until he was lost at the turn in the road. Angelos had shut himself in his room. Father was pacing up and down. Some time passed. Then I said to him:

"I am going to the Ministry myself. I'll sit in a corner and wait for him." I set out on foot for Philellinon Street. There on the second floor of the Ministry I found a little sofa and sat down.

An ambassador, friend of Father, saw me.

"You want to find out about your brother? The oral examinations are going on now. Come to the big hall. There are lots of people there." I entered the hall very shyly and sat down at the rear. An iron band was squeezing my head. The examiner appeared to me a dragon about to swallow my brother. George's turn came. He answered with confidence. He spoke easily about his subject. At one moment he turned toward the rear of the room and saw me; he smiled. I felt a great relief. It was over.

I can see George before me, saying sadly, "If only Mother were alive." I was thinking the same. We went to her grave with some flowers which she loved.

George entered the Foreign Service. The most pressing of his immediate needs was solved. His relation to Father was easier. Quiet spread through the house, as when they stop the engines on a ship. We had caught a favorable wind and were under full sail. I felt relieved, but not for long. It is not a simple thing to ask a poet to earn his living, especially if he has a personal pride in doing well the work to which he is committed. George, as in poetry, so also in diplomacy, was extremely conscientious and responsible.

"My true work is something else," he said to me in the evening. "I must find the time which I need for myself, for my personal work. What I can count on is time in the night." And he added a sentence which later appeared in his verse: "I am not one of those young men who spend their souls in order to sport a monocle."

I have always felt somewhat ashamed in the presence of the very poor. Only during the occupation did I in some way share their hunger. But when a talented man has to fight for his bread, I find the world is out of tune. I think it was in 1935 when we had gone to Chios. The young people told me about the poet, Angoulés. They had sacked him from the nomarch's office where he was working. Now at night he fished and wrote poetry.

> In all the forms
> that thought can know
> I've carved your image,
> Satan, in my hell.

If he was lucky in fishing, he would have food the next day. Otherwise he went hungry. I could not get my mind off that situation. I went back to Athens discouraged. I approached people of influence. No help anywhere. One minister said to me from the loftiness of his bureaucratic mind:

"But Madame, all these poets, good or bad, are useless people."

That was too much for me. Father had been right when he chose to conceal his poems under a pseudonym. Fortunately, Angoulés recovered his job in Chios.

1927–1928

Early in 1927 Angelos passed his examinations for his degree in law. He had enrolled retroactively under a regulation which made it possible for him to finish without loss of time. Now I was the last to qualify for my degree. But how could I concentrate? So much work and worry at home. Mother's friends thought it their duty to give me lots of advice — I must lock the cupboards, keep count of the sheets, watch the food. But why? Old Athenà, the woman who helped me in the house, was kind. She said to me sympathetically,

"Don't waste your time, Miss Ioanna, with housekeeping. Much better for you to study and finish." I agreed with her.

But still I could not concentrate. Mother was always there. Death is an episode. But we the living, go on. The blood tie is not severed just because someone suddenly leaves us. The dead are always asking our love. It is not they who are different; it is we. As our memory searches the past, we learn things about them which they themselves hardly suspected. And we envelop them in the heart felt warmth which, in our weakness, we could not offer them in life.

I considered being coached for the law examinations at a tutoring school. The presence of a third party would help control my galloping imagination. But perhaps the professorial circle would consider it degrading? I asked Father about it.

"In the recitations, I would have some check on my progress," I suggested. Father agreed at once. I sensed that George had been talking to him.

I entered the main room of the tutoring school as inconspicuously as I could. Very slender — just a rod wrapped in black. The teacher and the students rose to their feet. Absolute silence. I blushed, greeted them awkwardly, and sat down. It was a hard moment.

In April 1927 I too took my degree.

Now in the evening George was working at translations. Beside his bed were always the volumes of Solomos, of Makriyannis. He took note of every vivid word. He worked over his own syntax, a simple syntax.

He was attempting a translation of *Monsieur Teste* by Valéry. He was looking for the suggestive word, the resounding word, its relation to the other words within the text. The phrase *"je me terminais"* bothered him. His choice was for *"I was coming to the end"* while I preferred *"I was finishing."* One morning he telephoned me from the ministry:

"I found it: 'the *miser*'."

"It's all right," I answered, "but why not the *'hoarder'*?"

Anyone listening might have thought we were talking in code. How could he imagine that the discussion concerned the word *avare*!

The Evening with M. Teste was a difficult exercise. Valéry uses the perfection of the French language with utmost skill. How to render this subtle text, with all its nuances, in Demotic Greek? George worked diligently, without haste, like the woodcarver we saw working on the iconostasis in Metsovo. He often read aloud to me passages he had especially noted.

"Finding the phrase is nothing. What is difficult is making it your own, once you have found it."

It is a great comfort to feel you are not alone, that the great authors of the past are there beside you, they too with their troubles.

We waited impatiently for evening, George to work at his translation of Valery, I for the discussion when he came to a pause. There was only the one word with which he could express the meaning, the feeling. When he found it, great joy. I remember the phrase: *"je rature le vif."* I proposed to say: "I cross out the lively." George objected:

"In Greek it doesn't make sense." He considered it in context and concluded: "I cross out living things."

Every evening he worked at sharpening, clarifying the foggy passages in his Demotic. Does the reader ever think of the writer's track over stones and dry branches in order to arrive at the quiet road of good, simple expression?

For a long time Father had cherished the dream that we would travel together. Now the obligation to Mother did not tie me down. He wanted to show me his Paris. He enjoyed making plans, to what theatres we would go, in what corners we would dine. Accustomed as I was to the Paris of the students, I was a little put off by that of "the establishment," but I was glad it gave him pleasure. Till now all my concern had been devoted to my Mother. I realized that Father too was thirsty for love. Later, in spite of our separation after his second marriage, I tried until the end to add to his life what sweetness I could.

George also wanted us to make this trip.

"As soon as you arrive, telephone to Jacqueline. You will go to see her. You will tell her about me. You will tell me about her the things she does not write. You are the only one who can understand."

Of course I did as he had asked. On my first day in Paris, I telephoned and went to her house. I always liked the women who loved George. But when I saw Jacqueline, I suffered for her. Perhaps because of all I knew. Perhaps because all her sorrow was gathered in her big eyes. She spoke little and she did not complain, but when she spoke his name, the warmth of love filled the room. I don't remember her words, but the memory of her sadness has never been erased. Jacqueline believed that George was a poet, that the meaning of his life was poetry.

"He is unhappy when he is not writing," she whispered. She wanted to help in every way, whether by her presence, or by their separation. I listened to her gratefully. We met many times. I wrote to George and he answered:

Cybele Street, Athens, 24 July 1927
Today at noon I received your letter. Thank you for what you have written, thank you from both of us. You cannot imagine how complicated my life is. Surprises on all sides, here, there. At least I am managing to get back into life! Someday I'll write to you about all this. Better still, I'll tell you about it . . . I have read Valéry's speech and I recommend it to you . . . Excellent . . .

It was the first time I had left Greece since the Asia Minor disaster. Finally I would see it from a certain distance with a relative maturity which I feared as a dryness of soul. I remember saying to George:

"When I no longer have the courage to jump off the balcony for the sake of an idea or for a human being, then I shall be old."

In August Father sent me to stay with an English family near London. Marian, the mistress of the house, was a quiet, cultivated woman. She helped me to appreciate England with that sobriety which conceals much feeling and much will power.

At the end of September I returned to Athens with Father. Angelos was doing his military service. George received us with his old warmth. He pressed my arm, whispering a verse of Apollinaire:

>Si jamais je revois cette femme,
>Je lui dirai je suis content.

adding, "I was ready to burst from loneliness and work. We have so much to say to each other."

Actually, every evening, because Father went to bed early, we talked interminably until very late. He asked again and again about Jacqueline. He recited verses that were going around inside his head, but had not yet found their place in a poem:

> God! what a struggle it is for life to keep going,
> as though it were a swollen river passing through
> the eye of a needle. (p. 75)

"Do you like it?" I smiled, and George went on, feeling himself at ease:

"Shall I tell you how I passed the summer? I drank lemonades made from green lemons."

There was now some optimism in the political situation. In April 1927, Venizelos had gone back to Crete. He said emphatically that there was no question of his return to political activity, that he was going back because of his great nostalgia for his own land. But living in the heart of the country, he came to understand more deeply how the people, exhausted by the instability, the uprisings, were thirsting for his leadership. When he came to Athens for a short time, he tested public opinion, and saw that his prestige was enormous.

The coalition governments had failed. The small Venizelist parties were more obedient to Venizelos than to their own leaders. Agreement among the political figures, the only possible basis for normal political life, could not be achieved.

Therefore, on May 23, 1928, when Venizelos announced his decision to campaign, there was enthusiasm throughout the country.

That winter Father had many concerns. He was in regular contact with Venizelos. He was preparing his second volume of lectures. He was preparing his summer courses for the Academy of International Law at the Hague. It was fortunate for him that his children were not giving him any trouble. He wanted me to pass the doctoral examinations. To please him I had already begun work on my thesis: *Nationality and Marriage.*

"Next summer you will go again to England," he told me. "As a doctor of law, knowing two foreign languages, you can have an appointment at the League of Nations at a good salary."

I had no objections. I much preferred these ideas to talk of a son-in-law. I did my legal apprenticeship in the office of Maridakis and Tsatsos. From childhood, Mistos Tsatsos was like a brother to me. That was when I first met Costakis, my husband.

Now something else important slipped into our life. A real woman, of great musical cultivation and great sensitivity, fell in love with George. She was married, somewhat older than he, and she understood the drama of his love affair with Jacqueline. She drew close to him gently, without jealousy, but with love, with femininity, with admiration. She was honest with him. Above all, she did not ask him to be faithful. George accepted her love gratefully:

> and you were my fate's woof
> you, whom they'd call Billio. (399)

This painless love story of George's, along with the other one, lasted for years. The woman "whom they'd call Billio" was a great help to him. After a while she disappeared into silence.

How charming, how quiet the picturesque, civilized house of Professor Fokas at Kefalari. There we spent our summer. We had three rooms looking out on a large garden. From the dining room a little stairway led to the second floor, a fourth room, and that was mine.

When Father left for the Hague, we three children established ourselves there.

There are memories that disturb you, memories that make you want to take to the mountains in the hope that the wind will blow them away. There are memories warm with love where you take refuge. And there are still others that exercise in the heart an aesthetic grace, a spiritual enchantment. Certainly disturbing events do not cease to exist, but the element of beauty is stronger.

Such is the memory of the summer of 1928.

The house was hidden among trees. In front of one of my windows rose Mount Penteli. In front of the other, a little road through pines, cypresses, and roses led to the garden gate. We three were by ourselves, free, without pressures. Not a single legal book. Only the texts we loved. At that time we were reading much in the classical authors: Homer, Aeschylus. Angelos had leave from the army; he discovered Sophocles' *Ajax.*

Morever, all three of us were in love.

Each had his own room. We had given George the one with the biggest table, the most comfortable armchair. He would come back from the Ministry, from the suffocating heat of Athens, and open his double doors toward the garden.

> The skyscrapers of New York will never
> know the coolness that comes down on Kifissia . . .
> (p. 75)

The atmosphere of that house, so I believe, relaxed all three of us. I was silent for hours at a time. The cicadas, the nightingales, were to be heard all around us.

New friends poured in every day. There were comfortable chairs in the garden. The outer gate was always open. Our friends sat with us or by themselves, as at a club. We felt no obligation to be together all the time. Nor would it have occurred to us to lock the door. We saw them when it suited us.

My friend, Dora Vourloumis, asked John Theodorakopoulos questions.

"What is love?" — and he answered in Platonic terms: "The reach toward form." Then George: "Philosophy mixes me up. Let's go to Kokkinara." So we set out for the tall cypresses. We went into the little church of Saint George. There George would light a candle and study the frescoed walls like an icon-painter. At the exit, we could sit on the stone wall and be lost in thought as we watched the sunset.

In August 1928 the elections were held.

Venizelos won triumphantly. He could hardly believe it himself. Of 250 seats, the Liberals won 223. He wrote to his wife, "In reality, the Greek people have made me a parliamentary dictator."

I remember George saying sadly,

"If we had had such a majority in 1920, much would have been saved."

The beautiful summer ended badly. George was the first to suffer from dengue fever. There was a serious epidemic of the illness that year. His temperature was forty degrees. He was burning up. He was a big man, and I was very slight. I could not move him to change his bed. He tried to move himself, but in his fever he did not understand what I was saying. One evening he slipped from my arms and fell to the floor. I was desperate. How could I lift him? Angelos' leave had ended and he had returned to his unit. Where would I find a man to help me? Maybe one of his friends would be in the garden. I opened the door and there stood Mistos Tstasos. Together we got him back to bed.

Then Angelos broke his arm in training. They put it in plaster and gave him further leave. He arrived home, sleepless, pale. The bandages were torturing him.

I tried not to think of my personal drama. False hopes were wearing me out. All those months in Kifissia I had not seen the man I loved. I heard that he had gone to Vienna to forget me, that his betrothal to a rich girl was being arranged.

On this clear August night I was sitting alone in the garden. My brothers, fatigued by their convalescence, were asleep. I heard footsteps. Who would it be at such an hour? Would it be he? In the silence I could hear my heartbeat.

"You have come to tell me that you are to be married?"
"How beautiful you are, Ioanna!" I smiled.
"You don't want to answer me?"
"Life doesn't exist without you."
"We had better talk of other things. Crossroads are always hard. Tell me about your trip."
He spoke to me briefly about Vienna. I stood up. I sensed that he was kissing me for the last time. I held him close for a moment, then let him go. For some hours I walked up and down in the garden. I was hardly aware of my tears as they fell.

A few days passed. I had not told George of that evening call. He lived my sorrows as I lived his. Why burden him?

One noon after lunch, I was taking a nap. I still remember my dream. I was wearing a long red velvet gown. I was trying to look at myself in the mirror. The mirror was broken. I heard a crackle. I opened my eyes. George was standing over me, looking at me anxiously. He was holding a newspaper.

"He is married?" I asked quietly. He nodded his head. He seemed so unhappy that I felt the need to comfort him.

"George, situations you can't change bring their own courage. You finally close your door on hope."

I did not seem to have persuaded him. I went on:

"Shall we take a walk to St. George's?"

On the way I whispered to him Nena's line:

"And curses with time may turn into great blessings."

He only smiled. Then, with quick steps, burdened with thoughts, mine of love past, his of love to come, we went up toward the cypresses.

I was strong when I was near George. The bearing of his soul, a balm for mine. We didn't talk more of this matter. Mistos Tsatsos, who knew the particulars, was indignant, and wanted to say something, to do something. It was Angelos who answered gravely:

"A private affair." We all smiled. Angelos' phrase "a private affair" had become legendary.

Then I too fell ill with dengue fever. I had a bad case. For six days I lay motionless in bed, burning with fever. George came early from the Ministry and sat silently beside me. All the friends gathered around my bed. I opened my eyes and saw all the boys looking at me in agony. Costakis with his dark imagination thought I was dying, and dying of love. He wrote me poems of despair:

> What are you, so pure and faithful,
> doing in this savage world?
> The headless ones are raiding the stars
> and burning the flowers.

George was angry.

"Let Ioanna be quiet. Knock off, philosopher." He took them all downstairs and closed the door of my room. In the midst of my fever I could feel him protecting me.

As soon as I was on my feet again, with great effort I went down to his room. I took him by surprise. Quickly he made me comfortable in his armchair.

"George, read me something."

Who could know what had been happening on Professor Fokas' big table? On it George had been working well.

Our home was very lively during the autumn of 1928. Every Monday evening the group gathered with John Theodorakopoulos to read Plato's *Symposium*.

Venizelos had asked Father and the jurist, Ractivan, to work together in setting up the Council of State. Ractivan would be the first president and Father one of the founding members.

In the evening I would be with George again. After our meal, we would sit for a little while with Father and then retire, each of us, to his room. This private hour, uninterrupted, entirely one's own — what a delight! The night progressed. Noises outside came to an end. From George's room I heard the sound of paper being crumpled. At that time I read the *Oresteia* over and over. Its poetry would not let me be sleepy. Grief, irrevocable fate, tragic shock, mortal man so weak and yet so great — and then, the joy of the beauty and the magnificent poetry. How much there was to learn from the frugality of the ancient language!

"This is the perfect school," I said to George enthusiastically. Pure poetry, nothing more. I couldn't stand verbosity of any kind. Superlatives, diminutives, adjectives. This amused George:

"You'll end up a real Pythia. Think to whom you are addressing yourself. . . . Forget Aeschylus a moment and listen to me:"

> On the highway like the forked embrace
> of a pair of compasses, . . . (p. 403)

I could say with certainty for what young lady every poem in *Turning Point* was written. Women liked George. They had no idea either of his love for Jacqueline or of his tie with "the one they'd call Billio." He was self-contained and secretive. There were plenty of small conquests, small emotional episodes, but they were of no consequence.

> The veranda had grown dark
> Beside us the hurried flapping of wings. . . .

He wrote those lines for a brunette who had loved him. She was always looking at him with admiration, out of her great melancholy eyes.

He was ironic about events, and above all about himself. How he fought against his sentimentality! But did he really kill it? He hid it under stones and weeds, but if something grave occurred, he was mastered by strong feeling. At least when he was with me.

He was a man who spoke little, and listened much. But when he was angry about injustice, especially political injustice, he reacted vigorously.

1929

The great blessing of the years 1928–1932 was the rare sense that we had a real head of state. He brought a forceful intelligence to bear on every problem. The foreign policy of Venizelos was prudent. He signed the treaty of friendship with Turkey. He solved the questions concerning the exchange of population. When in 1929 Cyprus revolted and asked for union with Greece, he undertook to calm its patriotic people in order to safeguard our relations with England.

Internal affairs were so creatively organized that there were no longer any unemployed. For the first time the northern plains had flood control. Thousands and thousands of acres became arable. Networks of roads. Thousands of school buildings. The establishment of the Council of State and the Agricultural Bank. Lands and funds for the refugee farmers. In every way the government aided their rehabilitation.

Father had great plans for the summer. The Institute of International Law was to meet in America at Briarcliff Manor near New York. Each member was invited to bring someone from his family. Father wanted to take me with him, and organized my summer around this plan. In June I was to go with Angelos to London. In September I would return to Paris, and from there Father and I would set out for New York with other members of the Institute.

Edouard Herriot, former prime minister, Mayor of Lyons, leader of his party, was to visit Greece in August. George had been appointed to act as his escort. He was considered the most suitable member of the Ministry to receive and accompany him. We were all pleased at the prospect of new experiences.

Angelos and I started for London. We enjoyed this trip together very much. Angelos discovered in himself a great sympathy for the English. Their self-control matched his own. And at last he would see *Hamlet*, a work he greatly admired. We went directly to the family with whom I had stayed in 1927.

From London I wrote regularly to George. Passing through Paris, I had seen Jacqueline. Her situation was pitiful, and it worried me. She wanted to go to Greece to see George again.

Father was preparing his book, and George was helping him. They both had a weakness for fine editions. Father loved beautiful old bindings, and when a book chanced to fall from his hands, he picked it up quickly and caressed it as if it were a living child.

> Sunday 16 June 1929
> Your letter came just now at 5:12. Father is in his office preparing the table of contents for the printer. It is beyond description — the tension and trouble this involves . . .

> Thursday 27 June 1929
> All these days and the letter remains unfinished. Meanwhile, I have your card from Paris and yesterday your letter from London. You cannot imagine how hard it is for me to read what you write about Jacqueline. It draws my attention to that painful spot inside me which has never ceased to hurt. In the end, this is the human calling . . .

He wrote to me about Costakis Tsatsos whom he saw regularly. He was invited often to Kastella where Costakis was living with his mother and his brother, Mistos.

> In the afternoon I went with Costakis to see Palamas. Katsimbalis came later . . . I had very much enjoyed Palamas on another evening when Costakis and I went to see him at his home. . . . His narrow study was lighted by an oil lamp. The old man sat in a rocking chair beside the table, and he was telling us that, in the long run, poetry is a game. He reached a point where the expression on his face was the pure reflection of his inner being (or so it seemed to me). It was marvelous — but what a drama here in Greece where so few men are at one with themselves! . . .

On another evening he had been at the seashore with a woman, and he wrote:

A little boat was making trips back and forth. We took it. . . . How lovely it was on the evening sea. The wind was fair. The boatman was telling us the story of his life. The lights of the boat were blinking. The wind as it blew brought with it something of the free life out there on the open sea . . .

Father left Athens and George was alone. My friend Irene would go by the house now and then to look after him.

On the 14th of July I had a few words from him:

Why don't you write? I've lost you . . . I wander around the house. . . . It's boring, but it's restful. . . . Anyway, write to me.

Haiku

The house awake
by my side in the night
is always groping for sleep.

As far as George was concerned, however much I wrote to him, it was little.

Cybele Street, 19 June 1929, Friday
My dear, Last Monday I received your letter, and today, as I was coming home, another one. Please do me the favor of writing even when you have no important events to tell me about. There are days when I am so immersed in my solitude that I can hardly breathe. . . . But the truth is that now I have a better opportunity to see what a stranger I am among men and how fragile are my relations with them. Sometimes I think that the reason for this may be my lack of tolerance. At other times I think that the fault may lie in my relation to myself.

An undated letter from this period is concerned only with information. He was preparing to meet Herriot at the border. He was ordering a jacket. He was reading books related to the trip.

Herriot will stay fifteen days, and I hope we shall make several excursions. I shall send you a card from every place we stay, provided there is a post-office. I really would like to write to you at length, but in the autumn I shall pay you back with interest. . . . If you knew how much I miss you. . . .

I had a card — 13 August 1929 — from Salonika, and another from Delphi on the 20th.

I'll be traveling by car from the 16th. The itinerary: Monastiri, Florina, Edessa, Thessaloniki, Kozani, Larissa, Lamia, Delphi. Tomorrow we leave for Athens.

On the 25th of August word from Mykonos, and on the 28th from Olympia.

On the 14th of September, I received a long letter in answer to mine. He reminded me of some great times in the past. Everyone was putting questions to him about the visitor. He had made the proper report to Father about this sight-seeing tour, and didn't want to go over it again.

The day before yesterday I wrote to Father, little sister . . . My travels drained me, both physically and nervously, but yesterday I had to go back to the grind at the Ministry. . . . I went back somewhat reluctantly, and with a sensitivity, perhaps exaggerated, which I had not felt for years. . . .

On the 9th of September, three years had passed since Mother's death, and he went alone to her grave in Kifissia.

. . . The air was clear as if coming from a mountain spring, and a strange feeling caught me by the throat. I am writing to you from the living room, which I have changed into a work-room. . . . Through the open window, the sunset, a royal one. All the shades of red poured out over the mountain. The mountain itself, of an immaterial gray, has gathered into its beauty three or four shining little houses, thrust down at its feet. I want to cry out in my weakness. Many things bring me to the point of tears, and this is a bad sign. But it will pass . . . The day I was in Kifissia I went also to Irene's house and found her alone. We talked about you. She is an admirable and unaffected girl, and I like her very much.

Aunt Maria, Mother's sister, invited him to Spetsai, and John Theodorakopoulos to his village near Sparta, but he preferred to stay alone.

It's a strange thing the way this tour with Herriot weaned me away from my Athenian habits. . . . Athens, as I have always said, is the worst place in all Greece. To come to life again, you must go back to the provinces. Let's hope that in the coming spring we can make two or three small trips together. In any event, we must go to Crete. Three thousand years ago, it was Paris, and one senses this immediately. Absolutely unrelated to classical art. You will see this when we go there. . . .

In England Angelos and I were studying Shakespeare. We were discovering him line by line, scene by scene. Hours passed like seconds. We read *Hamlet* over and over. I think Angelos knew Shakespearean English better than the language of today. And when we learned that they would be presenting *Hamlet* at Stratford-on-Avon, we set out for the poet's native countryside. It was a short, easy trip. And what a happy fate to be able to hear this work in this setting! In the bus as we were returning, the problem of existence was haunting me again. Angelos' comment: — "Alas, poor Yorick!"

At this moment the play of memory on the heart is cruel. The lines so loved by Angelos flow by, sad prophecies. From that period and until the last years of his life, he worked on his translation of *Hamlet*. He found there his metier.

Finally we succeeded in seeing R. C. Sherriff's play, *Journey's End*. We had been trying all summer to get tickets. That evening both the play and the suffocating atmosphere in the theater took our breath away. All the action, which takes place in the trenches, is between English officers. Not a single woman. The anguish of the generations between the wars, in spite of British reserve and control, took us by the throat.

Coming out, we breathed deeply again. Angelos asked: "Why are men more afraid of death than of life?" And I answered him pensively,

"Who knows? Perhaps they are more afraid of the way in which they will die, for that too is life."

That summer I studied and loved Blake and Yeats.

In Paris I parted from Angelos with sadness. We had been happy together. He was to go to Germany to continue his studies.

I stayed on a fortnight with Father and saw a great deal of Jacqueline. Then we started for Cherbourg to take the boat for New York.

In the autumn of 1929 when I discovered America, that harsh, reckless country was for me a fairy tale. Sometimes everything converges to make an experience pleasant. On the steamship, *George Washington*, every one was truly civilized and cultivated. The learned professors were unaffected, affable. And among us, the young, there was an immediacy, a spontaneous understanding. As the ocean encircled us, a sense of community bound us together. In the serenity of this group harmony, I discovered the infinite. I stayed for hours on deck, searching for a nonexistent shore at the end of the horizon. I breathed deeply. My being expanded. I was the first human being, ready to begin the world. The lines of Laforgue went round in my head:

> Le coeur de l'oeuvre immense
> Vers qui l'océan noir pleurait,
> C'est moi qui l'ai.

The revelation of ship-board culminated in a further experience after debarkation. On a small steamer we moved up the Hudson River to Briarcliff. We glided through thick woods in colors of rust and gold. I was dazzled by these flaming trees. And the warm tenderness of the fruitful earth embraced us after we left the ocean. Its sweet breath — I wanted it never to end.

At Briarcliff we were lodged in an old castle which had been brought from Europe. Within, it was an excellent, comfortable modern hotel. I opened my window. Again the vast golden forest was spread before me. I was as happy as a child. My poor father beside me saw with emotion this glorious nature as it was reflected in my eyes.

Back in Athens again, I found George plunged into waves of inspiration, one after another. He was more sure of himself. He had begun to work on *Erotikos Logos*. He had settled on its rhythmic form, the 15-syllable line. But his composition of a poem was like a fabric which he would weave and ravel out and start again. This quest for aesthetic expression was itself a continuous expression. Evenings he would read me some of his lines. The next day I would say:

"Did you go on with those lines, George?"

"No, I was changing the old ones."

Thoughts of Jacqueline tormented him. He often asked me about her. The impressions I brought from Paris were painful to him. The only means of soothing the pain of love was to give it form. A beautiful poem. From time to time he would speak to me phrases which he might use later:

> in my breast the wound opens again.

That autumn I lived only for George. I had missed him greatly during the months of my absence.

Again now, as I think back to that time, his mood carries me away. Scattered rhythms, poetic ideas were working in us, consciously and subconsciously. I had shaken off the old romanticism. The ancient authors and Shakespeare had been a great help to me. I sensed that George was going in the right direction. And I went on postponing my thesis.

Again now, certain of his verses waken my memory, like the fragrance of Mother's linen handkerchief:

> Our love was not other than this:
> it left came back and brought us
> a distant eyelid lowered far away (p. 99)

George read simply. Even the suspicion of bombast was betrayal. Others approve understatement intellectually and try to achieve it. In George, and even more in Angelos, understatement was an inner function before it became an artistic one.

1930

After the holidays, I made up my mind to finish my thesis. I brought together all my material from the past year. I arranged it, and began to write. Before the coming summer, I wanted very much to finish the manuscript and defend it.

But then something important happened. Costakis Tsatsos began to give clear evidence of his affection for me. Every morning Nikolis, the old clerk from his office, would arrive with flowers, poems, letters of many pages. It was lucky that Father and, above all, George approved of Costakis. Angelos was away, but from boyhood he had had the closest ties with the Tsatsos family.

As the months passed, I found myself being touched by Costakis' passion. It was genuine and mature. I spoke to Father.

"Since you want it, my child," he said wistfully.

I sensed that he really did not want me to marry. But in spite of that, he knew that it was his duty to help me. He became even more austere. He never left me alone with Costakis. Evenings he would never go to bed until Costakis had left. That was his duty.

I would wait for George to come home. He would sit by the lighted stove and talk until late. Plans and then other plans for the publication of *Turning Point*.

"What do you really think? Shall I print it?" Uncertainty was gnawing at him.

"George, don't keep asking. Since we both are sure that the poems are good."

"I'm going to look them over again until autumn. That is the best season for publishing a book."

Finally at the end of the academic year of 1930, I successfully defended my thesis. At last I had my doctorate. Father was happy. Of course I dedicated it to him.

On the 21st of June I married Costakis Tsatsos. We went off to Skiathos.

Marriage has its dramatic element: it is the end of one life. At least in my circumstances this was true. I said goodbye to Father, pale from emotion. He looked at me, his eyes full of tears, with the expression of a small child forsaken on a dark road.

I was tempted to throw away the veil and the ornaments, to fling myself into his arms, and to say to Costakis: "I'm not going anywhere. I'm going to stay here."

George also looked wan, but at the moment he saved me. With words half serious and half joking, he changed my mood. I looked back at him rather anxiously: "We'll be waiting for you on Skiathos, you understand? Don't be long in coming, George."

And I wrote to them at each of our stops.

Saturday 28 June 1930
Dear little sister, Last evening I read your letter at table. I feel that you are happy and that comforts me in your absence. . . . It will be great to spend some days on Skiathos and I hope it comes about. This past week has been a strange one, something latently abnormal about it, as when one is a little feverish or nauseated, or changes climate. I don't know quite how to explain it. At first Father was very emotional, to a degree I had not expected. Sunday morning when I got up and found him sitting on the sofa in the living room, I could hardly bring myself to look at him. The room was still full of flowers, but our mood was out of tune with all these cheerful signs. . . . Later Elli and Irene came by, and the house brightened up. What delightful girls they are! . . . . On Monday Father came down with fever, stayed in bed for two or three days, and went out only yesterday on the eve of his departure. . . . Tassos and Eleni invited me to dine out with Bellina. . . .

Father sent me a clipping from a French newspaper. It was Diderot's letter to his daughter when she married. A beautiful text of the period. Father had underlined: "Je te laisse aller avec une peine qui ne saurait se concevoir . . ."

Costakis loved George. If he had not, life would not have been livable. He said to me spontaneously: "Let's wait for George so that we can go together to Kastro. As soon as he comes, we'll go to Papadiamantis' house."

I searched the sand for shells. I scoured the old boatyard for wood worn by the waves and for iron fittings from old boats. With these I decorated George's little room. It had a big window looking out on the sea and the masts in the harbor. When the great day came, we went to Bourtzi to wait for him. There it came, the proud island boat, and George smiling on the deck. I waved my white scarf like a flag. At last he was here, carefree, near me, near the sea.

When we were not on the great beach, we were clambering over the slopes of the island, on foot or muleback. We climbed to the highest point on Skiathos. The whole sea belonged to us, while from the distance came the unbroken melody of sheep bells.

Every evening our friend, Old Sotiris, came to see us. He was full of stories. I loved to hear him and to watch him as he spoke.

"The child a birdie, the old man a hawk." . . . and I saw my brother following him with the innocent gaze of a child, drinking in every word. He was, so he told us, "Saturday's child". Evenings he played the violin at the crossroad, and the nereids danced around him, beautiful, nimble.

"Oh, if only I had better eyes to admire them!"

Old Sotiris, a natural poet of unbridled imagination, also a born story teller, had lived outside wedlock with Yerako, the only woman he ever loved. Sometime before 1881, the Turks took him prisoner to Volos, and during his absence, Yerako married. When he returned years later, he found her middle-aged, forsaken. Her husband had been lost at sea. But for Sotiris, his Yerako was the most beautiful woman on the island, and he was never again separated from her.

While he was in the Turkish prison, he had tattooed himself with pictures of boats from his island. He pulled up his sleeves and showed them proudly.

We had discovered him while we were walking among the truck-gardens. He asked us for a cigarette. As we did not smoke, we had none, but next day we took him two packages.

He was as pleased as if we had given him a treasure. He took us into his garden and gave us beans. He trusted us, and thus we became friends. When George came to know him, he put to him question after question, and listened intently to his answers. His words were manna to George. He cared only for Sotiris and Homer because that summer his book was the Odyssey.

How his roots deepened when he was near sea-folk! We went often to the old boatyard. Some men were caulking the caïques, some were painting them. George sat among them, chatted with them, learning the details of their craft.

There was an old boat, biggest of all, abandoned, sinking day by day deeper into the sand. I stroked the hull which had sailed many seas before ending up on this little beach.

We tried to forget the worries which stalked us in the city. Only once, when we were alone, he murmured:

"If only Jacqueline were here."

Beautiful days — only an instant. George had to go back to Athens. It was possible that he would be a member of the Greek delegation to the League of Nations in Geneva.

15 August 1930

My dear: Yesterday I received your note. My trip to Geneva is now certain. I shall leave on the 29th of the month, perhaps even earlier. I am happy that I shall see you before I go. Yesterday, via the Potamianos Agency, I sent a suit for Sotiris, blue trousers and jacket. Unfortunately, there was no overcoat to be found. Mistos had none. But tell him there will be something before winter. . . . I shall expect you in a week. . . . Greet Sotiris for me, and say that I'm telling my friends about him. . . .

From Skiathos we returned to Father's home on Cybele Street. Father was away and George would be leaving. I looked for a small apartment where Costakis and I could settle down. Unfortunately there was no vacancy in the apartment house on Cybele Street. It would have given me comfort to be near Father. Finally we found something on Spefsippou which suited us.

George sent me a few words from Brindisi. It had been a good passage. "Sea like glass, moon, and now and then boats under sail presenting sudden seascapes. . . . Let's hope that all goes well."

But then a letter which disturbed me:

1 October 1930
Little sister, What shall I tell you and what shall I not tell you? Last weekend I was in Paris. You know what that meant. I wish you were with me to lift a little the enormous weight I feel upon me. In the forty-eight hours I was there, I think I shed all the tears I had in my body. It was as if a veil fell from my eyes, and I was shown a pack of creatures that had been sleeping and growing strong for many years now. I am in pieces. I shall try to go again to Paris if only for a day. . . . I shall arrive in Athens Wednesday evening between five and six. Do me the favor to be at the station . . . so we can have dinner together that evening. . . . I miss you. Don't say anything about my arrival until just the night before . . .

He had seen Jacqueline again, and he returned in despair.

That autumn his daily walk was the climb to Spefsippou Street. Early in the morning I would go to Father's to look after his household. At that hour, I would find George in a hurry and half asleep. But in the evenings at our house it was peaceful. Costakis was working. The Law School had proposed him for a professorship in the Philosophy of Law.

George and I discussed the use of the name Seferis. I liked it because it was simpler, but not a pseudonym. And my imagination responded to the mermaid as his emblem: earth and sea — a single element.

One day he brought me samples of paper to choose from. The cover he chose was dark blue, subdued, expressing his modesty, also his uncertainty about this first published utterance.

"What do you say? Shall I print it?" he began again.

"George my dear, I see your book before me, I hold it in my hands. When will you see your publisher?"

Then, like the tide in flood, the figure of Jacqueline returned. He concluded:

> Everyone in the ship is dead,
> but the ship follows the purpose . . . (p. 415)

1931

It was a great moment for me when, in 1931, George published his first book, *Turning Point*. He came to Spefsippou Street holding two copies.

He sat down beside me:

"This is Number One for me, and this is Number Two for you. I'm not inscribing it for you. What do words amount to? What we have in our hearts is infinite."

I took in my hands the little book, somber, elegant. I fluttered the leaves, caressed it. There was a lump in my throat as I whispered with effort:

"This is just the beginning." He smiled. These were the words he was waiting to hear.

"I say that love is a wild place."

All those who write know the agony they live through until they hear the first words of praise. Buried for a long time in the loneliness of their thoughts, at last they have given forth and are waiting for an answer. Then comes the critic — one who has at his disposal the column of a journal, publicity; the super-poet, the super-writer, one who sits in judgment. But he is only a man. He too has his limitations. How can he penetrate even the surface of another's poetic surge, tormented, toiled over, on which float so many unstable elements?

Many critical articles seem to me like the sermon after the Mass. Logical comments after the full offering of prayer.

In *Ethnos*, the comment on *Turning Point* was, as I recall, somewhat ironic. In *Ergasia*, Aristos Kampanis merely listed it with other collections of poetry. But Katsimbalis was a unique friend, George's true champion. He admired the new poet and praised him widely. Andreas Karantonis, a young critic, began a book entitled *The Poet George Seferis*. Theotokas wrote a first-page article in *Proïa*. Most significant of all, the aged Palamas sensed the true poetic quality of the modest little book. He wrote and told George this, and his judgment was a source of great satisfaction.

I still remember Alexandros Papanastasiou bounding up the stairs of our house, declaiming:

> The secrets of the sea are forgotten on the shores
> (p. 425)

and adding, "the most beautiful line in Greek".

In the summer of 1931, George was appointed vice-consul in London.

In Kifissia before he left, we christened our first daughter Despina. From the moment she was born, George adored her and called her Despo, Mother's name.

'We shall celebrate her name day on the Fifteenth of August as Mother did," and he looked at her a long time as she lay in her cradle.

But by the Virgin's feast-day he had gone.

V
1931–1934

LONDON

Here we come to a landmark. George was now his own master, quite separated from his home. His struggle to conquer the truth in poetry was focused and intensified; he was functioning on his own and with self-assurance. He now believed in himself.

Absorbing new elements were entering both our lives. He had the responsibilities of his official post. And I became a mother.

And we were not indifferent to politics as a means of improving the life of our country. The beginning of Venizelos' fourth year in power gave us the taste and the hope for great things. Most of our friends — Father's and Costakis' and my own — were at the same time poets and politicians. Father maintained his old tie with Venizelos. Some of his professorial colleagues were also entering political life.

Between George and me there was little room for discussions alien to ourselves. In our letters we seldom referred to political episodes and crises. He could learn about these events from the newspapers. What he wanted from me was that sure understanding of his poetry, the reflection of himself to keep him company in his solitude.

Now, as vice-consul in London, he was living through some of England's most critical hours.

In mid-October 1929, the great economic crisis struck America. Values dropped 40%–60%. Titles changed owners. Catastrophes and bankruptcies followed. No one was prepared to confront so widespread a disaster. President Hoover's efforts, at least in the beginning, were futile. In 1931, the unemployed numbered 8,000,000. Neither dividends nor rents were being paid.

It was natural that the reaction should be felt in Europe. England's position was difficult. Factories were closed. Unemployment increased there also. The dole upset the budget. The pound fell.

Venizelos was in a very difficult position. In the turmoil of the financial crisis, he was the guide of a small, poor country, one surrounded by implacable enemies. In spite of all the measures that were taken, the situation worsened from day to day. Bank deposits decreased. Maximos, a well-known economist, belonged to the Opposition, but was right in his proposal that the repayment of the debt in gold be suspended. It was one point of view. Father, in close touch with the Prime Minister, knew that Venizelos wanted to avoid this solution: "If I save our international credit, I shall be able to obtain a new loan and all will be well."

Contact with George in London was uninterrupted.

28 September 1931, Gower Street (addressed to Costakis and me)

. . . . I have filled my letter with economics. That's the way it always goes. The moment a man is about to rediscover himself, a brick falls on him and he is incoherent for a while. The martyrdom of Tantalus.

Courage, Costakis. . . . Did you see the poet? (He refers to Palamas.) His letter was to be published in *Nea Estia* on the 15th. Did it come out? If you see him, give him my warmest greetings, and my gratitude. . . What does Despina (his infant niece) say about the English crisis? Is she growing? Write me about the games she has discovered since I left. I kiss her tenderly . . .

He asked me for *Noumas*, for *Nouvelle Revue Française*.

Palamas' letter about *Turning Point* was published in the September issue of *Nea Estia*. I went with Costakis to thank the old man. He was sitting in his low armchair, knitting his brows, his long bony fingers spread on his knees. Before I had time to say thank you, he raised his eyebrows and his bright glance enveloped me.

"Seferis is a poet," he murmured.

And he allowed a moment of silence to pass as if he wanted the full meaning of that phrase to sink in. Then he asked me:

"What did you name your daughter?"

"Despina."

"Beautiful, and it goes well in poetry."

I could have stayed for hours in that room with the lowered light. How happy we were when later we became neighbors, he on Periandrou Street and we on Kydathineon.

12 October 1931 . . .
Evenings I am trying a translation of *Propos sur la poésie* by Valéry. It interests me as language and makes me pause at every line and think about things which I may later publish. Tell me, have you seen Katsimbalis? You can't imagine with what friendliness he writes me, every so often, and sends me a pile of periodicals. . . . He sent me an amusing critique on *Turning Point (Politika Phylla)* where they accuse me of bringing about a social reaction.

George Katsimbalis lived with his parents in their old townhouse on Syntagma Square. Personally I loved more the house on the hill in Marousi where they spent the summer. Zacharias Papantoniou called it *Three Winds*, and rightly so. The second floor was surrounded by a broad veranda. It caught all the winds from Attica. On the first floor, the dining room with the fireplace. Beside it the study. Outside, round-about, the hill with the pine trees. This house was most charming and I asked George Katsimbalis to let me have it some summer when he was not planning to occupy it. He offered it to me for the summer of 1940. There we spent our last months of freedom.

Meanwhile, Cyprus had revolted and demanded union with Greece. We were obliged to preserve in every possible way our good relations with England. The opposition papers were implacable.

Now for the first time I was regularly sending the newspapers of both parties to George. He wanted them and read them in his office. In his living quarters he was with difficulty maintaining some peace of mind for his personal work. It was not easy, because he was always deeply involved in events in Greece and in Cyprus. On October 25th he wrote to me:

. . . Send me as soon as possible *Estia, Kathimerini*, and something from the yellow press. Indeed send me any journal that writes significantly about Cyprus. . . .

London 2 November 1931
In the evening I usually do only work for myself from 9 to 1:30 a.m. It is my only refuge, though the truth is — it often cultivates my bitterness. As you know, no one writes Greek easily, and since I don't write easily any way, the difficulty is doubled. Let's see if I can manage another small volume when I return. . . . I have learned not to ask of a man more than he can give. . . . You can't imagine what a good, loyal friend Apostolidis is. . . . Another source of help to me in my exile is Katsimbalis. He writes me with so much devotion and concern — it's unbelievable. How I hope he will some day realize how much he himself can contribute to Greek literature. He is the only one I know who has for years followed all that was going on in Greece with care and diligence, with love and enthusiasm. With a good staff of two or three people, he could create a periodical that would make its mark. . . . Now he is preparing to publish a work by Karantonis. In his last letter he tells me it will be about 150 pages. I would not be up to writing that much. One evening before I left, he read me a part. I was astonished at the chap's critical mind. . . .

 Below, some notes, and these lines:
 Now I long for a little quiet
 all I want is a hut on a hill
 or near a seashore (p. 119)
That first book of Andreas Karantonis was written with great sensitivity and deep poetic penetration, and it influenced many people.

George received it. But how to judge it objectively? How to judge himself? From the moment he published *Turning Point*, it became alien to him. He could not look back.

28 December 1931 Little sister . . .
Karantonis certainly has great talent. He must go on working. But the question is how will he manage given the limitations of his life. What I say to you here has nothing to do with what he says about me.

He heard lots of music. He was reading T. S. Eliot.
At last the apartment next to Father's on Cybele Street was vacated. We moved there immediately. What a relief!

1932

23 January 1932
. . . . I have missed you. If you could know how much. Sometimes I think happily of the day when I shall go back and find you. . . . You will come to meet me at the station, and it will be wonderful. What will have happened by then, only God knows. Come what may, I shall be glad to return home . . .

Later on the same day he wrote a long letter to Costakis:

Dear Costakis, For some time I have been wanting to write to you . . . I no longer live in the dissolving despair that tortured me so many years, nullifying every force, every act, before it came to birth. I don't know whether this is good or bad. Sometimes I imagine that I am in a state of intoxication. Such a state that if they were to tell me that a comet would pass this evening and reduce the earth to splinters, I would go to my window and enjoy it without any feeling of horror or fear. . . You see, in art beauty depends on detail, and often repulsive detail. The beautiful is the All. This cannot be explained, and this is why the arts do not die, and why no one can work according to a formula . . .

In this period he read St. John of the Cross for the first time. It swept him off onto unsuspected roads in an agonizing movement upward. Later we talked a lot about that experience. Though he had no inclination toward religious mysticism, he developed his own erotic mysticism, and by a different route arrived at a similar feeling. John of the Cross wakened in him his old mystical urge, the erotic reach toward the inconceivable.

23 February 1923:
Little sister. . . . something else that I experienced during the first years of my return to Greece, was the labo-

rious, the implacable problem of separation, operating with the certainty of a clock. How much one must forget himself or alter his natural habits in order really to keep in touch when he is far away! Sometimes I consider the experiment I made then for approximately two years, *comme un voyant blême*, to accomplish just this. When in the evening I returned to that superhuman task, I have the impression that I am going through an attack of mysticism. The objective doesn't matter. What counts is the effort. This is why human actions after a certain point of intensity begin to look very much alike. Distinctions are easier in mediocrity.

And he quoted to me T. S. Eliot:
> Because these wings are no longer wings to fly
> But merely fans to beat the air
> The air which is now thoroughly small and dry
> Smaller and dryer than the will,
> Teach us to care and not to care
> Teach us to sit still.

1932 was a painful year for Greece.

George tried to keep himself out of the whirlpool of the general crisis, but it was impossible.

At the beginning of March he wrote to me:

> . . . Now recently I have had more intense worries over the crisis, almost unbearable. I think a great deal about our country . . . As early as last January they reduced our salaries. A few days ago I learned that they would soon begin to pay us in paper currency. Whatever happens, I'll manage. . . . If one day I come to a dead end and see that I cannot live here, I'll ask for a transfer, either to Athens or to some cheaper place. All that matters is that man should be saved.

The prosperity of the country was his constant concern. Often he said to me: "As for me, it doesn't really matter. I am poor and I shall remain poor. I have made up my mind that I shall always have more liabilities than assets."

On March 12, 1932 he wrote uneasily:
I am considering with deep concern the problem of Greece in every eventuality. When he has time, ask Costakis to

write me a letter about politics, internal politics, I mean. . . . Fortunately, Katsimbalis writes to me regularly, but I want Costakis' personal opinion.

That spring at the League of Nations in Geneva, Venizelos himself presented our case. He asked for such economic aid as was absolutely necessary. His statement was honest and to the point. Father had heard him and he told me: "I felt his personal tragedy, tragedy for all of us."

The decision of the Council was negative. The Prime Minister returned discouraged to Athens and declared a moratorium. Nothing else was possible.

For George old memories of student life returned from time to time — the crowd of the big city and at the same time the loneliness. But the new lifestyle of independence gave him some serenity.

> March 12 1932
> Of one thing I am sure — that the two of us will not change, however many years pass. Do you know how much that helps me? . . . .

Again he asked me about my little girl, Despina. When he returned, she would be able to talk more, he could play with her. Although she was only a few months old, he wrote to her:

> 14 March 1932
> Little one, shall we start English together? Listen:
>   'The day is ending, the night descending
>   the heart is frozen, the spirit dead;
>   but the moon is wending her way, attending
>   to other things that are left unsaid.'
>   (D. H. Lawrence)
> Your mother may say it to you this way, (and he wrote it in rhymed Greek.)
>   Kisses to you from the odd one of your family,
>   George

Recently I had had the feeling that little by little George's love for Jacqueline was becoming more cerebral, less emotion and more thought. I sensed that his being was refusing to suffer more. It was nothing definite. Our hearts are so incalculable. A sudden surprise, and again we collapse into the past.

21 March 1932
Little sister. . . . I received your letter. I am writing only two words to ask of you the following: write me immediately whether the letters I send you are opened *when you are alone.* If not, do me the favor from now on to take pains to open them only when you are alone and *not in the presence of others.* You are the only human being on whom I can rely, to whom I can speak when reason no longer helps me. You can communicate this to Costakis; he will certainly understand this need of mine. These are the preliminaries. In two or three days I may write you many things, or I may write you nothing. . . . But don't be worried about me. It is nothing. Just a somewhat harsher counterattack from the past. . . .

Later I learned that Jacqueline had gone with her mother to London and spent some time with George.

16 April, 1932, London
Little sister, As I wrote to you twenty days ago, Marie Louise and her daughter came here. They left last Thursday. May God help them — and me! I suffered feelings impossible to describe to you now. I lack the appetite, the desire to go back, but it takes a lot of courage to go on living. The only important thing to tell you is that it is all over between us, definitely ended. . . . Ten years of my life, and they were blessed years. I do not complain. . . . We are free now, the one from the other, with great mutual trust and inner solidarity. . . . I have truly aged during these fifteen days.

So it was. Time and separation had furrowed his heart and feelings. The warmth of desire had faded too. Each one had gone his own way. George was entirely dedicated to poetry, to the fashioning of his language. Jacqueline spoke very little Greek. She could hardly follow the course of his life, nor would she feign interest, as a Greek woman might have done. The points of contact were being wiped out. This mountain, haunted by love's passion, was sinking slowly under the silent, inevitable pressure of time. Whether through the forces of life or through death, whatever is ours is moment by moment drawing away from us. But they had known a great love, and its shadow fell over their hearts. Each felt for the other unlimited tenderness.

All this time George was working on *The Cistern*. He sent me some lines from it. The burden of his pain came through in these verses even more than in his letters:

> Alone, and in its heart such a crowd
> alone, and in its heart such labor
> (p. 439)

and in that unique line:

> Man's body bends to earth
> so that thirsty love remain;
> (p. 439)

The Cistern is this experience of resignation, of loneliness to the very depths of his being.

Meanwhile, three letters written very close together were full of bitterness and hope and matters concerning the Service. He also wanted to help Father. Together they were recovering the harmonious atmosphere of the old bond that had earlier united them.

Costakis' mother had fallen ill in her big house in Kastella. How could we leave her alone there? We decided to spend the hot months with her until she should be well. The veranda toward the sea was cool. All the little boats sailed by. Despina could play happily there.

Now George was able to write to me of his great discovery:

> 29 June 1932
> Every man must make up his mind: in his life there will be two or three things that will torment him until he dies, but for whatever he wishes to create, his soul, if you will, these torments will be his materials. . . . But I so long for Attica. The pines and the sea. These two things are before my eyes every day, like mythological creatures, in their changing aspects always new. A man must be away from his country at a mature age if he is to understand the *Odyssey*. The last time I read it in its entirety was at Skiathos — the most rewarding days of my life. . . .

So he came back to his old sorrow, the ravishment of Ionia, interwoven with the fear that yet another member might be detached from the body of Greece, and he judged mercilessly the politicians who were handling public affairs.

His real self functioned harmoniously only when he remembered the Greek earth. That earth of ours was the solid motionless center in the midst of a senseless cyclone.

> Always before me there is a pine with green-green needles. My soul, idle soul, with what eyes do you look at the pine, bending toward the boat in the wind, toward the sea, toward the world? The ocean is a book with unwritten pages, endless, one with the sky and the boat, like our hearts, still beating gently as they seek blindly for a mooring with a touch of the wind, a butterfly. . . .
>
> These unfinished lines came to mind, and I write them to you because, so they say, the unfinished lines are the best ones.

A picture of Skiathos? I read them many times, and I always loved them. Within me they produce an expanding tenderness, like faith, and also that complete response which beauty wakens. All of George, unaffected, simple, in this human homesickness of the Greek.

> Here there exists no contact that is more than skin-deep. . . . I have no complaint with life. I manage to live each moment, the simplest and often the most tortuous, as a gift from God. I cannot imagine greater good fortune. . . . Sometime we shall speak of this. . . .

Perhaps these words were only an attempt to achieve a day-to-day equilibrium during the oppressive atmosphere of *Mr. Stratis Thalassinos:*

> We found ashes. It remains to rediscover our life now that we've nothing left. . . . (p. 147)

In any case — and this was the important thing — he was working well: *Mr. Stratis Thalassinos, The Fires of St. John, A Night on the Beach.*

Now he returned to *The Cistern*. He was learning how to save some time for himself, in spite of the demands of his profession and his everyday concerns.

We were trying by logical means to preserve ourselves against the angry waves within us. We struggled in the changing sea around us, and our souls were forced far off course. If only we could lay hands on some piece of wood to serve as a tiller. A utopia. Why not? In love as in art, logic is a misfortune.

Jacqueline was considering marriage. Her mother saw it as an act of desperation. George suspected this also. He went immediately to Paris, remaining there from Friday to Tuesday. He returned somewhat relieved. The wedding did not take place. He wrote me nothing of all this. Perhaps because they were the secrets of other people, he did not feel free to tell me. He reported that he had seen again El Greco's *Crucifixion* which he greatly loved. Again he complained about the time he was losing.

>5 August 1932
>. . . . the profession I chose with its continual changes and the suspense which they create is perfectly designed to prevent me from accomplishing anything. . . . I no sooner get settled than the scene changes.

What was destroying him, what was preventing him from putting a line on paper, was nervous tension. In order to escape it, he would always give in. At that time, along with everything else, he was worried about me because I was expecting my second child. He gave me endless advice. There was no serenity for him.

At sunset on the broad veranda at Kastella, I watched the charming ships as they went to and fro. I envied the butterfly hovering over the flower pot. It lived a day, a century, in the sunshine as it went from rose to rose, drinking in beauty.

"Kiss Despo for me," George wrote in every letter. Little Despina beside me was building castles with her blocks. At such a sunset in August Dora, my second daughter, was born.

Elections took place on the 25th of September, 1932. The composition of Parliament did not give us a stable government.

>13 October 1932
>Little sister. . . . It is strange not to have a moment of tranquility when I am independent. So free and so disturbed. To be a human being is not easy. . . . The only literary interval I have had recently was a discussion about *The Cistern* with Katsimbalis and Karantonis. Even if nobody likes the poem, I have given it to be printed, a few copies only for some of my acquaintances and friends. For me it was a matter of literary honesty. First, because I have

worked over the poem and finished it as best I could. I do not mean to say that it is perfect, or that it is without weaknesses. But its weaknesses and defects are my own defects. I don't find it right to behave like the merchant who puts his best wares in the window, and tries to unload his worst merchandise in the darkness of his store. In the second place, the poem does not please those who supported *Turning point*. I thought it honest to show them that even they could be wrong. In the third place, today in Greece unfortunately we cannot take public opinion into consideration. Once we decide to publish, we must go by our own criteria. And these criteria come from the conviction that we kave worked to the best of our ability.

Katsimbalis, who is brilliant and loves me as few do, wrote me in a recent letter "you have betrayed all of us who believe in you." I think I would have betrayed them if I had done the opposite of what I did.

I was worried as I read this letter. I did not want George to feel isolated. The response to a work of art is a very important thing, even for the strongest, the greatest. I was afraid he might abandon the struggle, even for a short time. I liked *The Cistern*. For me it was not difficult to say so again, with all the warmth of my heart. I added, "Your whole value is in being yourself." And I reminded him of a sentence of Millet: "I find it absurd that men should wish to appear other than they are."

In Paris, Jacqueline's father died, leaving her nothing. She was now independent but very poor. But she was beautiful and did not lack suitors. As soon as George learned the news, he telephoned to her from London.

He was disturbed:

How can one clear up anything on the telephone? To go to see her would be worse, and I cannot muster the strength to write. What would I say? No human being hates words more than I do. . . .

The truth of that last sentence touched me deeply. At least in correspondence, words, however measured, turn out to be unbearable — especially those written in deep feeling. This is the experience of years. How I longed for a living dialogue — to see his eyes, to hear his voice!

At the Consulate in London, only two remained. There was much work. Rumors of recall were circulating.

As for us, we returned from Kastella to Athens. Costakis had been elected Professor of Philosophy at the University of Athens, and was preparing his inaugural address.

I began receiving our friends again. We met as before and wrote all our news to George, each in his own way.

Father had saved a little money and was eager to find a lot on which to build his family a house. The drachma had lost half its value.

When the boys were away, Father would ask my opinion. He easily found property on Patission Street and in Kolonaki, but for me the real Athens is only the part near the Acropolis. Father was angry:

"You are being difficult and you will spoil the whole affair."

But when he found the lot in Kydathineon Street and saw how happy I was, he too was pleased. At that time it was a quiet, picturesque area. Opposite, a Byzantine church with cypresses. At the end of the street, the Parthenon, the sacred rock with the cave of Pan. For me this cave was a symbol of ourselves. It is strange, but Ghika's portrait of George in 1972 brought back to me that impression of the cave.

I knew the neighborhood well. I wandered through it on my way to Anafiotika, to Metochi, to Tricherousa. At the end of Yperidi Street, there was an old mansion with its own chapel in the garden. There, behind the chapel, a gigantic cypress rose toward heaven. This tree was the pride of the Plaka. But the house was sold, and its demolition began. I was terrified. What would become of the chapel, the cypress? I begged my friends, Myrivilis, Phteris, who had columns in the newspapers to write that this corner should remain unspoiled. They did write, more than once. But one terrible day the cypress was laid low. It covered the whole of Yperidi Street. I cannot forget my despair. I sat down on the thick trunk, weeping, sobbing. Passers-by stopped to ask what was the matter. I went on crying. Who would understand me? All of them seemed to me barbarians, like a skin disease on this unique earth.

The building of our house began immediately. Father wanted it ready in the autumn of 1933 when perhaps George would return to Athens.

1933

6 January 1933
Even with the most regular correspondence it is impossible to overcome the separation.

He was working on *Notes for a Week*: the longing of the Mediterranean Ulysses locked up in London. The overcast white sky. The river which does not flow, which has "forgotten the sea." And always the memory of lost love, the regret over a big mistake.

. . . who am I going to play? Who will I kill? . . .
(p. 161)

28 January 1933
This morning I received your letter, little sister. . . . However much time I have, I feel it will not be enough. That is why I am never bored. I ask myself if this is the last year I spend here. . . . I feel deeply the desire to return. It is important that I should see you all again. . . . But above all, no plans . . .

Again his thoughts went back to Skala, to Grandmother's garden, to the fountain, to the well.

But how is it others can forget so easily, and go on living? He was lingering in the closed, charmed world of memory.

He sent me these lines as if he were whispering a secret we had in common:

The garden with the fountains that in your hands was a rhythm of the other life, (p. 15)

I began to think of his return, and there came to mind those first years in Athens after Paris. They were hard years, but this time, it would be different.

Wednesday 22 February 1932
Little sister, I was much entertained by your recent letter. I

> felt that if I were to sit down with it near the fire, there would come back to me many of those long conversations we used to have when we found ourselves together with no distractions. And sometimes when I take up my pen to write to you, I think of all those letters I wrote from Paris when I tried to describe to you the smallest fluctuations in my psychology. Many years have passed since then, and much life. I have become stronger. You have become a mother. Many things which I despised in my youth I now look at in a gentle and affectionate light. Other matters that I considered important, like my despair for example, I now know how to put aside. I have come to believe, contrary to certain others, that a man who knows he will die cannot be without hope. It has been a long road, and a hard one, because my sensibility was unbridled. There had to be many battles and many crises. Now I have learned to observe them from a greater distance and a greater height.
>
> During this period I was fortunate in having close to me two or three human beings who, knowing me, came to know themselves better, and whom, in a sense, I may have formed. You are one of them. And you are the only one for whom I have no regrets as I have none for myself. Of others I sometimes think with some remorse that they might have been happier not knowing certain things . . .

He was thinking of Jacqueline. She had written him a pitiful letter.

> Whatever happens, it happens from necessity. But this does not prevent the human drama from being always lively. But who knows, perhaps if it were otherwise, man would have no value.

During this period in London he wanted very much to know T. S. Eliot, the greatest English poet of that generation. His friend, Basil Photiadis, knew Eliot well and promised George an introduction. Unfortunately he fell ill, and the letter was late in coming. When George finally received it and telephoned to Eliot's house, it was learned that he had gone to America for six months. But George no longer had the old impatience. He had learned to wait.

And how right he was. In 1951, when he was again in London as counsellor to the Ambassador, he met Eliot and they became friends. They knew and admired each other's work. At that time Eliot was living on the riverbank in Chelsea with John Hayward, a paralytic of amazing vitality who went to parties in a wheelchair.

George loved London.

"Either London or Athens," he wrote to me, referring to his service.

> 21 March 1932
> . . . If there is ever a question of my transfer, have it in mind that I don't want to be sent elsewhere. I'd prefer to serve again in Athens for a while.

> Monday of St. Thomas 1933
> . . . I can and I am working better. The recent fog and cold nearly killed me this year. It is the first spring that, by some strange luck, has not been unbearable. . . . This year with the spring I began to recover. . . . I long for you more than you can imagine. . . . Write to me if you want anything.

During the winter of 1933 Father was Rector of the University of Athens. He had been elected to the Academy as well. It was very convenient for me to live beside him. He often needed something or other, and I was nearby. He found loneliness hard to bear.

The building of our house proceeded. Father greatly enjoyed it, and worked closely with the architect. Angelos came back too. Costakis made his inaugural address at the University with great success.

George asked me for the Greek newspapers and I sent them regularly. Katsimbalis mailed him *Today* and *The Circle*.

And as always, I kept asking him what he was writing.

> Friday (Spring, 1933)
> Little sister, I have just come home and found your letter. Spring is really bursting forth. It is warm, and most agreeable to watch the trees putting forth their leaves day by day. With such delight, with God's true joy. I was in the park after lunch. I watched the children in their bright colors playing on the lawn, and I thought of you with your babies . . . Am I writing, you ask? At this moment I can write absolutely nothing. It isn't that I don't try. I just cannot. Literature presents certain obstacles for me. First, there are those which are inherent in the art, and second, there are those that are topical, connected with the current

intellectual atmosphere of Greece, and perhaps with my absence and lack of touch with men of letters there. These are secondary obstacles, of course, but all of them I must overcome if I am to make progress. Not everyone is easy, and probably I am pathologically difficult. I know this and I confess it as a sin. . . . I have no wish to collaborate with *Idea*. I wrote my reasons to Theotokas in the winter of '31–'32. I don't get on with Melas . . .

At that time he was having unimportant disagreements with some of his friends, and this embittered him. But how right he was about Melas, and Theotokas was the first to recognize it.

. . . If you could only know how far away *Love Song* and my other lyrics seem. It is as if they were written by a stranger. . . .

Pessimistically in the following letter:

7 June 1933

From conversations with my colleagues, I gather that, in spite of my zeal, they will not leave me much longer here in the British Isles . . .

This was the harsh beginning of the experience of professional uncertainty. It would torment him all his life.

Early in June 1933, there was the tragic attempt to assassinate Venizelos. He had lunched at the Benaki house in Strophyli and was on his way home. The killers pursued him the length of Kifissia Boulevard as if he were a thief. Their bullets riddled his car. His wife was wounded as was his chauffeur, and one of his security guards was killed. Worst of all was the psychological trauma suffered by Venizelos himself. He never recovered from it, and the country paid dearly for it.

Political passions had reached their zenith.

We took a little house in Kifissia for the summer. The building on Kydathineon was progressing rapidly. Father and I had to supervise it. There had to be strict economies if we were not to exceed the estimate. I could not be far away from Athens.

About George, no one knew anything. Was he to stay in London? Would he come back to Greece? Would he be sent elsewhere?

Wednesday 1933 (summer)
I would like to take leave and spend half the time with you in Kifissia, the other half on some island. It would be wonderful. We would chat without interruptions, and I would find again certain human values, and at the same time Greek nature which I so long for. . . . Keep sending me newspaper clippings, also interesting reviews.

This was his only allusion to public events. I was anxious about him. What were they going to do with him? Was he to stay in London?

5 August 1933
. . . I am waiting with eagerness and impatience for us to talk together without stopping — the moment is drawing near. In the meantime, have a good time, without thinking too much about what would be advantageous, at least for me. Whatever happens will be all right. It is enough to have the great blessing of health and, from time to time, God's gift of work . . .

18 September 1933
. . . Let me say that I am pleased to be in London and would like to stay. If, however, the service thinks someone else should come here, I want for family and personal reasons to return to Athens. The only request I made was that they should give me leave with my recall.

Then suddenly, unexpectedly they came up with the decision to send him to Cardiff.

I wrote to George. He was trying to keep a cool head, but clearly he considered it a demotion:

I did not enter the Diplomatic Service in order to be a Harbor Master for four years.

He was rebellious and I did not know how to calm him down. I could never bear to ask any favor for myself, but could I for George? After all, the only thing he wanted was to come back to his own country, and that was no favor. What could I do?

Who would be inclined at that moment to help a Venizelist vice-consul? Good work counted for nothing. It was a matter of balancing conflicting interests.

I began to sense then that being a public servant was a form of slavery, always having to put up with the caprices of ministers and secretaries.

Both George and I were frightened by the inconsistency of these orders. Uncertainty had shattered the charm of London.

I came to understand then that my own nature and my upbringing had left me with a vulnerable spot, my sincere faith in human beings. Every time I discovered their guile and self-interest, I was bereft. I had no means of defense except withdrawal. But I had also most loyal and devoted friends. One of them came spontaneously to my aid. Cardiff was cancelled. I breathed again — and wrote immediately to George.

> 14 October 1933 — Saturday
> Little sister. I just received your letter. I hope that what you write me is definite, that they won't change again at the last moment. For the time being, I am at peace and preparing for my return.

I too could not wait for that return!

George was still suffering from the blow of the nomination to Cardiff and wrote to me:

> 25 October 1933
> . . . It is hard to stay in a service made up of individuals who change direction according to the wind of the moment. . . . If I find a little calm in our new house, I imagine I shall be able to work in a more humane way, in a way more in accord with my nature. . . .

There were various letters about errands. In his last letter he is so impatient that the place can no longer contain him.

> 14 December 1933
> Little sister . . . Cold and foggy. My house is upside-down, uninhabitable. Write to me if you don't want me to do something stupid.

In November 1933, the house on Kydathineon Street was almost finished. A few small things remained to be done. We kept it heated night and day in order to dry it out.

At last I began the moving. Books and more books. It seemed to me that they would never empty Father's big bookcases. He himself trembled lest one book should fall and the corner be damaged. . . . "Ioanna, I want you yourself to look after them. Don't leave the men by themselves."

There were Costakis' books too, and George's, and those of Angelos.

We moved the holy icons with great care. When I had placed the iconostasis and hung Mother's vigil-lamp near the silver Virgin, all the old prayers, all the present ones, all the memories and all the hopes were there.

Christ was again in His place in a house which, for the first time in Athens, was our own. I was following Him. If it should be His will, I prayed that we might take root in this soil, like the lemon tree in our garden, playing with the wind in front of my window.

What is a home but a shelter on our road to an Ideal? And this home, on the heights of old Athens, as Myrivilis said, was a shelter. It gave cover to our struggle for poetry and, I hope, to our struggle for Mankind.

1934

Early in 1934 George returned to Athens. I found him more handsome, more elegant. His instinctive concern for others had increased. There was something slightly official about him, but we soon found ourselves just as we were before.

I shall always remember that winter. The house on Kydathineon started off with a wind favorable to poetry. The Mermaid Madonna on her dolphin was sailing with us.

On Father's legal manuscripts the margins were filled with lines from *The Bridge at Arta*. Costakis was deep in his philosophy, but he was also writing poetry. Angelos was shut in his room translating *Hamlet*. He had not yet been appointed to the ministry of Security. And in the evening, George was working on *Mythistorema*.

Each had his privacy, but still was not alone. At the rear of our house, an outer stairway joined the two apartments. Father and the boys came up whenever they wished. And every so often I went down below to them.

On his way to the Ministry, George would come by and describe his day to me. I liked it when he grumbled because he had not worked well the night before. This little time together was precious. In the early evening, after I had said goodnight to the small ones in their beds, I would run down, and then, if he was there, he would read to me.

> On winter nights the strong east wind drove us mad,
> In summer we were lost in the struggle of the day
> which could not die. . . .

"What do you think of it?"

He was his own best critic, but he always raised a question. May I be forgiven for referring often to the poems. They are the clearest memories remaining to me from every period, and they help to transfer to this text something of that old atmosphere.

By that time he had conceived his own forms of expression. More than ever he needed time for himself.

I liked choosing a house for the summer, a house that suited us, that fitted into the landscape. The house we took for the summer of 1934 was beautiful, a house on the old harbor at Spetsai. Like a promontory between two seas, like a ship. And Old Lefteris' boat leaned against the wall. George counted the hours until he could join us. It was the first leave he had taken after London. After so many years of confinement at a bureaucratic desk, his pent-up need for air and sea was uncontrollable. In the noonday sun he was himself part of the sea.

Angelos was with us too. Afternoons, when I did not want to leave the children alone, Costakis, George, and Angelos would take off early and make the circuit of the island. I would meet them at Brélo.

There in Spetsai Angelos fell in love with Roxane Pappas, the girl whom he later married.

That autumn came the painful day. Jacqueline was married. George was plunged in sorrow, deep and gentle like a lagoon. He knew that this story had come to an end. It pervaded *Mythistorema*, and the outcome gnawed at him bitterly.

Who will lift this sorrow from our hearts? (p. 19)

Now Jacqueline also slowly became a metaphysical yearning, like Skala. An urge to return to something you neither can, nor any longer really wish to, bring near. Yet there is that knot in your heart.

I knew that sunset would be the hard hour for him. I went down and found him in his study, sitting in the dim light with the lamp extinguished.

"It was good of you to come."

I sat in the other armchair. Now and then we exchanged a word or so. Then, as if to himself:

"All this is unhealthy. Let's see what the children are doing."

Despina and Dora gave him great joy. They climbed on his knees, and showed him each new thing they invented.

With time he had some comfort in the thought that Jacqueline would be happy. The responsibility he had felt for her was lighter. Her husband, a fine musician, would give her a good life. Dubious consolation.

And so:

> We set out again with our broken oars. (p. 31)

This line had become our refrain in every big disappointment.

Costakis' mother was not well. The doctors disagreed. Her sons decided to take her to Vienna where a famous doctor put her in his clinic for treatment.

At the end of 1934, we had a message from the doctor that she was worse. Costakis left immediately for Vienna. We brought her to Kydathineon Street. Hard hours. Doctors, nurses, oxygen. But every morning our children hugged her in their little arms and said "Good morning" to her. And she smiled back at them, happy.

In the evening George would come up. In the rare intervals of hopeful quiet, he would insist:

"You are very pale. Let's go for half an hour to Phaleron. It will do you good."

So we would take a taxi and get to the sea. There we would walk for a while. The breeze of December was icy, but welcome, and it braced the spirit. And the dark dome came lower in a friendly way.

VI
1935–1941

POETRY AND POLITICS

At the beginning of 1935 the review appeared: *New Letters*. Thus one of George's old dreams became a reality: Katsimbalis was creating a monthly literary periodical.

Friends of all generations gathered in our home: writers, poets, scholars.

George was living in his own apartment below, and often joined us.

Our discussions were unadulterated pleasure. We knew how to listen. We knew how to give and take.

I was worried about the publication of *Mythistorema*. These first publications of George's were a work of the heart. The slightest detail was as important as the most substantial. This demand for perfection was innate in George and he kept it to the end of his life. But at that time George was questioning more than ever. Investigation of intellectual subjects is a great source of delight. It shows that we are constantly seeking new ideas.

The tragic revolution of Venizelos in March 1935 had an inglorious outcome and it limited our pursuit of literary matters. It was followed by the persecution of the liberals. The real leaders, Venizelos and Plastiras, were abroad as were their staffs. Thus those least responsible bore the brunt of the rage.

The fanaticism was so extreme that members of the opposite party no longer spoke to me though they were warm friends. Every day at the Polygon, I followed the trial of the aged Sophoulis and of our good friend, Papanastassis. It was a great relief when we learned that they had been released.

I wanted to leave Athens as quickly as possible so as to hear nothing, to read no newspapers. I also wanted George to come with us. He too was dismayed at seeing his country the pawn of irresponsible people.

The hot days had come. We decided on Mount Pelion, the village of Zagora. A beautiful mountain side, facing Mount Athos, covered with chestnut trees. On the right and left of the flagged road leading to the village stood magnificent poplars as if framing gates to other worlds. The Athenians and their political discussion could hardly reach us there.

On Pelion we tried to find ourselves again. Costakis finished his book on Palamas. Now and then with a deep voice he would intone the lines:

"Shepherds, at the city's gates, the wolves, the wolves!" and my little girls made it a refrain in their play: "The wolves, the wolves!"

George wrote from Athens:

Sunday
The country is utterly disjointed . . . Recent events are not likely to take us off the road to ruin.

I had promised myself I would see Antonio (the poet D. I. Antoniou, Captain Mimis) performing his duties. So I took his boat on Thursday evening and returned yesterday at dawn. I saw many islands without leaving the bridge, among them Naxos, Paros, and Santorini where men do not build houses but rather dig them out of the pumice. At Syra there was time for a half-hour walk. It's a civilized town, perhaps more civilized than Athens. Going up a steep flagged street with Captain Mimis, I heard a piano playing a Chopin *Prelude.* Below was the sea, the moon, calm and clear, and the fragrance of sage being burned in the ovens. My companion was much moved, and murmured mysterious verses. . . . I in my beret, he with his gold braid and his trembling voice, must have seemed like characters from a schoolgirl's novel.

That much only until we can talk. At Zagora I shall devote myself to Dante only, for 'tout le reste est pourriture.'

George came to Zagora on horseback, like St. George. Not a word about politics — our tacit understanding. At night we felt the broad waves from Horefto bringing us the ocean breeze. It is there that George wrote *Sirocco 7 Levante.*

>seeking the sea's sleep
>slipping towards the sea's sleep. (p. 105)

He dedicated it to his good friend, Captain Mimis.

George loved the sea passionately, but he also greatly loved the mountains. We went all over Pelion, on foot or mule-back. A beautiful woman visited us. One morning, on their horses, her long hair flowing, she and George disappeared into the forest. Scandal in the village. At sunset, in the Square, the women gathered 'round me much agitated: "The chestnut trees are on fire, Kyria Ioanna, the chestnut trees are on fire!"

It was 5 August, 1935. I know the date from my journal. He did not wish to waken me when he left, so he wrote there some lines by Ephtaliotis:

> Days which with you would be pearls
> without you are lost in the depths of time,
> lost and useless, like the pebbles
> little children toss into the sea.

Home again. Athens was seething. The return of the king appeared certain. The plebiscite took place on November 3 in a strange atmosphere. The democratic leaders did not recognize the results as legal, but the King and the Crown Prince landed at Phaleron.

When the political scene is uninterruptedly irrational, man cannot insure his continuity except through the permanent value which he feels within himself, that is, through his own spirit. For George this instinct of self-preservation was sublimated into poetry. I knew that the slightest irritation put an end to all inspiration, and I made every effort to see that problems should not enter his place of work. Once when he asked me something about politics, I answered him: "Never mind. Don't ask. You must get rid of these daily worries and live your own life. Otherwise you will die a dead man."

This amused him. He often quoted it when he wrote something new: "What do you think? Will I die a dead man?"

He worked and published. He wrote *Gymnopaidia*. He translated Eliot: *The Problem of Civilized Man, Murder in the Cathedral*.

1936

On his return, the King sought amnesty for all the political figures, and pardon for the military men who had been condemned. A new government was sworn in. The new Prime Minister, Demertzis, a superior man, issued a decree cancelling all the accusations against the revolutionaries of March first. Then he advised the King to announce parliamentary elections for 26 January 1936 as the only way to put an end to political chaos. They did not produce a sufficiently strong government. The spirit of collaboration did not exist.

Those were the last elections before the war.

It was then that we learned the sad news: Eleftherios Venizelos was dead. Night and day our people had been hanging on every word from Beaujon Street. Better news, God, some better news. But there was none. The country was plunged into mourning. Our house too. My father, my husband, my brothers, deep in thought, speechless. George and Costakis pulled themselves together to follow his bier to Akrotiri. This dead man, traveling far in order to lie in the Cretan earth, carried within him all our national hopes. For a brief moment he had unfolded our wings in the light of our age-old dream. Now suddenly we were overwhelmed by the painful, persistent memory which death evokes, by the vision of that greatness, and the fibers of our hearts quivered. George wrote in his diary:

> Friday 27 March 1936
> . . . Up there on the destroyer, the *Koundouriotis*, I can make out the leaves of the wreathes . . . There encased in steel, the old man's body, like a treasure from the sea, starts widening circles of myth: Aegeus, Theseus, black sails. The Cretans have draped everything in black. The walls by the water are black, and black are the sails in the wind . . .

Alone in Athens, I read his epitaph, words which he himself had spoken on a quite different occasion, the funeral of a political opponent. I could not get beyond the first phrase: "The dead man lying before us was a true man." — and further on — "with confidence in the people he was called to govern."

How right he was! Now that he had gone forever, I saw people, with frenzied devotion, ready to fall into the sea if only they could follow him to Akrotiri. How right he was! As the years pass, and I know this people better, I say that with pride.

On an April evening in 1936 our group roused itself to go to the lecture hall of Parnassos. Another great poet, Sikelianos, was to speak on Palamas. I had not heard him before.

I sat in the second row between George and Katsimbalis. Further along, Costakis and Theotokas.

His first words took me by surprise. So different from others. He gave his interpretation of the poet in long sentences which only he could properly utter, in his deep melodious voice. His every thought, his every concept transported us into the world of the sublime. As he went on, his voice grew stronger and stronger. Fascinated, we too followed the poet as he climbed Jacob's ladder. And surrounded by a radiance, we saw him wrestling body to body with God Himself.

I was overwhelmed. I pressed George's arm. He gave me an understanding smile.

"My God, are we human beings worthy of You?" I thought to myself.

After this great leap toward God, a deep silence fell on the gathering. The heavens closed. But nothing was quite as it had been before. We had touched His presence. Our yearning was pain. Mechanically we went along to the little room where Sikelianos had retired. Katsimbalis embraced him. I stayed shyly by the door. Every word would be a judgment. I would have to hear all those opinions just when I was at a peak of ecstatic contemplation.

Our little party went back to Kydathineon on foot.

"George, what shall I do? Shall I write to him? How shall I thank him?" He answered gravely:

"We have an obligation to encourage artists."

So I did write to him. Sikelianos later reminded me of some words from the letter:

"I see with despair this perfect hour being lost in the past. I fight against every moment which, with the strength of physical law, blurs its intensity."

He answered me with a package wrapped in thick paper and tied with a ribbon. It was Part I of *Carmen Occultum*.

That summer we went to Aegina. The house was a tumbled-down mansion that had belonged to Trikoupi. A large overgrown garden ended in a clearing near the sea. There were pines, tall cypresses, and some exotic trees. But one cypress surpassed the rest in strength and height. A wise tree, with abundant sap which coursed the length of its trunk into its rich dark-green foliage. Its roots spread deep in the earth, its top breathed the sea. This tree was my friend. At noon I stretched out on the warm earth, fragrant with the cypress cones bursting open in the August sun.

What good fortune to have for one's country such a beautiful earth! All the ancient myths came true. Nature with its own special light was full of gods and heroes. Whatever beauty, whatever strength we ourselves could not possess we found in those friendly creatures, in the rocks, in the winds, which, as they came closer to us, became our own. When I was in good humor, I called my cypress Bellerophon. Perhaps because it climbed higher and higher, perhaps because it was so strong. (*Iliad* VII, 156)

There were extra rooms in the house. Any friend who wanted to come was always welcome. Myrivilis was often a guest. Every morning at coffee he would ask:

"Have you thought of a subject for my column?" He was in a hurry to discharge this obligation so as to be free to enjoy the rest of the day. Costakis gave him lots of ideas, George remarked: "You are worse off than I. You don't have any holidays."

At noon the little boat left. Then we ourselves became an island, and our spirit traveled under its own sails. No radio, no newspaper, no haste. The sea protected us on all sides. We were impregnable.

Impregnable? Error. In the evening we heard the engine of a motorboat. It came nearer and nearer to the lighthouse, and finally arrived at the little harbor in front of our house. Angelos Sikelianos and Nausicaa Palamas from Phaneromeni.

Sitting in the garden among the trees, we heard him recite poetry in his deep voice. Children of Aegina climbed up on the garden walls to listen, and fishermen sat on the parapets.

Sikelianos had within him the divine grace of poetry and he lived it as a mission. His occult learning was inexhaustible. I have imagined that the ancient mystics were like him. He lived with the mystics of all centuries as if they were his brothers. From Dionysos to Heraclitus, from Christ and St. Paul to St. John of the Cross, Novalis, Rilke — all these were familiar spirits to him because they had had the same experiences. He could communicate with them with wonderful immediacy.

Evenings in the garden it was to them he referred. He quoted Heraclitus:

"You will not arrive at the limit of the soul whatever road you take, so deep is its meaning."

He spoke of himself, of the awareness of faith, and always he came back to Christ, to St. Paul:

"For whatsoever is not of faith is of sin." (Romans 14:23)

Not even for a moment did he want to lose contact with the divine substance of the world. He believed in its mystic harmony.

In the great things as also in the common ones, he sensed life's deepest meaning, the symbol. He wrote to me one time these lines:

> Sweet, sweetest death!
> The wood of the Cross lives
> and at its apex blooms the wild rose.

That summer George and Costakis became close friends with Sikelianos.

Throughout my life, certain coincidences have made an impression on me, almost as if they were secret messages.

In 1951 we celebrated the nineteen hundredth anniversary of the Apostle Paul's travels in Greece. Professor Hamilcar Alevizatos organized a pilgrimage officially sponsored by the government. Representatives from all the Christian churches of the world took part. Archbishops, bishops, theologians. Costakis was then Minister of Education and I was invited, a privilege I gladly accepted.

We embarked on a ship and followed the Apostle's itinerary exactly. I took with me only the Epistles and some biographies of Paul. In this floating monastery, we began the day with the liturgy and ended it with vespers. Throughout the day there were religious discussions and lectures. I still remember Prof. Clavier supporting Paul's Hellenism by his use of the Greek word "conscience". The Apostle used it, though the word did not exist in Hebrew.

In contemplation also I sought to follow Paul. He saw the light. He said of love "it seeketh not its own." What is there more?

On we went: Philippi, Apollonia, Thessaloniki, Berea, Nikopolis. Suddenly, outside Lefkas, newspapers came aboard. On the first page, the terrible news: "Sikelianos is dead." I withdrew to a corner of the deck and supported myself by the railing. I could hear him saying to me:

"Like Digenis, I wrestled with Charon. I saw the ultimate darkness." With his every phrase he added to the substance of poetry. What an infinity a single human being can embrace! Now he is gone. But where? What mystical world is waiting for him?

At Nikopolis I found some wild flowers. As we left, I scattered them on the sea of Lefkas where Sikelianos was born.

At that time George was counsellor to the Greek Embassy in London. He too grieved, and spoke on the radio with love for the great poet.

That summer George met the woman he later married. She was spending the summer on Aegina with her husband, Andreas Lontos, and their two little daughters, Mina and Annoula.

At the end of July, Papanastassis came to see us. A friend had loaned him a small sailboat and he persuaded us to go with him to Spetsai — two days in the blue of sea and sky.

Those were our last good moments.

On August 4 the dictatorship of Metaxas was proclaimed.

The King had not succeeded in forming a stable government. He installed John Metaxas as dictator.

How would we ever be delivered from this intolerable Greek slavery?

Costakis' brother, Themistocles Tsatsos, was sent into exile. I hurried to Athens to say goodbye to him. We reached his boat just in time, before it left for Anaphi, his place of banishment. He was in irons, handcuffed, on deck with others. Civilians and gendarmes came and went. I embraced him and murmured a line from Souris, the satirist: "I would like to be a member of parliament or at least a brigand."

Mistos laughed. "You know, Ioanna, they took away my book on Constitutional Law. If you could find it, I'd like to have it with me."

I went back to the quay. A gendarme was guarding a pile of books. I saw the book I wanted immediately, and took it in my hand.

"This belongs to Tsatsos, and he needs it," and I showed him Mistos' name on the flyleaf.

"You cannot take it. He is a Communist."

I insisted: "How can he be a Communist when he teaches at the University?"

He called the officer in charge. Finally a higher officer came and gave it to me.

We felt spiritually exhausted. I went back to Aegina with George. One noon the postman brought me *Autumn 1936* from Sikelianos with the line from Pindar:

"The Muse grows greater, proclaiming the truth." In that hour of senseless enslavement, that line of pure poetry brought tears.

George was assigned to Koritsa. He did not want to go. The dead-end loneliness of Albania was unbearable. But he had no choice.

For days the opening of a door, steps on the stairs, an unexpected voice would startle me into thinking it was he.

Koritsa, Wednesday evening, 18 November 1936
My third night here. Yesterday I did not go out at all. I was trying to fix up, somehow or other, a couple of corners in this nondescript house full of the most gaudy colors."

Then he wrote of his journey.

... After three hours of boredom from Edessa and beyond, I had some moments of pleasure when, toward the end of the evening, I got out in a muddy ditch and found myself facing the wind from the mountain; beeches, beeches. I could imagine the flanks of Pelion at the end of the summer all in that color of dark gold. Then night fell, and I crossed the border. . . . Give my address to Karantonis. . . .

In another letter:

... Desiccation . . . How can one wait for nothing?

Koritsa, a plain surrounded by mountains, like a frying pan, as George said. One of the most difficult posts at that particular time. Against the background of depression which dictatorship brings to free men, he struggled vainly with his loneliness and his longing for love. Women were always important in his life. Great love or persistent desire, one or the other always mastered him. Only the first years after his separation from Jacqueline were ascetic years. Those he endured because of the fervor of his love, but the feminine element always pursued him. In summer it came on the waves to the islands, on the breeze from the chestnut-clad mountains. His erotic disposition like the bee was forever searching for the honey of the feminine. And the alchemy of his poetry gave to each woman the quality of that hour.

> even that buffalo on the Macedonian
>   plain, so patient,
> so unhurried, as if knowing that
>   no one gets anywhere, (p. 205)

He asked for leave, but it was not granted. Should he resign, be a free man?

"Have a little common sense, George." Thus Costakis wrote to him.

"Common sense smells of carrion," he answered, and, being a literary animal, he sent Costakis a charming short story, *Mme. Dongo Tosca*, full of repressed sensuality.

The greater part of thirty-five letters from Koritsa is concerned with his work, with orders for things he wanted sent to him, and with women. Has anyone ever thought of the situation of the first Christian in a desert land, studying the Scriptures? For George the heart of life was on the border between beauty and the abyss. He fought temptation by writing, sometimes amiably when the climate of life was gentle, sometimes ironically when the climate was harsh. It was the only way he could work.

On New Year's Day he sent me a long letter, a kind of accounting:

> Little sister, I have filled six pages with orders and errands for you. Don't faint. Read them slowly and give me a lift. Help me to endure my exile. . . . I am glad to see the end of 1936, a suffocating year. I am reckoning the inheritance it left me: sins . . . Five days ago I was haunted by these lines:
> and the water frozen in the hoofmarks
> of the horses. (p. 177)
>
> Man is entirely surrounded by his torments, the aches of his body, demands, irritations, erotic desire. The phrase makes its way, seeking to achieve its own alchemy. I have never before tried as hard as I have recently to work at this obstinate and painful thing called art. Your material is your own being and you chop away at it from one side and the other until it speaks. You must try and not try, you must be on fire, you must — oh, the devil with it! In spite of all this, I have begun to work, although asceticism is no help to me in my labors. I sent a poem to *New Letters*. It is called *A Word for Summer*, and there were two or three other poems. You will be seeing them. Seferic literature, crazy, incomprehensible, passionate. . . . so let Costakis calm down. I'm doing my best. . . .

I sent three letters by diplomatic pouch but they were very late.

> 25 January 1937
> Every month you will see my article in *New Letters*. There will also be one or two of my poems. I shall go on with them if God gives me the quiet needed for the unbearable spiritual gymnastics of writing poetry. Write me your opinion. . . . Basically the writing of prose is a discussion, and how can you do it without an interlocutor? . . . . No one but you can remain stable while being near me. . . .
>
> But in Athens I felt suffocated. The uncertainty, the insecur-

ity of organized dictatorship did not suit me at all. I read a lot of history seeking comfort in comparable circumstances. But in vain. What is terrible is the present because the present is our responsibility. . . . Angelos became ill — unbearable pain in his stomach, the beginning of his ulcer. He sat all drawn up, without speaking. I sent George all the things he asked for, also a nice little wood-stove which arrived half broken.

A Word for Summer was well-received — so his friends told me — and I wrote to him about it.

> Koritsa — Thursday 4 February 1937
> Little sister. . . . I am happy that *A Word* made a good impression, though I am not entirely pleased with it. I like *Epiphany* a thousand times more. But I know it is a bad sign when you love things you have finished, and I am therefore mistrustful. Logically, *Epiphany* should be the poorer poem. . . . Any way, I shall continue until they amount to a volume (if it's at all possible) to be called *Sketches for a Summer*. I now have the security needed for writing poetry, and I know how to work. Favorable opinions naturally warm my heart and move me, but they do not influence me . . . What interests me more now is prose — and I began late to write that. It's a question of finding a style. For the time being, I'm groping, trying things out. In *New Letters* I shall have a column called *Essays*. Write me your opinions about this even if they are unfavorable. Actually those are the ones that interest me most. . . . Tell Costakis to have a look at the essays. Find the issues of the 23rd and 30th of January, *Modern Greek Letters*, and cast an eye at *The Formation of a Generation* by Terzakis and Theotokas' answer. I sent a letter about this to Photiadis. . . . Tell Costakis and Triantaphyllidis to get involved in this. . .

Evening we would get together in Kydathineon Street, sometimes only a few friends, other times more. Panayiotis Canellopoulos was reading his novel to us. On Friday, 5 February 1937, the party did not break up until 2 a.m. Had so much time passed? I was not yet in bed when the bell of the outer door began ringing frantically. It was some of our friends back again. Kapetanakis, pale, upset, stammered: "The men from the Security Police arrested Canellopoulos."

Next morning at the headquarters of General Security we were not allowed to see him. They exiled him to Kythnos.

On February 20th, George asked the Ministry for permission to spend a few days in Athens. There were many reasons why he wanted this leave.

> . . . I'm enclosing an envelope for Saltaferas (his colleague at the Ministry) and I ask you to admire the certificate from two dentists. One was formerly a repairer of watches. . . .

Fortunately he received his leave and came. A break, an interruption in the separations, and, above all, a chance to collect his thoughts. Perhaps the only way to combat temptation is to commit the sin. On his return he was able to confront snowbound Koritsa quite calmly.

> 6 April 1937 (to Costakis)
> The truth is one seeks not to get away from a place, not to travel, not to see again the people one loves, not even to create something. At bottom, one is seeking to get out of oneself, and perhaps the criterion of a man's worth is the way he manages to get out of himself.

George Katsimbalis was going through a difficult time in Paris where his father was gravely ill. He was a charming man and all of George's friends were devoted to him. He was our friend, a man of great sensibility, also a poet, and there was no "generation gap" between us. From early years my brother George had loved him dearly. When he learned of the death in Paris, he found an outlet for his sorrow there in his isolation by writing something about his old friend.

> 15 April 1937
> Dear little sister,
> I am glad you wrote to me. . . . You will have received a short article I wrote about Katsimbalis. I wish it were better . . . So time passes, and I feel that what is accomplished is never enough. I lost many years getting accustomed to my life, learning how not to waste time. . . . I went for a walk this evening. I love the green fields in the dull light, and the mountains lost in the cloudy sky. They seem less solid and you get the feeling that you are less imprisoned. . . .

He tried to establish himself more agreeably in Koritsa, to change his house. He found something he liked. If he could add a second floor it would be quite good. Would the Ministry agree? He sent me photographs and plans so that I could discuss the matter with our architect friend, Basil Douras. Basil was an artist and had excellent taste. I would send George his ideas.

George was beginning to settle down, to feel more at ease, to be able to work better. His literary instinct was functioning productively. He thought a great deal about his friend Katsimbalis, mourning his father's death.

It poisons life to have to think constantly about public affairs. Perhaps in no other country at that time did one feel so keenly the relentless combat of good and evil. We were constantly getting bad news of one sort or other. They were abolishing the Scouts, a new Metaxas organization called EON would enlist the children.

After Canellopoulos' arrest I had lugubrious thoughts every time Costakis was late. Father saw war coming again and mistrusted Metaxas' friendly attitude toward the Germans.

My only wealth was my friends. Myrivilis came often and sat by the fireplace. He offered a quiet companionship of few words. He was never immoderate, but his imagination was untamable. Later he wrote me letters, letters inspired by the knowledge that their recipient would respond to their truth.

"The book goes toward men, and strikes at their hearts. When it is worth while, the doors open wide and the artist enters in to enjoy the warm alien heart as if it were his own. This is a miracle we ought to sit down and think about. Because if we start counting one by one the good things of life, and if we weigh properly the joy they offer, we will discover this truth — that the greatest blessing God has given to men is Man."

Kapetanakis often kept us company. It was he who brought us Sikelianos' new poetry.

Koritsa 30 April
Little sister, If we take this attitude of speaking lightly about serious concerns it is because we have bandaged our hearts and grown up, as Comrade Mathios Paskalis proclaimed. Fundamentally we know that there are many

things much more important than our humble existences which are, in the last analysis, nothing but a form of matter (and interesting only as matter).

In my deep melancholy, I thought to myself: the life of love exists; the struggle of work exists; there exists too the invincible attraction of beauty. All the rest — time's deception till Death comes. Perhaps the meaning of life is death? I turned this elusive idea over and over in my mind, trying to comprehend it, to reach it by roads outside of logic.

Throughout 1937, George contributed something to every issue of *New Letters* — poems, prose, translations. An immense comfort to him.

25 May 1937
Little sister,
I've divided the world in two parts, — above, dreams with the sun and the sea and nymphs; below, dreams with the dampness of the cellar and capering demons. . . . The evil of boredom is that it involves the sense of eternity quite as much as does the enthusiasm of love. One must try to establish an equilibrium, and one feels that if one does not die to be born again, nothing will change.

Easter passed. Everything about it made him melancholy, choked him. The funeral bells of Great Friday, the rather miserable *epitaphios* with so few flowers. As he described it to me, only the little earthen pots being sold around the churches sounded a note of novelty.

Baud-Bovy translated *Mythistorema* into French. He showed the translation to Marcel Raymond, the well known French critic who succeeded Albert Thibaudet at the University of Geneva.

2 July 1937
Baud-Bovy writes me that Raymond wants to publish the poems which they like very much. They asked my approval and naturally I gave it. I write this to you because I know how much your brother's glory interests you. Moreover, your brother will be left only with glory, considering the road he has taken. At least, that is what my Zodiac indicates. . . . If I had hair, it would be my fate to have my hair blow in the wind . . . Now that I am bald, I must accept the decision for a more humble destiny. Why do I

say all this to you? *'Have you ever been lonely, have you ever been blue, my dear, my sweet little sister?'*

That summer George came on leave again. Many problems. Bad days, good days. He went to Pelion and I saw little of him. But he sent me a charming diary written on sheets from his notebook. That is another matter, a secret which might have become history, but did not.

Final months at Koritsa.

How often our reactions were the same! It was an interesting phenomenon: psychological crises produced high fever in me. Doctors did not admit this, but George knew about it, and he wrote me that he suffered the same way.

12 September 1937
Yesterday I was seized with a chill, and I had the impression that I was in the lowest circle of Hell — there where it is the tip of an inverted cone — all ice, with the gnashing and grinding of teeth. . . . Usually things attack my body first and then my spirit; this awful chill came from a wave of memories. You see you are not alone. Try not to let these things disturb you. . . . I do not understand the novel. Sometimes it seems to be one of the fabrications of our epoch. Does even a good one leave with us more than we get from a short poem? I think not. . . . I love to receive your letters. They bring me some companionship. I need them. . . . I have finished copying and arranging *Book of Exercises*. It makes a volume of a hundred pages more or less, and I haven't yet decided whether or not to publish them. I have still to write a couple of pages of introduction. Next year I must bring out a volume of essays. Will Athens leave me time for it? . . .

Who will understand the poet's abyss which for a moment is lighted up by expression? George returned to Athens loaded with the flowering fantasy of his nostalgia, but it withered in his fingers, stripped of its leaves: *The Return of the Exile* or life without mercy.

> Raise your head a little
> so that I understand you.
> As you speak you grow
> gradually smaller (p. 217)

Why do we rebel against the human condition? Why this refusal to accept mediocrity, injustice? From what perfect world did we come with these claims, renouncing patience and submission to life? Only when we leave the firing-line behind and draw near the end are our hopes and our resistance subdued. And we dare to call this annihilation wisdom and experience.

1938

In Athens George established himself in his first-floor apartment, Kydathineon 9 A. He was able to organize his private life in his own way. By an inner door from the main entrance, he went up to Father or to me for whatever he might want. His work was going well, and he continued to appear in the pages of *New Letters*.

In 1938 Angelos married Roxane Pappas. They lived together some years and then, during the Axis Occupation of Greece, they were divorced. Warm-hearted Angelos adored his little boy. To be deprived of him drove him to despair. In his distress he wrote:

> Naked, tied at the back of the chariot of the past,
> Skamander or Astyanax, he still
> recognized me, and called out: 'Father,
> come, let me wash your bloodstained body' . . .

His nature was even more tragic than George's, and he faced persecution unprotected by armor. He did not deign to defend himself. His heroes were Ajax and Hamlet. His life, wounds in the heart of all who loved him.

Throughout the terrible period of the Occupation, we lived side by side. His imprisonment was agony for us, but his courage greatly helped us.

Always smiling, full of humor, he was never a burden to anyone. My little girls adored him. When they were free, they would seek him out. The little one amused him:

> Certainly our Doritsa
> is not haughty —
> her nose just turns up. . . .

Hand in hand we waited for the great day of liberation. But the Civil War of 1944 brought us to our knees. The first night of the slaughter, in front of Angelos' window, — a beardless youth, dead. The blood in his open wound was still fresh. Reeling, I turned to Angelos, so pale. Was it for this we were liberated? He later wrote his prayer:

> Blood and soil on the ruined asphalt,
> and the fixed eyes of the murdered lad
> reflecting the cold Christmas moon.
> God, have mercy. Turn up the wick a little
> and give us some light in the dark
> where we are killing one another.
> Let us see each other's faces.
> Let the murderer know his victim.
> Here, Lord, rest Thy hand. . . .

He left for New York in 1946. The first years in America were unbearable. For him, but also for me. I heard his voice in the roar of the sea: "Here I am, poor wreck, driven away by that magnetic storm of a dusty winter, unable to pray in a foreign language . . ." These are words written in English from New York.

He died one night in January 1950. He fell asleep there in California, at Monterey, reading Plato once more. But this time it was forever. The book was found, lying open upon him at the page in the *Phaedo* where he speaks of the immortality of the soul. Not a wrinkle on the sheet gave evidence of any break in his serenity.

At that time a postal strike in Athens had isolated us. George, counsellor to the Embassy in Ankara, learned the news first. He telegraphed Mistos so that he could stand by me. Costakis, himself deeply shocked, was shattered by the thought of my despair. Then George was able to send me a letter by an aviator friend.

> Ankara 25 January 1950
> A few hours ago I received the terrible news that we have lost Angelos. . . . My pain is very great, here alone. . . . I am in no condition to write to you at length. . . . Be brave . . .

I was frozen to the deepest places of my heart. Angelos — so far away, always so far away. He had written to me a few days earlier with wishes for my name day. He spoke of his little boy. At last he seemed happy in Monterey. The climate there had a softness like our own. He was teaching Greek to the officer-candidates in the Army school. Everyone loved him.

He was "lost"? What a strange message! How was I to interpret it? I clung to the fireplace until late at night, trying to embrace the flame. Something alive. My yearning for Angelos was a heavy cloud which cut off the breath of the earth.

> 4 February 1950
> Ioanna . . . Today I received your telegram. I think of you constantly. Angelos' drama has concerned me all my life.
> Do please write me whatever you are able to find out. . . . For the present, we have two things we must do. First, we must think about his child. We must keep him as close to us as possible so that we can help him. You have been doing more about this than I, but now I too want to do what I can.
> Something else I have taken very much to heart — how shall I say it? — the question of his memory. I want to look after his papers and do what I can to bring out the little book he wanted to publish . . . (*Sima of Angelos Seferiadis*, Ikaros, Athens 1967)

He wrote down for me all the information he had received from Monterey. There was also a letter from Henry Miller in October 1948 describing an evening when Angelos had gone to see him. And here is part of the last letter from Henry Miller: "I got word of his death, a shock to me. I had been expecting him to visit me again, and I sent messages to him through mutual friends. I supposed he was just too busy at the school."

I remember well with what tragic dependence George and I wrote to each other all that winter. We were climbing, each in his own way, the same wild, lonely path.

> 13 February 1950
> Little Stelios must sometime learn about it. It would not be right for him to grow up with the idea that his father was indifferent to him . . . You must tell him. It is a great support in life to be spiritually attached to some person with love and admiration and faith. Sometimes it is a talisman for the conscience. . . .
> I go on in this snowy place, saying to myself that if I stop

for a moment to admit my pain, the wolves will devour me. . . . I am thinking about this boy who had suffered so much in his life — except for you, I think no one knew how much he suffered — but then he died the sweetest, kindest death in the world, not even a breath of air as he died. A simple ray of love gone elsewhere. . . .

When, little by little the dreadful nightmare of his loss faded, we were again and always the three of us, together: "*Yet we are three.*"

And even today, Angelos in the earth of California, George here near his mother, and I still on Kydathineon Street, we are forever the three.

George tried to conceal his grief by doing interesting things with his life.

He decided to go back to Smyrna, to Skala. How did he find the courage to see dead the best of himself, the place he had yearned for years to revisit? The ordeal of the winter seemed to have intensified his longing, to have wakened in him a painful attraction to those years.

His letter of July 21, 1950 is the first text of *Another World* which he later published. A symbol of the living death of a land caught in the impasse of our era.

George's journey to Cappadocia that summer of 1950 drew him somewhat away from his dark thoughts. He talked to me many times about the churches of the area. When he skipped some detail, he would start over again. He explained his photographs. I could listen by the hour. In my mind's eye I saw Christianity persisting there among the rocks. In the little light which fell upon the Byzantine colors of the figures, men and nature had worked together to create a harsh discipline.

But always there was Angelos.

He sent me some lines of poetry. In everything I sensed his bitter grief over the loss of his brother.

> I thought of playing a tune and then
> I was ashamed of the other world
> the one that watches me from beyond
> the night from within my light (p. 357)

The mystery of love where life and death melt together like the lead of 'Klydon' so that separation does not separate.

Later, with the passage of time, things seemed to become normal, but only 'seemed.'

Then I too left for Paris. I needed to see Father.

I said nothing about Angelos. One evening, looking very old as he sat in his armchair, he spoke as if to himself: "That boy doesn't write. I wonder what he is doing?"

I stroked his dear, fleshless hand.

"But he never wrote much," I whispered. There was silence, as if he was afraid to ask more.

He did not live long after that.

On August 4, 1951, he died quietly. We were not in time to say goodbye, neither George nor I. Every summer I had gone to see him, and each time I left him with aching heart. He was much aged. Far away from his children, his friends, in the suburbs of Paris, he must have felt himself deserted. His second wife was a good woman, and she looked after his physical needs, but for the restless spirit, that is not enough.

His loneliness was the greater because he had so many ties. The fate of those we love weighs more heavily on us than our own.

And these graves in foreign soil. The tradition is burial in the soil of one's homeland. Tradition? Or rather an emotional need of those who remain?

George was then counsellor to the Greek Embassy in London. In the beginning we tried to communicate by telegram.

> 18 August 1951
>
> Ioanna, I just received your letter. This suddenly awakened self of ours, biologically united to those who have gone, suffers terrible pain and bitter sorrow. One seems to be carrying their sorrows too which perhaps they did not understand. It is curious but I did not feel this way about Mother. As I recall, the infinite tenderness of the earth took over and dominated all other feelings.
>
> You would do well to write to Teresa (Father's second wife) about gathering and putting together all Father's papers.

Much later he wrote me of his one request:

> If you can do so easily, write to Teresa to keep and not sell that painting by Ioannidis (a painting of a monas-

tery). . . . It is the only memento I can keep from the old house. . . .

I wrote to Teresa and she sent it immediately.

In April of 1938 Costakis had published his essay *Before Setting Out*. It concerned art and poetry. George undertook to reply and a lively written discussion developed between the two of them: *Dialogue on Poetry*. Intellectual Athens divided into two camps — that of Seferis and that of Tsatsos. People stopped me in the street to ask me to which one I belonged. I expressed amusement and managed to stay out of it. Actually, I was pro-Seferis, but I did not want to seem at odds with Costakis.

Octave Merlier said to me, "It is certainly remarkable that one lives on one floor and the other on another floor of the same building, but they carry on their discussion in writing!"

That was when George began to write *The King of Asine*. How he labored over that poem which I so loved!

Father's book on international law was out of print. In May work on a second edition was started. By September copies began to flood the storerooms of Kydathineon Street.

That summer for the sake of the children we spent a month on Pelion and later ended up in Kifissia. Poor George had stayed in Athens. I wrote to him regularly.

> 7 July 1938
> Your letters are coming and I am reading them greedily. . . . Here on the plain of Athens it is hot, and men are turning into not very attractive juice. The literary quarrels continue . . .

From Kifissia I went down regularly to Athens to take delivery of Father's books. One morning I stopped counting them to cast an eye at a newspaper. I jumped up in dismay. The last package fell from my knees. Without warning, Metaxas had made a law reducing the age limit for University professors from 70 to 65. Father had just completed his 65th year. I was staggered. All those copies spread on the floor were like dead children. So much pointless work, so much money thrown away. And how would Father take this news there in Paris, alone, facing the great emptiness of retirement when he was still so full of life, with new plans and programs in his mind. One of his phrases came to my head: "I don't want their help. It's enough if they do me no harm."

He did not deserve this blow. There should be a margin of a year before such a law took effect. But no. The law of the jungle: your death — my life.

Father never returned to live in Greece. He taught international law in Paris, at the Sorbonne, where he was warmly received. He married again, a French woman, Teresa.

This was a painful story, both for him and for us. We lost our father while he was still alive.

1939

We waited for the war. Every day at the Red Cross Hospital I followed a course in nursing, and we began practical instruction. A delightful Red Cross nurse showed us how to change the bed linen of the wounded.

"Such gentle movements you have," she said to give me courage when she saw that I was depressed. To thank her, I made a special effort. She was killed while carrying out her duties during the Civil War of 1944.

The declaration of the European war found us in Kifissia. We had a simple little house with a courtyard. One morning at five, the whole place was shaken by loud knocking. Half asleep, I threw on something and opened the door. There stood six men.

"Security Police."

"But what do you want at such an hour?"

"Tsatsos."

"He isn't here."

"Where is he?"

"Kydathineon Street."

"Search."

They searched the house. I opened the door of the children's room softly. They were sound asleep. The police did not notice the telephone curled up under a big cushion.

The moment they were gone I called Costakis.

"I knew about it yesterday, but I wanted you to sleep well," he said.

In a vehement letter to the exiled Canellopoulos, Costakis had expressed his wish for the victory of the democracies in that critical period. Metaxas considered this a personal affront, and banished Costakis to Skyros. I left my children with Mistos; I took leave from the hospital; and I too left for Skyros.

But the island was so beautiful! What a place to be exiled! I stayed as long as I could.

On my return George came every day to Kifissia to see me. It was often three in the afternoon when he arrived, exhausted with the heat. He was determined that I should not be left alone. He read aloud D. H. Lawrence's *Ship of Death* which I very much liked. He talked to me about André Gide whose acquaintance he had made.

From Skyros, Costakis, with his customary facility in writing, sent me ten-page letters. The censor of the gendarmerie needed months to spell them out, and of course I never saw them.

Later they transferred Costakis to Spetsai. There he rented a large room in the house of Bouboulina. One corner was the bedroom, another the study, a third a kind of bath. Henry Miller found him on Spetsai. He was curious to meet this convict who was reading Plato and Aristotle. He looked all around the room and finally found him covered with soapsuds, in the corner of the room devoted to the bath. Katsimbalis gave a colorful account of the episode.

1940

In April 1940 I had a warm letter from Henry Miller, writing from New York. He could not believe that war was encircling Greece. He told me that he kept hoping, as if he was trying to reach out and protect from chaos this country he so loved.

From our first meeting at George's in 1939 and afterward in my own home, I always felt that Henry Miller also had travelled the road to Damascus. The divine light was the sound of his own voice among the voices of the books which he had read. And his voice, for him, was life itself, the whole of his humanity. In this wide-ranging humanity were the hidden sources of his art. He gave himself freely, sharing his spirit with appealing forthrightness. Even his memoranda, for he had given George a little notebook with his impressions. He had written to me from his hotel in Athens: "I have finished the little notebook which I have been preparing for your brother, Seferis. I shall re-read it so as to enjoy it before I send it. There are things in it which you will like." George and I often referred to that notebook. I still remember a conversation in January 1971 as we walked in the National Garden. We talked of Henry Miller, about his recent news, and we were reminded again of the little notebook which had by then been published. On that same morning George talked again about the plan which he never abandoned — to leave the Nobel Prize money to his country. "I think I have found the people for the Board of Trustees. At last I shall be able to establish my educational foundation."

The sky turned black, came lower. We were speechless as we looked from one to another. Devastation, war, moving southward. What would become of Greece?

At dawn on 28 October 1940, George came up to our home. He had just come from the Ministry. I had not slept. I was expecting the worst. To find a little peace I was sitting in my children's room, listening to their rhythmic breathing as they slept. He bent over their beds for a moment. As he turned to leave, he looked at me with brimming eyes: "We are at war. God help us."

Later that morning he went to church and stood silent beside me before the icon of Christ. Nothing to wait for, nothing to prepare. Only a thick sadness, but still a hope.

A call to arms throughout the country. Girls in the villages were offering their dowries to the army. Silken sheets, woven for the first night of love, were being sent to hospitals, perhaps to become shrouds. In the cities women became nurses. Mothers wept. Victorious war songs resounded, but we were all hopeless, waiting for death.

1941

And now the Nazis. Their bombers strafed our army. Disorder, anguish everywhere. The government went into exile.

"George, you are leaving? When shall I see you again? How shall I know what is happening to you?"

Suddenly we were both old. We no longer had Greece.

Before leaving, George married Marika Zannos.

Angelos, Costakis, and I, nailed to Athens, sank together into the most tragic and the most responsible ordeal of our lives: the German-Italian Occupation of Greece.

Enough. This memory has torn my heart.

As I re-read these pages, I see that I have said nothing. A speck of love cast into the chaos.

Truly we possess only what we have given away.

GEORGE SEFERIS

Biographical Note

George Seferis was born in Smyrna on February 29, 1900, the son of Stelios Seferiadis and Despina Tenekidis. His father was a university professor of Law, both in Athens and in Paris, and he enjoyed a world-wide reputation in the field of international law. He was also a poet and translator of Greek tragedy.

Seferis received his elementary education in Smyrna, and passed his childhood summers at Skala, old Klazomenae. When he was 14, he moved to Athens with his father and mother, his younger brother Angelos, and his sister Ioanna, who later became the wife of Constantine Tsatsos. In 1917, he received his diploma from the First Classical Gymnasium of Athens.

In 1918 the family moved to join the elder Seferis in Paris, where he had for several years been practicing law. Paris was to be the poet's home for six years. They were years torn between poetry and law studies, but in 1924 he received his degree in law. He then spent almost two years in London with the special purpose of perfecting his English. In 1926 he returned to Athens to qualify for the Foreign Service, where he served until 1962. In 1941 he married Maria Zannos.

His thirty-six years of government service alternated between assignments in Athens and posts abroad. His first foreign tour of duty was at the Greek Consulate in London. He was consul at Koritsa in Albania and served as counsellor to the Greek Embassy in Ankara and London, respectively. He was ambassador to Lebanon, Syria, Jordan, and Iraq, and later to Great Britain for five years, from 1957 until 1962. During the Axis Occupation of Greece, he was with the Government-in-Exile in Egypt, South Africa, and Italy. During the

Regency he was Director of the Political Bureau for Archbishop Damaskinos and at the time of the deliberations on Cyprus, he was a member of the Greek delegation to the United Nations. In 1969 he made known his opposition to the dictatorship in a published declaration.

Seferis was the recipient of many honors, among them an honorary degree at Cambridge University and the Nobel Prize for Literature in 1963. He was a member of the Princeton Institute of Advanced studies in 1968–69, during which period he also lectured at Harvard and other American universities.

He died at the Evangelismos Hospital in Athens, on September 20, 1971. He was escorted to his grave in the First Cemetery by thousands of young people for whom, even in advanced years, he had been an eloquent spokesman. During the decade since his death, his writings have enjoyed great popularity and have also been the subject of much discussion by scholars and critics. He continues to be recognized as one of the most important leaders of the new Greek poetry.

INDEX

Adam, Peter 71–72
Aegina 226
Aesop 7, 8
Aesop (Theodore de Banville) 36, 57
Aix-les-Bains 23, 56
Ajax 56, 238
Ajax (Sophocles) 174
Alevizatos, Hamilcar 227
Alevras, Andreas 14
Alexander the Great 7
Anacreon 10, 86
Anagnostopoulos, Athan, translator, *A Poet's Journal* vii
Andreadis, Andreas 78
Angoulés, Photis 168
Ankara 239
Antoniou, D. I. (Capt. Mimis) 222
Apollinaire, Guillaume 52, 172
Apostolidis, Heracles 198
Aristotle 246
Aronis, Nikos 78, 102
Athenagoras, Patriarch of Constantinople 128–129

Bataille, Henri 45
Baud-Bovy, Samuel 235
Baudelaire, Charles 63, 77, 91, 155
Beethoven, Ludwig van 54
Beirut 90
"Billio" 173ff
Blake, William 183
Boecklin, Arnold 105
Bourget, Paul 80
Boutmy, Emil (*Le Parthénon*) 78
Briarcliff, New York 179, 184
The Bridge at Arta 215
Byron, George Gordon, Lord 10, 16, 148, 157

Cambridge, England 127
Canellopoulos, Panayiotis 232, 234, 245

Cappadocia 138, 241
Cardiff 212–213
Carrière, Eugène 100, 137
Charitakis, Sophia 115, 117
Chios 168
Chopin, Frédéric 222
Chrysostom, Bishop of Smyrna 32, 112
Clavier, Etiènne 228
Clos, André 73
Constantine XI, Emperor of Byzantium 7
Constantine, King of Greece 20
Constantinople 128
Corfu 22
Crete 224
Crystallis, Constantine 46
Cyprus 127–128, 197, 252

d'Aurevilly, Barbey (*Diaboliques*) 86
da Vinci, Leonardo 155
Delacroix, Paulette 26
Delphi 131
De Max 25, 36, 77, 96, 107
Demertzis, Constantine 118, 224
de Musset, Alfred 37
de Vigny, Alfred 63
Douras, Basil 234
Dresden 105
Durrell, Lawrence 65

Electra (Sophocles) 10
El Greco 205
Eliot, T. S. xi, xii, 198, 200, 209, 223
Ephtaliotis, Argyris 223
Erotokritos 60, 75
Euripides 11

Forster, E. M. 127
Frantzis, George 112

Gallipoli 23ff

Ghika-Hadjikyriakos, Nikos 207
Gide, André 246
Goudis, Demetrios 19, 92
The Great Idea 8, 111, 122
Gregory, Bishop of Cydonia 112
Gryparis, I. N. 46

Heine, Heinrich 59
Heraclitus 65, 227
Herriot, Edouard 179, 181
Homer 86, 203, 226
Hugo, Victor 79

Ioannidis, Evangelos 242

"Jacqueline" 140–144, 154, 161–163, 171, 190, 202, 205, 206, 209, 216
John the Baptist 67

Kaiser, Walter vii
Kalvos, Andreas 138
Kampanis, Aristos 191
Kapetanakis, Demetrios 234
Karantonis, Andreas 191, 198, 205
Katsimbalis, George 46, 65, 180, 191, 197, 201, 205, 233, 246
Katsimbalis, Kostas 104, 233
Kavvadias, Dr. Alexander 163
Keats, John 36
Keeley, Edmund vii, xii
Keyes, Sidney 43
Kierkegaard, Søren 122
Kifissia 115, 116, 163, 166, 173, 182, 192, 211, 245
"Kirsten" 57ff
Kondilis, George 166
Kordatos, I. K. 156
Koritsa 229ff, 234ff
Krikos, Mrs. Maria 19
Kythnos 233

Laforgue, Jules 52, 76, 91, 149
Lautréamont (Isidore Ducasse) 52
Lawrence, D. H. 201, 246
Louth, Scotland 138
Luminais, Evariste-Vital 87

Mackail, J. M. 78
Makriyannis, General John 162, 170
Malakassis, Miltiadis 100, 118
Malraux, André 73
Mavilis, Lorenzo 24
Merlier, Octave 243

Metaxas, John 228, 234
Miller, Henry 65, 240, 246–247
Mimnermus, 10
Monterey 239
Moréas, Jean 46, 62ff, 88, 130
Mussolini, Benito 148
Mycenae 100
Mylonas, Despina Tsatsos — (niece of G. S.) 192, 201, 205
Myrivilis, Stratis 207, 214, 234

Normandy 51
Nietzsche, Friedrich 159

Oikonomopoulos, Irene 182, 187
Oikonomos, George 33, 85

Palamas, Kostis 46, 78, 100, 159, 180, 196, 222
Pangalos, Theodore 157, 166
Papanastassis, Loukas 221, 228
Papantoniou, Zacharias 118, 197
Paraschos, Cleon 66
Pelion 222ff, 236
Periodicals:
    The Circle 210
    Ergasia 191
    Estia 197
    Ethnos 91
    Kathimerini 197
    Modern Greek Letters 232
    Nea Estia 196
    New Letters 231, 238
    Noumas 196
    Proïa 191
    Revue Critique 100
    Today 210
    Vomos 64
Phaleron 19, 48, 217
Philyras, Romos 53ff
Phteris, George 207
Pindar 229
Plastiras, General Nicholas 132, 148
Plato 246
    Apology 63
    Symposium 177
    Phaedo 239
Plutarch 152
Poe, Edgar Allan 75, 107
Politis, N. 78
Poniridis, George 52, 55, 102
Pougollon, Mme. Marie Louise 142, 143, 149, 202
Prometheus 88

Racine, Jean 25
Ractivan, Constantine 177
Raymond, Marcel 235
Rhamnous 34
Rilke, Rainer Maria 227
Rimbaud, Jean 51
Rodokanakis, Platon 64
Roethke, Theodore 48
Rostand, Edmond 24, 102
   translations by G. S. 26
Runciman, Sir Steven 138

Saltaferas, S. 233
Samos 8
Savvidis, George 127
Scheherazade (Rimsky-Korsakov, N.) 153
Sceaux 83ff
Seferiadis, Angelos (brother of G. S.) xv, 6, 11, 15, 18, 23, 50, 85, 103, 105, 107, 121, 135, 156, 161, 169, 238ff, 240, 251
Seferiadis, Despina Tenekidis — (mother of G. S.) 3ff, 9, 14, 22, 53, 77, 81, 85, 87, 104, 108, 121, 132ff, 146ff, 161ff, 251
Seferiadis, Maria Tenekidis — (aunt of G. S.) 115
Seferiadis, Roxane Pappas — (wife of Angelos) 238
Seferiadis, Socrates (uncle of G. S.) 11, 14, 31, 50, 85, 115, 118
Seferiadis, Stelios (son of Angelos) 238, 240
Seferiadis, Stylianos (Stelios) (father of G. S.) 6ff, 23
   and George 55ff, 76, 89, 133, 162ff, 167
   and Ioanna 106, 134, 170, 187
   associate of Venizelos 8, 23, 55, 173, 177
   professor and scholar 9, 145, 152, 179, 210
   old age and death 242, 243
Seferis, George
   LIFE (to 1941)
      boyhood at Skala 12ff, 251
      departure for Athens 18
      secondary schooling 19
      journey to Paris 22ff
      law studies 26ff
      French language 45ff
      growing conflict with father 56, 76
      influence of Jean Moréas 45ff
      poetry vs. law 81–82
      the doom of Ionia 109–158
      final year in Paris 154
      law examinations 50, 89, 145
      first visit to England 155
      return to Greece 161
      mother's final illness 163ff
      diplomatic competition 167
      Herriot's escort in Greece 179, 181
      publication of first book (*Turning Point*) 191
      early diplomatic assignments: vice-consul in London 195
      counsellor to Greek Embassy in London 228, 251
      assignment to Cardiff and cancellation 212
      consul in Koritsa 229ff, 251
      counsellor to Greek Embassy in Ankara 239, 251
      holiday on Pelion 222
      Italian invasion 247
      marriage to Maria Zannos 249
      departure with government-in-exile 249
   LATER EVENTS
      death of Angelos 239ff
      death of father 242
      honorary doctorate at Cambridge 127
      the Nobel Prize 73, 252
      manifesto to dictatorship 130ff
      death and funeral 150ff, 252
   POEMS CITED OR QUOTED
      The Altar, 99
      Another World 126
      Book of Exercises 236
      The Cistern 141, 203–206
      Description 141
      Dosmena 6
      Epiphany, 1937 232
      Erotikos Logos 140, 184, 211
      The Fires of St. John 204
      Flight 185
      Gymnopaidia 223
      The King of Asine 125, 243
      Last Stop 125
      Last Words of a Suicide 26
      Letter of Mathios Paskalis 132, 172, 174

Memory I 241
Mr. Stratis Thalassinos Describes a Man 124, 204
The Mood of a Day 190
Mythistorema 124, 141, 208, 215, 221
Narration 124
Neophytos the Prisoner 131
A Night on the Beach 204
Nocturne 96
Notes for a Week 208
Piazza San Nicolo 166
The Return of the Exile 236
Santorini 124
Sirocco 7 Levante 222
Sketches for a Summer 232
Slowly You Spoke 173
Turning Point 186, 191, 196, 197, 198
A Word for Summer 124, 231, 232
TRANSLATIONS BY G. S.
The Revelation of St. John 48
Murder in the Cathedral, T. S. Eliot 223
The Problem of Civilized Man, T. S. Eliot 223
Seferis, Maria Zannos — (wife of G. S.) 228, 249, 251
Sèvres 27, 28, 55
Shakespeare, William 183
Sherrard, Philip vii, xii
Sherriff, R. C., *Journey's End* 183
Sikelianos, Angelos xvi, 225–228
Simeonidis, Dora Tsatsos — (niece of G. S.) 205, 238
Skala 3, 10, 12–17, 23, 31, 33, 47, 58, 85, 97, 99, 125–127
Skiathos 187–189, 204
Skliros, George *Our Social Problem* 156
Skyros 245
Smyrna 3, 9, 28, 31, 85, 111ff, 116, 119
Solomos, Dionysios 24, 100, 163
Sophocles
  Ajax 174
  Electra 10
  Oedipus 10, 16
Sophoulis, Themistocles 8
"Sotiris" of Skiathos 188–189
Souris, George 229
Spetsai 216, 228, 246
St. John of the Cross 199, 227
St. Paul 227
"Suzanne" 35–37, 51, 53, 84

Taine, Hippolyte 95
Terzakis, Angelos 232
Theodorakopoulos, John 174, 177, 182
Theotokas, George 211, 232
Thessaloniki 182, 228
Triantaphyllidis, Manolis *Our Orthography* 156, 230
Tsatsos, Constantine (Costakis) (brother-in-law of G. S.) viii, 73, 173ff, 196ff, 207, 214ff, 243ff, 251
Tsatsos, Ioanna Seferiadis — (sister of G. S.)
  family life at Skala 12ff
  fun and games with G. S. 14–15
  move to Athens 18
  journey to Paris 22ff
  end of World War I 26
  freedom of Ionia 32–33
  to Mycenae 100
  to Venice 105
  to Dresden 106
  rediscovery of Paris 106–107
  the doom of Ionia 111–112
  refugee relief 113–114
  illness and recovery in Kifissia 115ff
  decision to study law 134
  privation in Athens 138–139
  Corfu bombarded 148
  return of G. S. to Greece 161
  mother's illness and death 163ff
  first degree in law 169
  Paris with father 170ff
  legal apprenticeship 173
  trip to America 179, 184
  completion of doctorate 186ff
  courtship and marriage 186ff
  wedding trip to Skiathos 187–189
  birth of Despina 192
  birth of Dora 205
  family dwelling built in Plaka 207, 213
  summer on Pelion 222ff
  death of Venizelos 224
  impact of Sikelianos 225–229
  dictatorship of Metaxas 228
  father's final departure from Greece 244
  war in Europe 245
  invasion of Albania 247
  Nazi Occupation 249
  LATER EVENTS
  death of Angelos 239ff

   St. Paul pilgrimage and death of Sikelianos 227
   Nobel award to G. S. 73
   death of G. S. 150–152
   visit to Patriarch 112

Tsatsos, Themistocles 19, 173, 175, 229

Valéry, Paul 170ff, 197
Vaphiopoulos, George 61
Venizelos, Eleftherios 8, 55, 81, 149, 172, 175, 179, 195, 201, 211, 221, 224
Verlaine, Paul 86
Vlachos, Angelos 59
Vourloumis, Dora 174

Warner, Rex vii, 138

Xerxes 6

Yeats, W. B. 183
Yiophyllis, Photos 66

NOSTOS BOOKS ON MODERN
GREEK HISTORY AND CULTURE

Yannis Ritsos, *Eighteen Short Songs of the Bitter Motherland.* Translated from the Greek by Amy Mims with illustrations by the poet. Edited and with an Introduction by Theofanis G. Stavrou.

Kimon Friar, *The Spiritual Odyssey of Nikos Kazantzakis.* Edited and with an Introduction by Theofanis G. Stavrou.

Kostas Kindinis, *Poems: Reinvestigations and Descent from the Cross.* Translated from the modern Greek with a preface by Kimon Friar.

Andonis Decavalles, *Pandelis Prevelakis and the Value of a Heritage.* Including *Rethymno as a Style of Life* by Pandelis Prevelakis, translated from the Greek by Jean H. Woodhead. Edited and with an Introduction by Theofanis G. Stavrou.

John Anton, *Critical Humanism as a Philosophy of Culture: The Case of E. P. Papanoutsos.* Edited and with an Introduction by Theofanis G. Stavrou.

Ioanna Tsatsos, *My Brother George Seferis.* Translated from the original Greek by Jean Demos with a preface by Eugene Current-Garcia.

Nikos Kazantzakis, *Two Plays — Sodom and Gomorrah* and *Comedy: A Tragedy in One Act.* Translated from the modern Greek by Kimon Friar. Forthcoming.

Theofanis G. Stavrou, *Angelos Sikelianos and the Delphic Idea.* Forthcoming.